The ⬚⬚⬚⬚ Diaries

Volume one : Keith Haynes

A proper unaccountable account of a young un'

For You I Will Give

A CIP catalogue record for the title is available from the British
Library www.bl.uk

ISBN: 9798492526023

ASIN: B0CK8YWS6R

This is a semi fiction, non fiction work based on the experiences
of Ken Barnes, an officer of our times. Names, places, locations
have been changed to protect the guilty.

Senyah Publishing
Independent Publishing
Made with Love
+44 7922
565473
ISBN: 9798492526023

9 798492 526023

Imprint
Lost Dog Books

Thanks to Dan Collins at Monday Books for his initial and second edit of this book.

Of course, without doubt I have many people to thank as I pondered and delayed this project. It's what writers do. For now I will let those that know, to know, And for those that think they know, to do just that.

About the Book

Being a detective isn't easy. When your name is Ken Barnes it just gets harder. Having sucessfully navigated the first steps to move on to the Criminal Investigation Department in his home town force big questions present themselves to him every day. In amongst the heartache and stress he delivers an hilarious take on what he describes as his "daily bread Yardie drug dealers, collapsing constables, flying babies, exploding office furniture and lunacy on scales only personal experience could recall are all contained within these pages. There's so much more of course. It's a true (as it can be) account of a real life British detective. Now retired but seeing humour in almost every scenario in his recollections this diary contains the truth, the whole truth and possibly some shadier areas of nothing but the truth. With his candle taken to the darkest corners of the investigations he was involved in as the stupid just gets stupider, and the weirdness just gets weirder he describes adeptly the characters involved so well you can smell them. And that in the majority of cases wasn't a pleasant experience.

About the Author

Keith Haynes

Keith lives and writes in Andalusia, southern Spain. Having been in the country since 2016 he has found time to run a successful website, play shows around the world with his band, Picture Frame Seduction and run a very successful football website on Swansea City. They say retirement is easy, daytime TV is not an option, enjoying his life and home with wife, Angela is most certainly a daily objective.

Contents

Step One

THIS WAS ALL I'd ever wanted.

It was a bitterly cold day, unusually so. The sky looked grey and full of snow, a biting wind nipped at my hands and face, and my feet were numb in my Reeboks. It didn't help that the only other things I was wearing were a pair of Levis and a Smiths 'Meat is Murder' t-shirt.

I stood on the steps of our brand new headquarters, shoulders hunched, staring at a piece of paper.

At the top was the force crest – this was way back in those dinosaur days of September 1990, so there was no fancy, expensive logo, no 'Working Together To *make the community* Safer For YOU'.

Underneath the crest were the words, 'Notification of examination result'.

I'd been in the Job for six years.

Lots of walking around in my dark blue uniform, in my big shoes, with my big hat.

Lots of driving around, blues lights on, blue lights off, creeping round the backs of houses, and arguing with drunks.

Lots of nights, lots of bad food, bad banter, and bad sleep.

Stomach aches, headaches and ball aches.

The building above me made aching noises of its own in the freezing wind. Back then, it was a pristine, slightly futuristic structure, built to house those who had long forgotten what a cold, ten-hour nightshift feels like, and who had long forgotten the stab of fear that sometimes comes with an urgent shout on the radio.

I looked at the piece of paper in my hand.

It told me that I had passed the exam – that I was eligible to take up an attachment in our Criminal Investigations Department, the CID, as an 'aide'.

An aide-ship was a kind of temporary try-out – if one became available – so as the lads in suits could decide whether you had what it took.

I was on a rest day, and I'd just popped over from home to get the result. Three months of intense study, in between my uniform shifts and long hours as cells relief, reception relief, and radio room relief, and long-lost response driver… were they about to pay off?

I'd been expecting a lot of waiting and messing around at the hands of the admin woman in the force HQ. She was a lady of some repute, a thin, middle-aged secretary to a senior officer, and a superintendents' charabanc if all was to be believed. Of course, all is not *always* to be believed, especially in the police. But when I'd walked inside, not five minutes before, she hadn't ignored me and walked away – I was a mere PC, after all – but had greeted me with a familiar smile, a small despatch note signed by the new boss, and a wink.

'You've passed, Constable Barnes!' was all she'd said.

Maybe she's got plans for me? I thought, shifting uncomfortably on my feet. *Oh dear.*

''Ey up, youth,' came a voice to my left. 'What you doing out in this weather in your t-shirt?'

Wreathed in warm breath, wrapped in a Burberry scarf and a bright yellow Stone Island jacket, it was my old crew mate, Duffy.

A tall lanky lad in his mid-twenties, he was an amateur boxer, and absolutely fearless with it; he packed a hell of a punch. Great in a bundle, never took a backwards step. First to the bar, last to leave. All the clichés applied to Duffy, though in his case they were true. If you've got a police-issue skirt on and a pulse, chances are you've probably woken up next to him, or at least a version of him. The Old Bill is – or was – littered with guys like Duffy.

'I've passed, mate,' I said. 'The CID entrance exam. I've passed.'

If I sounded surprised, that's because I was – by the fact that I'd passed, and by the fact that I'd passed with a mark of ninety-three percent. I'm still not sure how I managed that.

'Well, that's it, youth,' said Duffy, with a grin. 'You're off to the dark side. Mark my words, your work here is done.'

'You reckon?'

'Your vocation lies elsewhere,' he said, mystically. 'You'll be on top of their list.'

He seemed pretty confident, and if *he* was confident the chances were he was right. Duffy had sources all over the force; if it was worth knowing, he knew it. In police terms, he was a superlative gatherer of information – if there was a whiff of a hint of a rumour of a story at the most outlying nick on the force area, Duffy would ferret it out. In theory, this made him a tremendous asset. The problem was his idea of information worth gathering was who was shagging who, when, where, and how. If he'd ever applied his ability to actual police work, he'd have been a legend, but I'd yet to see it.

'Me? On top of their list?'

'They're desperate, Barnesy,' he said, with a laugh. 'Get yerself an account at Burtons and don't look back. You'll be hanging out of that admin Doris before long.'

He laughed longer, and louder, and slapped my back.

I looked again at the piece of paper in my hand.

'I'll see you, then,' I said, and we went our separate ways.

I got back to my car – a beige, four-year-old Ford Sapphire with brown velour seats – and fired the ignition.

My head was all over the place, to be honest. I had expected at some point to get on to 'the department' – our term for the CID – but you could wait months or even years for a position to open up. This was frustrating, but at least it gave you plenty of time to get used to the idea. Duffy hadn't done anything to settle my nerves.

I headed out of the car park and drove off towards the dentists. I'd recently had two quite decent teeth knocked out by one of the esteemed Thompson family – young Barry, to be exact – and needed to get myself sorted out. Back then, dental treatment was free for cops – a privilege and something of a relief, given the way various members of our client group like to keep the dream alive by punching the fuck out of us on a regular basis.

Moves were afoot to remove this and other privileges, and the Police Federation – the closest thing rank-and file officers have to a union – were in the process of doing absolutely nothing to fight this. Toothless tigers, said some, and so would I be if I kept getting my head kicked in like this.

Into the dentist's chair.

Say Ah!

This won't hurt, much.

Bad breath and inane chatter. Spit and rinse.

Think about life in the department.

After a novocaine numbing on the inside, I joined the wailing, numbing wind on the outside and called in to the nick on my way home to see if anything was afoot, especially on the CID front.

In those wonderful days before the arrival of email and mobile phones, the pigeonhole was your link to the Job. Mine was usually stuffed with a collection of demands, wants, and desires – none of them mine, and almost all of them from our patrol sergeant who we affectionately called 'Beaky'. If they weren't from Beaky, they came from the relatively recently-formed Crown Prosecution Service, making a point that you had forgotten to write a date of birth in the correct way on your statement. There is a world of difference, apparently, between *July 1*st*, 1990* and *01.07.90*, and it's enough to mean the difference between a nasty man going away for six months and him walking out of court grinning at you.

I wasn't a big fan of the CPS, and I'm sorry to say this attitude hasn't changed much after a further thirty odd years. They are a body of bureaucrats and lawyers whose job is to prosecute offences in court on behalf of the public, via the broken noses, dented cars, and puke-ridden cells of the police. As far as I was – am – concerned, they had ditched their brief, made up their own rules, and completely forgotten that we were meant to be on the same side.

I had joined the police just after judges' rules disappeared, and PACE (the Police and Criminal Evidence Act 1984) was introduced. The Act revolutionised the way we could search, arrest, and interview suspects, and fair enough in most cases it gave coppers like me some protection.

Everything had to be recorded, and appropriate custody times were introduced. Before PACE, you dumped your man in custody with a statement form and a declaration to sign; the quicker he signed, the quicker he got out. Often, a felon would be left to stew over their misdemeanours while you spent the weekend at home with the family. It wasn't right, and it led to miscarriages of justice. But having to record everything in triplicate, or more, meant more chance for errors, and more opportunities for the CPS – who were now presenting cases at court, instead of the prosecutions Inspector, as had been the case – to be total tossers.

I rooted through my pigeonhole; the usual blather, but nothing from CID.

I sighed, and went to the Coach and Horses.

* * *

DUFFY WAS IN the report room as I walked in the following morning.

'Here he is, lads,' he said, with a beam. 'Detective Ken Barnes has graced us with his presence. Come to gloat about your exam pass, mate?'

He was loving it. First with the news, as ever.

'Nice one, Duffer,' I said. 'Is there nothing you don't know?'

He acted surprised at my response, winked at me, and moved it up a gear. 'Has the DI been in touch on the bat phone, youth?' he said.

'Not yet, mucka. But he's bound to ring now you've said it, so just tell him I'm at the footy Saturday.'

He chuckled and walked out of the room, and I followed him out to the car. Duffy was going to miss me, I knew that much, and it was going to be mutual. We'd been crew-mates for three years, colleagues and friends who had fought and laughed alongside each other, and on two occasions nearly died alongside each other.

We had delivered death messages, taken charge of crime scenes before the professionals turned up … wrestled hard men, taken punches and kickings, been sworn and spat at, been grabbed and beaten, smashed, ran and chased, driven, and screamed in terror at a hundred miles an hour.

It had been a laugh, and certain deserving people had benefited, too – the nice people who call us when they're scared and lonely, and of course wanting reassurance. The real deserving members of the public – MOPs – who work hard and live straight. They're easy to spot, and they had – and have – our one hundred percent support. They're why I was still a copper after all those years.

Mrs Lilly was just such a case. A frightened, retired old widow of little note who lived in a lovely old house in one the richer parts of town, she'd paid her way all her life and now had little to do but sit and think about her husband, who had been dead for seven years. She got more knocks on her door offering new driveways, fixed roofs, and gardening services than the rest of us put together, and – and I know this will shock you – some of the tradesmen offering these services were less than honest.

A while back, an informant had passed on the news that Timmy Thompson was targeting her. Timmy was a fat, ugly, waste of skin, granted, but he was clever enough in a scheming, bastard sort of way, and he was slowly moving in on Mrs Lilly's bank accounts and pin numbers. His *modus operandi* was to lurk around her house, slowly gaining her confidence. Back then, chequebooks were easy to find in a drawer, and all they needed was a signature. A couple of cheques could be nicked from the back of the book, stolen and kited (cashed in) with a dodgy signature thereupon. Mrs Lilly wouldn't find out for months – people who had a few bob sometimes *never* noticed the missing dough.

Duffy and I had had a quick conflab and had decided that the best way of dealing with Timmy was to catch him at it and front him up. An official operation littered with bureaucracy and paperwork, requiring Inspectors' signatures, observation points and agendas, wasn't our preferred tactic. And at the time as many cops will agree all the paperwork was pointless as when it was all signed off in about three days, the scheming toe rag would be long gone. Oh yes brother, me and Duffy would deal with it.

So whenever the radio was quiet, we'd drive down Village Lane, eyes peeled, hoping to get lucky. And back in the summer, as a scorching hot afternoon slipped into the sort of steamy evening beloved of rioters, we'd got exactly the luck we'd been after.

Who should we find on Mrs Lilly's driveway, lurking in the shadows of the trees in her front garden, but Timmy ! And what should he be doing but going through but … a bag? A *hand*bag, in fact, if our eyes didn't deceive us.

What an opportunity! And how very fortunate we were to be there right at that time, I thought … Lets see there's Timmy, us and plenty of time on a lovely summer's evening to discuss matters and get to know each other a bit better. What a perfect scenario. Even if he'd seen us, Timmy wouldn't have run. He couldn't outstrip us in our prime, not a chance, and he knew that the hands-on methods we used back then to detain fleeing suspects – lawful though they were – would hurt. Of course, some who don't run fight, but Timmy wasn't one of those. He was many things, but he only scrapped if the odds were well in his favour.

'Timmy, youth,' said Duffy, by way of introduction. 'Drop the bag, and don't fucking move.' Lets start by saying being polite never worked, talk to them how they would talk to you. Our friend had been so engrossed in going through its contents that he hadn't noticed the two big coppers walking up to him. Now he saw us, and his face was a picture – goggle-eyed horror is probably the best way to describe it.

'If you start, mate, you'll fucking wear this,' added Duffy, holding out his stick.

'Hey lads,' said Timmy. 'Don't you go getting the wrong idea. Mrs Lilly's upset, and I'm making sure she hasn't lost anything. I think she's been burgled.'

He held the bag out and adopted a Jesus Christ pose, offering no threat as I put my own stick away.

It was a promising response, well-delivered, and I will say this: many would have been taken in, had they not known of Timmy and his ways. Duffy went to lay hands on him, and I turned to the house, where Mrs Lilly had appeared on her doorstep.

'Hello officer,' she said. 'There's no need to worry. Timmy has been helping me out, that's all. I've been burgled, and he has been helping me sort out my things.'

I took my hat off – it was all very *Heartbeat* in the suburbs back then – and introduced myself. 'Hello, Mrs Lilly,' I said, with a smile. 'It's me, Kenny Barnes. I don't think this is all that it seems, I'm afraid. Timmy's a bit of a bad lad, you know.'

She smiled back at me. It really was a beautiful day, all bumble bees, roses and sunshine, enhanced by the innocence of this sweet old lady in her ninetieth year. 'Oh, no,' she said. 'No, he's turned over a new leaf. He told me so himself. And he's found God as well. He's been with the minister all afternoon at his cottage.' Mrs Lilly had been told a thousand times, over many years, of the ways of our local criminals, and she always responded in the same way, stating firmly that she wouldn't let them near her house ever again.

And, every time, they chatted their way back in.

She had lost about ten grand over the past five years that *I* knew of. It was frustrating. Like many of the elderly, she couldn't follow the safety advice she was given, she was very trusting, and she was quick to forgive – too quick in my book, if not in the good lords as well. 'He *isn't* helping you, Mrs Lilly,' I said. 'He's actually thieving from you, right now, while you watch him. He isn't making sure things are all right, he's going through your bag. This is what these people do.'

'Oh, but I *told* him to look through it, officer. He said he could locate some fingerprints and give them to you. He knows where to look.'

Somewhere behind me, Timmy hit the floor with a loud 'Oooofffff!' Duffy had found Mrs Lilly's bank card in his pocket, and had quickly restrained him. A moment or two later, handcuffed and whingeing, he was hauled back upright and led to our car.

'Careful with him now, officer,' called Mrs Lilly, a look of concern on her wrinkled face. 'He has an injury from the Falklands, you know.'

I smiled, but through gritted teeth. The only action Timmy Thompson had seen was in the city a few months back, when the *Afro gang* as they were known turned him and his brothers over and nicked a load of speed from the boot of their car. To be honest, that had been like taking sweets from a kid for the Afro lads.

'He served in the regiment, you know,' she added.

'I know, Mrs Lilly,' I said. 'I know'. 'Look, we'll just take him down to the police station for a chat and then I'll be back to take a statement. Is that OK?'

She smiled and waved and disappeared inside. It was all quite surreal.

Thompson was a well-handled lad, fully briefed and predictably, he said nothing in interview. The right to silence was nothing if not a precious bulwark against the bully boys of the State, after all. We charged him with burglary anyway, but Mrs Lilly died two weeks later and the matter never went to court. A DS (Detective Sergeant) from the CID told me later that the CPS wouldn't take it any further without a witness – not that she would necessarily have made the case, anyway. Honestly, what can you say to that ?

So: a thieving scrote caught, bang at it, and he walks away, laughing.

Standard fare from the CPS, I thought. *Any excuse to make* their *lives easier, and screw the victims.*

Of course, over the years I discovered that that's not always the case. As with the police, it's the individual that matters, and their professionalism, not the organisation. Oddly enough, the minister visited by Timmy reported losing two old Victorian watercolours valued at around two grand the very next day. Mrs Lilly had vouched for a nice young man who said he worked in a well-known London gallery. The young man had advised the minister to leave the artwork out in the garden overnight – apparently, the natural monoxides in the night air are famous for retarding the deterioration process from which all art suffers. You just need to do it on a warm, dry night – once a year is enough. It was just a sickening coincidence that some ne'er-do-well had passed by that very night and taken them.

'Rotten luck,' said the minister, shaking his head. 'Who'd have thought they'd be spotted, hidden away in my back garden after eleven o'clock at night?'

He was a bright man, too, but no matter how intelligent people are, there are those whose blinkers work so well that they won't even see the train that kills them until it passes over their body and slices off their fucking head.

Like all my interactions with various MOPS, good bad and indifferent, there is a saying we both should get used to: Honestly, you can't make this stuff up.

* * *

TWO WEEKS LATER I moved from C shift uniform to the CID in the city. I had a right old do out with my old shift, including various husband-seekers and friendless folk, before I casually slipped away. We were a mixed bag.

My pigeonhole was raided for the last time, and as I did so I noticed a new name tag on the front of my personal piece of private space: *PC Ray Davies*. Kinky to those that knew him better than me.I'll let you work that one out.

'Jeez,' I said, to no-one in particular. 'Talk about jumping in to my grave before it gets cold,'

'I know, son,' said a voice behind me. *Sergeant Beaky*. 'We survived for a hundred years before you got here, youth, and we'll survive for another hundred after you've gone. And that's a fact.' He smiled, and squeezed my shoulder. 'You've made a difference to a lot of folk, youth, and you'll do that as long as you care about the real people out there. Just remember, the majority will forget you and only a few will remember you. But it's those few who make this job the best job in the world.'

Beaky smiled, and walked away, and for the first time in five years he actually made a bit of sense. He was right of course, most of us will only be remembered for what we did wrong, not the good we did when the rest of the world was asleep.I made my move. Best get down to Burton's. They had a special suit offer on.

Something grey, double-breasted, with pleated trousers, I fancied.

Meet the Boys !

NOBODY WAS READY for the CID – certainly not the late twentieth century vintage.

Then, as now, its officers investigated the most atrocious, disgusting, hilarious, bizarre, ridiculous and upsetting crimes that people could commit.

The people who commit these offences do so because they are bored, or lazy, or nasty, or mad, or just because they can. Many of them are as well known to their local detectives as they are to their own kids, probably better.

If our regulars put as much time in to finding work and behaving like decent citizens as they do in burgling, robbing, and ripping off old folks, half the cops in the country could jack it in tomorrow and go and do something else.

My first experience of entering a CID office had been as a three-month probationer when I wandered in to pick up something or other and was promptly told to fuck off.

The next time was a year or so later, when I was asked to take something over to them, and was *then* told to fuck off.

The third time, a middle aged chap with a moustache and a friendly-sounding voice actually said, 'Come in, son,' with a smile.

'Er, okay,' I said, nervously.

'Tell you what,' he said. 'Stick the kettle on, eh?'

When I had *stuck* the kettle on, he pointed his finger at the door and said, '*Now* fuck off.'

I didn't take it personally. The ability to fuck off when told to do so was a core competency for the young policeman. Equally, the ability to fuck someone off in a variety of different ways was a learned skill, and not usually an inherent thing. My co-worker with the moustache had spent twenty years in the job fucking people off, and he now had it down to a fine art.

Our uniformed colleagues – and, as things stand, everyone in the police still starts as a uniformed PC (ish) there are some differences today – will tell you that they cannot investigate most offences because they haven't got the time, what with spending their lives tear-arsing around the county from one Facebook row to another. Although it was a long time ago now, I still remember my time under the iconic but thoroughly unsuitable custodian helmet – the official name for the big, Boer war-style, tit-shaped blue hat worn on the beat by male bobbies – and I know that life on the streets is a lot busier now than it was in my time, when we didn't have Facebook, and having a row with your best mate that ended in threats-to-kill all round at least required some physical effort. So I have some sympathy with them on that score.

However, nutters are born and bred no matter the decade.

On the other hand, many CID officers will argue, enthusiastically, that our uniformed colleagues are fucking useless, and lack the ability to investigate their own backsides, let alone a real job. There may be a grain of truth in this, but most are keen or at the end of an unproductive career too, though I've seen many uniformed officers who are more than capable, if given the time, of coming to a very satisfactory conclusion to any investigation. I might go so far as to say that some of them may actually be better at it than a good many CID officers, but then I wouldn't want to destroy the police or public stereotypes of the CID and the uniform branches.

Anyway, the fourth time I set foot in a CID office was on my first morning as a CID aide. And although I wasn't told to fuck off, it was still slightly surreal and more than a touch confusing.

* * *

I HAD BEEN told to report to a DS Tosh, a man I didn't know but had heard plenty about: he had attained a certain iconic status within our little corner of the *old bill*. More specifically, he was widely said to be an inhuman tyrant. Reckoning that my best approach was to look confident, even if I didn't feel it, I walked boldly into the office, through a fug of fag smoke, Brut33, chit-chat and belly laughs, and took the centre ground, ready to have it if needs be.

I recognised a few of the faces.

Lance Legge was there – a chubby little chap of younger years than me, the proverbial ultra-slick detective in dapper rags and a comb in his back pocket.

His sidekick Andy James was an even smoother character. A renowned lover of the ladies, he was wearing impossible to shine any further shiny shoes and had a glowing Embassy Regal balanced carefully in an ancient Watneys Red Barrel ashtray on his desk. (If this sounds a bit like an episode of that TV programme with DCI Gene Hunt, it is, because that's genuinely what it was like. In the world outside, clean-cut, floppy-haired metrosexuals like Jason Donovan and Chesney Hawkes were storming the pop charts; inside our little kingdom of criminal detection, people still had sideburns and perms and, probably, flares.)

I took in Andy's classic Burtons three-piece and kicked myself. *Should have gone for the waistcoat and breast-pocket hanky.* I made a mental note to go back for them.

'Hello mate,' he said, with a cheery smile.

'Hello, bud,' I said. 'I'm the new bloke. Is DS Tosh about?'

Andy smiled and nodded to the corner of the room. 'He's over there, mate, behind *The Racing Post.*'

He winked at me and picked up his phone.

Chin up, I walked across the room, carrying my overflowing box of precariously-balanced accoutrements, appointments, and other stuff. The fug was shading into Hamlet cigars and Old Spice, its subtle notes smacking me about the head and making my eyes water like a misguided student at a riot – and this at a time before thoughts of mortality crept in, when I was a smoker myself. The deafening laughter and chatter continued, though I think I saw one lad who looked a bit like he was working.

I found myself in front of *The Racing Post.*

I coughed politely.

Nothing.

'Hello, er, sarge. I'm Barnesy.'

Not a flicker.

I stood some more, and then some more staring at the Racing Post. *Garrison Savannah* was highly rated for the Gold Cup, apparently.

In front of *The Racing Post* was a desk.

I parked myself down on the corner.

That rattled his cage.

'Move, you fucking moron,' growled the voice behind the paper. 'That's my desk, that is, and unless you're the new sarge you need to fuck off out of it.'

I stood up smartly. I still hadn't had sight of the face, but the voice was enough: a deep, angry bark that sounded like it came from somewhere down Cornwall way. A place where they took no prisoners, except for shipwrecked souls whom they ate in the caves under the rocks.

And by hell was it loud.

A few faces turned my way and a few laughed, a few tutted, and the chatter began again.

'Sorry sarge,' I said. 'Only, I was told to report to you at two o'clock. Shall I come back?'

The paper lowered, and – through a thick blue haze – I saw DS Tosh in the flesh for the first time. He had piercing, gleaming blue eyes, a surprisingly youthful face, and a flicked hairstyle that was not dissimilar to that worn by Hitler, or the bloke out of The Human League. Not for him the common grey suit: he was dressed like a farmer, in a greasy Barbour, a green checked shirt, and a brown tie.

'Do you like fish 'n' chips, son?' he said, with a wolfish leer.

'Er, yes, sarge,' I said, nodding furiously. 'Yes, I do like fish and chips.'

It was good to find some common ground, to get the first hurdle out the way. Mind you, he could have asked me if I liked being smacked in the gob with a piece of two-by-two, and I'd have agreed.

He weighed me up for a moment, and then grinned.

'Good,' he said. 'Later on we'd better have some then, eh, constable? Later on, we'll get ourselves to that chippy on the estate and have us some haddicks and chips, haddicks and chips, for tea, for you and me.'

He almost sang the last bit and waved his fist in a Broadway musical sort of way. My feeling was that it was absolutely ridiculous, though I tried not to let on.

'Now get that kettle on, constable, and get me a cup of that tea stuff.'

The Racing Post snapped back up to obscure his face. From behind it came his voice again, the yokelish, West Country drawl now even more pronounced, and even more concerning.

'I loves them chips, me,' he said. 'I *loves* them haddicks and chips.'

I looked at the tea corner. *Better make that tea stuff strong, sugary and hot*, I thought.

* * *

THE KETTLE CLICKED off the boil, and I felt a presence behind me.

It belonged to a jovial-looking chap – mid-thirties, slight squint, pencil tucked strategically behind an ear.

'Hello, matey,' he said, holding out his hand. 'I'm Brookesy.'

Brookesy looked like he'd arrived late to a jumble sale – he was wearing a baggy jumper (yellow) over a checked farmer's boy shirt (red and black) and some crumpled cream things which, speculatively, I identified as trousers. The badge on his jumper said 'Housemartins'. He was lean, and had one of those interesting faces.

'Ken Barnes,' I said, shaking his hand. 'I'm the new attachment.'

He smiled and patted my back, leaning in conspiratorially.

'Don't worry, mate,' he said. 'We've all been here before, and we all know how you feel… even that grumpy twat.'

The words 'that grumpy twat' were accompanied by a nod in the direction of *The Racing Post*, but discretion – or cowardice – led him to lower his voice enough so as not to be heard.

'It's all an act, Ken boy,' he said. 'It's all an act.'

I nodded.

'Mind you,' he added. 'It can be a fucking scary act sometimes. Mine's two sugars, alright?' He gave me a thumbs up.

These words were prophetic. Not the bit about two sugars – though that was fairly constant too – but the bit about acting. Over the years, I would develop the greatest of respect, admiration and affection for DS Tosh – rude, aggressive and downright weird as he was – but that didn't alter the fact that he was permanently starring in his own never-ending episode of *The Sweeney*. And before The Sweeney started as well. Unusually in my opinion.

For younger readers, this was a 1970's police show set in the Met's Flying Squad – a team of detectives which chased all over London after armed robbers, fuelled by Bells whisky, Piccadilly fags, and late night rumbles – and its ripples had spread far and wide.

Of course, by the time I even thought of joining the job, John Thaw star of the Sweeney was poncing about Oxford in another far fetched detective series in a classic Jag, solving improbable murders by brute intellect while drinking real ale and listening to Vivaldi.

But in the real world, life was still imitating the art that had once imitated life – if that's not too confusing. Long after Jack Regan would have been given a ten-stretch for fitting up some blagger, officers were still flapping their gums about brasses and shooters, spinning drums and dropping knickers. All this whilst wearing sheepskin coats and drinking Johnnie Walker Red Label out of plastic cups – even if they had to hide the winces as they swallowed it, or craftily pour it into the pot plants when they thought I wasn't looking.

I suppose we all need heroes, and something to believe in.

And DS Tosh was no different.

Precisely none of which occurred to me as I choked my way through air that was thick with smoke and ribald laughter with that first mug of hot, sweet tea for the sarge.

'Here you go, sarge,' I said, placing it carefully on his desk. 'Best I can do.'

The Racing Post was lowered again.

He took the tea and slurped.

A moment's recognition.

A sniff, a further sip, and a smile.

'I likes'ee, officer Barnes,' he bellowed. 'I likes 'ee a lot.'

I smiled.

He smiled.

I smiled a bit more, and he smiled even more.

We were the smiliest detectives, albeit one of them a trainee, who had never detected at this level.

Then he slung his thumb over his shoulder. 'Now, fuck off out of 'ere and gets me some car keys.'

* * *

IT SEEMED I HAD passed my first assignment with flying colours, and two hours later – full of them haddicks and chips – I sat down in the office opposite my new co-pilot, Wolfie.

DS Tosh approached me, having lifted a large bundle of crime files from the top of a cupboard, and – dramatically blowing off the dust (did I mention the dust in this place?) – he slammed them down on my desk.

'Here Barnesy,' he said. 'You reckon you're a good copper, son… So good-copper this fucking lot, and write 'em up!'

He rubbed his hands together, clapping them and cackling.

I *hadn't* claimed to be a good copper, actually, but I didn't think it was worth pointing that out. I'll just get on I thought.

'They be *just* the jobs for you, Constable Barnes!'

I gazed at my immediate investigative future – a green cardboard bundle of crumpled papers and files which lay staring back at me from my desk, all draw-stringed and criss-crossed. Wolfie looked up, and looked down again. He sparked up a Red Band, and carried on writing a statement.

'If I were you,' he said, his head still down, 'I'd get yourself a strong cup of something and think very carefully as you work through that little lot, Kenny boy. Very carefully indeed.' His sharp intake of breath was followed by a loud exhale. Poignant.

Across the room Karen – our token female officer, it was pretty much a boys' club back then – stared at the scene: me, the files, then Wolfie, and then Tosh.

All sat in one corner.

One happy family – smoke, tea and me, with the look of the hopeless abandoned on my face. It felt like the eyes of the world were upon me, and, in a way, they were. I was being stitched up somehow, I was sure of it. It was the 'how' part I couldn't put my finger on. I had to work it out quickly, but without displaying any emotion and without any stress.

I now know exactly what Karen was thinking, but then I know a lot more today than I did back then. Back then – as Tosh would be keen to inform me over the coming weeks and months – I was *'just a boy in a man's world Barnesy, a boy in a man's fucking world.'*

The dust settled, the string was unravelled and, like my career to date, it was a very thin piece of rope indeed.

I began to read.

The crime files talked of arson, GBH, drugs and assault.

Horrible people stalking other horrible people, sitting out all night and watching each other as they played out their lives, and in two cases with themselves.

Threats of death and fire, sex and fuckery…

It all leapt out of those pages, the unseen undercurrents of our little city. No crime thriller would ever match these tales, because these tales were real-life tales.

You could not make them up.

I moved from job to job, noting the detail and scrutinising the information collected by Detective Constable This and Detective Sergeant That. I made notes and looked busy, but inside I was unravelling like the string in front of me.

Basic stuff, like the continuity of evidence and the summaries of information, was all over the shop. Nothing made sense.

It was very weird.

What the hell was 'larceny'?

And the procedure for each investigation seemed flawed, and was missing obvious things. As I ploughed on, it occurred to me that maybe this wasn't for me, after all. I spent the rest of that shift on those files, but fuck me if I could find the starting point on any of them.

Just what was DS Tosh expecting from me?

Wolfie looked up and grinned at me from time to time, as did Karen.

The odd detective (no pun intended) appeared and disappeared, stopping momentarily to look at my desk and tut or just sigh, as he returned with a tea or a coffee. They were all smiling, and I couldn't help noticing that one or two even looked to be sniggering behind their hands. One even looked at me with something that might have approached compassion, but it was probably wind.

Eventually, not sure whether I had finished – or even started – I looked up.

The clock said it was eleven, we finished at midnight, an hour later … I think. My wife wouldn't be up but she would be awake and hoping I was okay, and my two youngsters would be fast asleep, safe, cosy and secure.

The sarge was standing there, fag on, tea in hand, staring intently right at me.

'Well, Barnesy,' he said. 'What do you reckon then, boy?'

His green Barbour jacket was wide open, displaying his brown trousers, check shirt, and brown tie; he looked like a minor member of the landed gentry, or perhaps a head gamekeeper.

He took a sip of tea, and I took a look down at the open file in front of me.

I looked up, and then quickly looked down again.

Finally, I sat back. 'Er, Sarge…'

'Yes, Barnesy?'

'What the fuck is larceny, and why are all these files a bag of tits?'

'A baaag of tits!' Tosh screamed, splashing tea on the grubby grey carpet tiles at his feet. 'A fucking baaag of tits!' He burst out laughing. 'Here,' he shouted to the rest of the office, which by now numbered only four. 'Here, Barnesy says 'his, his, his work's a baaag of tits!' Mass laughter.

He spilled more tea, his laughter increased, and his voice got louder, as he yodelled and chokeled and slapped his thigh in what was evidently, for him, a moment of uncontrollable comedy.

'A bag of fucking tits, Barnesy?' he said, when he had recovered enough to speak properly. 'What *do* you mean?' He stopped laughing immediately and stared at me piercingly.

Oh dear. I started that 'Er' thing again.

'Er, well, er, it's, er…'

'Fucking *er*?' said the sarge. 'What the fuck does "Er" mean, Barnesy? Speak up! Tells me about the tits!'

He was getting more Farmer Giles by the minute; he was actually dancing from foot to foot, a mindless fucking Cornish yam. Was I the victim of some bizarre practical joke? Was he a theatrical lunatic just purporting to be the cops?

'The tits, Barnesy!' he yelled. 'The tits! Come on, Barnesy, tells me about the tits!'

I tried to explain myself. 'Well sarge, it's… er… Well, the whole thing seems dated, it's out of sorts, and it doesn't make sense at all.

Maybe this isn't for me, but I can't see the wood for the trees here, sarge, I really can't. Not at all.'

Suddenly, Tosh stopped jigging and talking about tits. He sat down, leant over towards me, and grabbed the files, wrapping them up in the string they had been bound in.

'Constable,' he growled, like a sinister Jethro, 'I'm disappointed in you, I really am. Them jobs should have taken you at least five days to get to grips with. That's the average. One took… 'ow long, Wolfie?'

Wolfie was putting on his coat. 'Oh, a month, Tosh. Three weeks, at least.'

'Yeah, Phil took a month to do 'is. And where's 'e now, Wolfie?'

'I think he's on foot patrol in the town centre, Tosh,' said my colleague. 'You know, wandering about rattling shop door handles.'

Wolfie illustrated this fate by adopting the look of a demented village idiot, and blended that with a chicken clucking, as he started walking oddly and looking out of the office window making odd noises and… Well, I got the idea.

'Yeah,' said Tosh. 'That's where 'e is, Barnesy, rattling them doors.' He mimed rattling a door himself, and adopted a gormless face by way of accompaniment. 'I'm rattling shop doors for a living,' he said, mock-forlornly. 'Rattling doors, that's what I does.'

I looked straight at Tosh, and then at Wolfie, and scratched my face. They were all clearly stark, staring mad. 'I'll be off, then,' I said, and stood up to go.

'Oh, you're going nowhere, boy,' said DS Tosh. 'You've got one more job before you can go 'ome, and it's not 'ere. You owes me and Wolfie 'ere a bit of your time, and that time is best spent at the other nick across the road. Come on, let's go.'

I hadn't realised there *was* another nick across the road. There was a multi-storey carpark, a chippy and the Brown Jug pub. But I dutifully followed the DS and Wolfie out of the CID office, down the stairs and across the road.

Five minutes later, we were in the Brown Jug, supping old timers' special ale, having found a space in the corner of the snug. It was a proper pub, no doubt about it. It had that not all bad stale smell of hops about it

Wolfie winked at me, and Tosh took a large gulp of the brown stuff from his pint. He neither looked at me nor away from me, he just gazed straight ahead.

'Welcome to the CID, new 'un,' he said, blowing froth off his upper lip. 'I loikes you a lot, I does. I sees a lot of me in you, back twenty year ago. I loikes you, new 'un.'

No further words were spoken for quite some time.

Just staring straight ahead.

I didn't like to say anything, as I didn't have a clue as to what might be appropriate, and neither Tosh nor Wolfie seemed to want to break the silence. So, we all supped our ales and stared straight ahead at nothing in particular.

The smoke swirled, and the bar chat around us continued – it was not dissimilar, in fact, to the CID office we had just left. The only difference was that now I felt an indescribable surge of hope, and a genuine feeling of having found a new and most welcome home.

Not in the pub – although that helped – and not, particularly, in the company in which I had recently found myself. No, I felt I'd found my path. I felt I knew, suddenly, what life I had decided to live.

I was on the CID, and, yes, I had sat the old timer's test of giving a new DC a shit load of shit files to try and investigate, and I'd passed the test. Sure, I was only the attachment for the next four months, and a lot depended on the big CID course I hoped to do after that up at headquarters, with other like-minded officers. But for now, after day one, I felt almost complete, smoking and drinking with my peers – yes, they felt like my peers – in the Brown Jug pub.

All together in the snuggy bar. Life couldn't get much better than this. I undid my tie, relaxed back in my seat, and smiled.

'Watcha smiling at, young 'un?' came the familiar pirate's growl.

'Nothing sarge,' I said. 'I'm just tired.'

'Don't call me sarge in 'ere,' he said. 'In 'ere I'm Tosh. I'm your buddy 'ere, and don't you forget it.'

Now he was staring right at me, piercing me with his eyes again, waiting for a response.

I raised my glass. 'Cheers, sarge,' I said, and smiled.

He hooted and Wolfie winked at me again as he blew the froth off another pint.

Information Received

I MANAGED TO GET through the next few days without too many blunders and fuck-ups. I made the tea, fetched haddicks and chips, and generally tried not to catch anyone's eye. That seemed to suit DS Tosh and the rest of them, who seemed to be easing me in gently. I certainly wasn't doing any actual detective work.

My first sniff of anything approaching what I was being paid for came early one afternoon, when the big grey phone on my desk rang.

I picked it up.

It was the central control room.

'Wolfie?'

'No, Barnesy.'

'*Who?*'

'PC Barnes. I'm on attachment.'

'Well, is Wolfie there?'

'No, he's, er… He's just popped out on a job.'

If you call nipping down to Ladbrokes with a tenner and a tip for the 3.30 at Goodwood a job, that is.

'Ah, down the bookies, is he?'

'No… What makes you say that?'

'Never mind. Right, I've got this bloke on the phone, wants to talk about an affray. Or an assault. Or something.'

The line clicked off, and there was a few seconds of dead air while the control room patched our friend through.

'Hello?'

'Hello.'

'Is that the police?'

'Yes.'

'Only, I was trying to call the police?'

'Congratulations, you've succeeded.' I said.

'Right. Well, what it is, like… But I've just explained all this to someone else?'

'Yes, but then they've passed you through to me.'

'Why's that, then?' A confused response.

'Well, their job's just to answer the phone and then decide who you need to talk to, really.' This felt like it would be a long conversation.

'So they think I need to speak to you, then?' Said the caller.

'That's right, yes. So how can I help?'

'Well, what it is, like… I was in bed this morning, yeah, and the door goes. So I gets up and goes down, yeah, and it's…'

'Hold on a sec,' I said. 'Can I just start by getting a few details from you, sir? Your name, please?'

'Why do I have to give you my name?' Was an alarmed response.

'Well, if you want us to investigate something – such as a crime, perhaps – I need to know who you are.'

'Why?'

'I just do.'

'But I don't trust the fucking police – no offence.'

'So why are you ringing us?'

There was a lengthy silence, while he turned this one over in his mind. Eventually, he said, 'I ain't no grass, see?'

'I never said you were.'

'Normally, like, I won't help the police. No offence.'

'None taken.' I looked at a discarded burning cigarette in an ashtray close-by and began to see the relevance of them.

'So I ain't grassing no-one up.'

'Understood. Your name, then?' I tried again.

'Dave… Smith.'

'Really?'

'Oh, fuck it. Alright, it's Dave Kelly.'

'Address?

'12b Mariner Avenue. Top floor flat.'

A street very well-known to me from my six years in uniform.

'So what's the problem, Dave?' I said, pen poised. Just then Wolfie walked in, whistling, hung his jacket over the chair opposite me, and made the universal 'fancy a brew' gesture.

'Well, like I said, I was in bed this morning, yeah, and the door goes. So I gets up and goes down, yeah, and it's only fucking Kev Jones. So he says to me, "Right, you bastard, your missus stopped my missus's kid in the street yesterday and told him he was a twat and he said…" This was proper Facebook stuff before it was even a remotely interesting idea.

It went on like this for quite some time; I tried to work out what the salient points were, and made a note of them – all the while knowing full-well that none of the parties involved would ever make formal statements (they ain't no grasses see) and that the whole thing was, in job parlance, LOB (load of bollocks).

But here's the thing. As he set down my mug of tea – the first that someone *else* in the department had made for *me* – Wolfie's eyes ran down my notepad and stopped near the top, at the words 'Kev Jones'.

He stabbed it with his forefinger. 'That bastard's wanted for that jewellery shop job a few months back,' he hissed, as I covered the mouthpiece. 'We haven't been able to find him. Keep this idiot talking and see if you can find out where Jones is?'

And so it was that Dave Kelly – who ain't no grass, see – led us straight to the guy who'd boshed a bloke over the head at Ratners and had it away on his toes with a couple of grands-worth of what the proprietor of that particular chain would soon describe as 'crap'. Crap it might have been, but that was still a robbery, all day long, and Jones was soon doing a four-stretch. Which is what we in the trade call a result. More on this very shortly.

* * *

WHAT REALLY MAKES a CID team tick is information.

A lot is made of technology in this regard.

In 1990, at the start of my career as a detective, we had just taken delivery of a rake of gleaming new terminals, then called 'CAD screens', which stored details of incidents and relevant intelligence.

We were tremendously impressed with them: at last, we were moving into the mid-1960s!

We also developed a unique way of referencing our age-old paper system of thousands of reports, incidents, and people. We might have fancy computers now, but, like all hoarders, we couldn't let go of our paper-based collection. After all, we might need it later.

But info – whether stored electronically, or in a dusty old filing cabinet somewhere in the bowels of the nick – has to come from somewhere.

There's CCTV, electronic trails, forensics and all that, which are all very well, and not to be sniffed at.

But *people* are where it's really at. They're the tangible information system.

A whisper here, a tip there, an address passed on, or a suspicious conversation overheard – it doesn't have to be massive, it's all about the jigsaw.

Put the pieces together, and, the next thing you know, you're locking up a gangland killer, capturing a gang of armed robbers, or cracking a big drugs ring.

Accidental informants like our friend Dave Kelly are a nice little bonus when they drop out of the sky with the last shower of rain, but they're obviously not enough.

Actual informants – people who move in the right circles, and keep their eyes peeled and their ears to the ground – are vital. Where would Starsky and Hutch have been without Huggy Bear?

I'd always prided myself on having good communication skills, and it had paid off many times. I like people, generally, and they seem to like me. I can chat with most folks about most things, and when it comes to work – in the land of 'getting information' – my approachable style and sunny nature usually ensure the person I'm talking to feels confident enough to speak freely, and I mean this for both witnesses and suspects. That's probably why I got offered that original CID attachment all those years ago.

Tosh was certainly very keen to check me out in this respect.

'Young 'un,' he growled, one afternoon, spitting bits of battered haddicks around the place, and picking at his teeth with his warrant card. 'Now then, 'as you got any informants, lad?'

'I've got a few, sarge,' I said. 'Nothing official, though,' I added, hastily. 'I mean, two or three, here and there. They just talk to me whenever they think I can help.'

I always studied his face for a reaction when I answered his questions.

It hinted as to what was coming next.

His face told me that he wanted to explore this further.

'I'm going to need to gain their acquaintance, Barnesy lad,' he said. "You needs to introduce me. We needs to get them on board, proper like, so we can *glean* them properly, and get to the root of their real problems. Do you know what I means?'

He liked the verb 'to glean', and used it in all the wrong places.

'I'm not sure they would talk to anyone else, sarge,' I said, almost flinching. 'I'm not sure that would work.'

I was expecting an uproar, and I got one.

'This needs controlling properly!' he yelled, slapping the warrant card down on my desk and leaning over me with his fishy breath and bulging eyes. "Get your big head in to the manuals, boy, and look at the procedures! We can't have you willy-fucking-nilly talking to cunts and scrotes and not logging it down or making a proper record in the right way! You okay with that, you fucking bozo?"

I couldn't say much by way of response, other than a meek, 'Yes, sarge.'

Tosh was right, of course. What he was actually saying, in his own inimitable style, was that each person who spoke to us on an informant basis had to be 'registered'. From there, they had to be controlled by a Detective Sergeant, and managed by the originating

Detective Constable. A record would be made of all contact, and we would always work in pairs.

This was so for two reasons.

The first was to protect the source. We'd keep everything on a need-to-know basis. I wouldn't necessarily know Wolfie's snouts, and he wouldn't know mine. That way, it's rare that anyone gets compromised.

The second was to limit the likelihood of corruption. Any information we received would be rewarded – usually with money, though sometimes favours might be done. Everyone is human, and when you have villains and cops talking in secret, and cash changing hands, the risk is obvious.

And yes, most proper sources *are* villains. You set a thief to catch a thief, and there's not much point using your local vicar as a source on a big row between biker gangs or crack dealers. You need to get stuck into the criminals themselves – and forget all that bollocks about not being a grass. Most criminals, no matter how big they think they are, or how notorious, will talk to us at some point.

Why? Well, they're cowards when it comes to bird: if they're looking at a proper jail sentence, they can't wait to tell you what they know so you'll put a good word in for them with the judge.

And if they're not personally in the frame, waving a few tenners in their faces – when they're sure no-one will find out – can work wonders.

There's also revenge. What better way to stitch up the bloke who's been shagging your missus, or who made you look bad in front of your mates, than to turn him in to the old bill?

Obviously, we have to be careful we're not taking sides in a war between criminal gangs or individuals – that could get a bit smelly. We're not there to be used for their ends – it has to be proper and honourable, so a lot of checks are made. But it's undeniably a motivation for some informants.

The upshot is that you can ram all that, 'I ain't no grass, see?' stuff right where the sun don't shine. It's mostly just a charade for the benefit of anyone who might be listening. All that said, my 'informants' at that stage weren't hard-core blaggers or general villainous types: they were more like a few nice people I'd come in to contact with over the years. One thing I was sure of, they wouldn't warm to a lunatic like Tosh. In fact, if they met him there was a fair chance they would call the police!

I had to have a careful think as to how to play this one.

* * *

AS IT TURNED OUT, the timing couldn't have been any better.

Pretty much as Tosh walked away, Duffy came bouncing in to the office in uniform.

I was pleased to see him. I'd been the CID aide for approximately a week at this point, but it seemed like years since I'd been sat in the car with him, chewing the fat, pulling over the odd driver, and blue-lighting it to pub fights in our own well-controlled, well-manicured way.

'Barnesy boy,' he said. 'Can I have a word?'

'Of course, mate,' I said, 'What's the problem?'

Duffy looked right and left and leaned in, conspiratorially. 'Timmy Thompson wants to talk,' he whispered.

I was amazed – not least by the fact that Duffy had managed to speak to Timmy in such a way that Timmy wanted to speak back.

'How did you crack that, mate?' I said.

'I went on that informant introduction course at the big house the other day,' he said. 'I saw him in the yard a minute ago and I thought I'd try out some of the techniques on him. I just went up to him while he was having a fag. I thought he'd tell me to fuck off, but once he'd started he couldn't stop. I had to tell the bastard to shut up in the end.'

Duffy looked genuinely shocked that his love of gossip and undoubted gift of the gab actually had a policing application and could work on criminals as opposed to just impressionable young women.

'Why didn't you just go for it yourself?' I said. 'Why involve me?'

'Ah, I thought I'd better get a detective to speak to him. You know, an expert.'

I looked around the office, grinned and said, 'Well, that must be me, youth.'

Had I not been so busy puffing myself up in my grey nylon suit, I might have thought about this more carefully, and then I'd have realised that Duffy was just passing on work. He either couldn't be bothered to deal with an informant, or didn't know how. He'd never had one before – unless you counted the ladies in admin, who spoke to him daily, mostly with their hands on his truncheon.

'Where is he now, Duff?' I said.

'Still in the fucking yard,' he said. 'Probably still chopsing away to anyone who'll listen.'

This was great: if I could bring Timmy in, it would save me the embarrassment of admitting to the sarge that two of my 'informants' ran local neighbourhood watch schemes, and the third was a teacher who knew my wife from aerobics.

All I needed to do was sign Timmy up, show I could deal with an informant, and kudos would be mine. I got up from my chair, feeling that glow we all get when we're on a roll. I felt confident.

'Lead the way, Duffers,' I said. 'Let's go to work.'

DS Tosh looked up from some paperwork across the office. 'Where you going, young 'un?' he inquired, genially. Smoke accompanying his words.

This was tricky. I'd been hoping to slip out unnoticed. Duffy was no help: he just looked at me like a frightened animal, and virtually bolted for the door. He didn't like Tosh. More to the point – he was petrified of him.

I decided to come clean. 'Just off down the smells, sarge,' I said. 'Timmy Thompson wants to talk.'

'Does he, by fuck?' said Tosh, raising his eyebrows. 'Then you better be getting yourself down there, son, and see what the prick wants to say.'

This was going better than I'd thought it might. He seemed almost enthusiastic; I had expected him to take over, or give it to a more experienced DC – not to trust the aide.

'Yes, sarge,' I said.

'Oh, and Barnesy?'

'Yes, sarge?'

'Don't make a cunt of yourself, and keep your head on.'

'Yes, sarge.'

The cells were a bustling, smelly mass of shouting, banging, piss, sweat, and hot chocolate. Young runners – legal reps – trying it on to gain an advantage with even younger uniforms. Two cell guards, both relief constables from the shift – that was me, a fortnight ago – running about with all-day breakfasts, hot drinks and fags. The custody sarge keeping a lid on his temper, but you just sensed that it wasn't far from blowing. The groaning and shouting, the moaning and barking from the confined souls in their cells, it was incessant, and the closest thing you'll ever see to a human zoo.

Shooting my cuffs and adjusting the new red hankie in my top pocket, I quickly found the custody board for Timmy, and signed myself in to the yard.

'A/DC Barnes to yard for cells debrief' it read, and I don't mind admitting that it looked bloody mint. Sadly, this was well before mobile phones, let alone mobile phones with 10 megapixel cameras, so I never did get a picture. Still, I blinked and preserved the image

on my own retinas for posterity.

Duffy was gone, his mission to quickly pass on the job and get on with another half measure was done. The yard camera would pick up the interaction between me and Timmy, but there was no audio.

I sensed a butterfly or two as I walked in to the yard, which was the outside on the inside – a small, windowless structure open to the heavens but corralled in by the rest of the nick. The walls were wet with recent rain, and the roar of the traffic on the main road outside bounced around a bit.

'Timmy,' I said, walking towards him and trying to look and sound more confident than I felt. 'How goes it?' it was a culmination of dark spaces and yellow light.

He was dressed like a forty-year-old ragamuffin, unshaven, overweight, and breathless in jeans, a black Harrington, and grey Dunlop trainers that had once been white. The same clothes, in fact, that he'd been wearing the last time we had met.

And the time before that, too.

His fingernails were black, and the sleeve of his shirt carried a smear of something brown and unpleasant. He wasn't *GQ*'s Man of the Year, put it that way. But he did know who did what around town, and where, and, most importantly, when.

So I was prepared to give him the time of day.

'Fuck me,' he said, on seeing me. 'He told me a proper detective was coming to see me, not a shop dummy. You're the wanker who arrested me for that daft old lady, ain't you? I told you I was innocent. It got dropped. And you fucking hit me.'

No-one had hit him, and it was Duffy who'd nicked him, but these sorts often get things wrong or just make stuff up to suit the moment.

'She died not long after that, you nasty cunt,' I said. 'That's why they dropped the charges. Now, do you want to make this happen, or do I leave now? I'm not bothered either way.'

I looked straight at him, close enough to smell his fag-ridden breath.

Timmy stared at me, and backed away slowly, gaining some space. The yellow light crossing his face. He took one last drag on his cigarette, and flicked it against the wall.

'Get me out of here and I'll talk,' he said, his voice echoing round the red brick walls.

'It doesn't work like that, Timmy,' I said. 'You're not in the Mafia, I'm not in the FBI, and neither of us are in a film. You don't dictate to us how it goes, we tell you. What are you in for, anyway?'

'It's bollocks, mate,' he said, bitterly. 'It's absolute rubbish. Some handling shit from a bit of stuff I found round the back of Tesco's, mush.'

With lads like Timmy, it's always rubbish, it's always found at the back of somewhere, and sadly it's nearly always believed by the CPS, (Crown Prosecution Service) the magistrates, or a jury. The amount of stuff people claim to find lying around our streets would give the impression we were living in Dick Whittington's London, only paved with tellies, old ladies' jewellery, and bacon.

'Alright,' I said. 'I'll speak to someone. You hang on here for a bit. You got a brief?' (Solicitor)

'No, mush.'

I locked the yard door and went to seek out the officer in the case. It was a lad called Mark Dickens, who I knew well from my years on shift, and I found him in the back office, supping a hot cardboard tea, staring morosely into space, and taking advantage of a few moments' respite from the constant shouting out front.

'What's the score with Timmy Thompson, Dicko?' I said. I sat down and gave him an opportunity to speak.

'Arrested on a stop-check, mate,' he said, slurping tea. 'I saw him driving, he hasn't got any insurance so I've pulled him for that. But then I've found a statue from a burglary in his boot. It was from that old lady's house in Village Lane.'

'She's dead, mate,' I said.

'I know,' said Mark. 'But what could I do?'

He was right. It was a good stop.

'Who's won the job?' I said.

'Some dickhead on the CID,' he said, with a chuckle. 'Some new lad. A fucking aide, I think they said. Tosher the tosser has sorted it.' He smiled, pointed at a bundle of papers and slapped my back. 'Best of luck, youth.'

Tosh had kept his finger on the pulse, he wasn't daft. In the short time it took me to make my way across the car park to the cells he had sprinkled his personal desires all over the job.

It dawned on me that Mark was Duffy's new crew mate. I felt oddly jealous, and shook my head. 'You bastard,' I said.

'Yes, mate,' he grinned. 'I may well be, but I ain't working with that fucking monster Tosh, and I *am* finishing on time. Have a nice day, Barnesy.'

He strolled out, whistling, and I fished up the papers.

I didn't read them: I didn't need to. not yet. I knew the score here, and Timmy didn't. I went to track down the custody sarge, who was doing a passable impression of a homicidal, PMT-addled mother dealing with a kitchen-full of toddlers.

Like all custody skippers, his whole life only had meaning insofar as he could get rid of as many prisoners as possible in as quick a time as possible. Justice was not irrelevant, exactly, but it was certainly a side issue. No custody sergeant wants prisoners in his (or her) cells; they bring far too many problems with them, and further to that they also bring a host of incredibly *odd* issues with them. Some kill themselves, some die for no apparent reason (both of which lead to the police on duty being accused of murder, irrespective of the evidence), and others harm themselves continuously, meaning a uniform has to sit and watch them whilst they spend their time with us.

Some just rant and rave, or press their cell buzzers permanently, or find other creative ways to wind up plod. In short, prisoners are a right pain in the arse and, believe me, if we could get away without arresting any of them we would.

But I could turn this to my advantage.

Timmy Thompson was a prisoner.

Ergo, he was a pain in the arse.

Ergo again, me and the 'custard' sarge could strike a deal.

* * *

ONCE I HAD EXPLAINED to the sarge that the old lady to whom the property belonged was dead, that we had a statement, but that we would have to run it by the CPS, he couldn't *wait* to give Timmy bail.

All done and dusted in ten minutes.

'I'll get him from the yard, sarge,' I said.

'Yeah, cheers, Barnesy,' he said. 'It's a shame all our jobs aren't as easy as this one, mate.'

He was smiling, he was on board, and the pent up rage was clearly subsiding. There was a faraway look on his face: nearly knocking-off time, and he could almost taste that ice-cold tin of Carlsberg, his tea on a tray in front of *Dempsey and Makepeace*, with that *blonde bird* and the smarmy Yank smashing it on the streets of London. Shame Mrs 'Custard' Sarge doesn't look a tiny bit more like the *blonde bird*, but if he plays his cards right…

Well, you never know, it's the little things after a shift in this hell hole.

'I'll go and get him now, shall I?' I said. 'Best get rid while we can, eh?'

I was right back in the confidence zone, bouncing towards the yard.

I opened the door. 'OK, Timmy,' I said. 'Chop-chop, let's go.'

Timmy looked at me with a new respect. 'Am I out, boss?' he said.

'You certainly are, my smelly little friend. I've worked the oracle, had a few words in the right ears. You're out on bail. Let's get the papers sorted, and then we can have our little chinwag.'

To all intents and purposes, Timmy saw this as a result, and me as some sort of miracle worker. Being a bit of a thicko, he had no idea at all how it had occurred, and it didn't cross his mind that it would have happened anyway without me – just an hour or so later, that's all. He didn't understand, and he didn't much care. All he saw was a bail notice, and sunlight.

'Nice one, boss,' he said. 'I appreciate this.'

'You'd *better* appreciate it, Timmy,' I said. 'I've had to walk over hot coals for you, I really have.'

'Don't worry, boss,' he said. 'I owe you, big time.'

One-nil to Barnesy.

Timmy was quickly processed and traipsed through the police station behind me. Carefully avoiding the more confidential areas, we made it through to reception and thence to the front office.

'You sit there, Timmy,' I said. 'My boss will be down for a word in a minute.'

A few moments passed, during which I tried not to inhale through my nose, and then Tosh walked in.

'What the fuck's going on here?' shouted Timmy, leaping up from his seat. 'What the fuck is *this*?'

'Calm down, Timmy!' I said, slightly nonplussed. 'This is my sarge, that's all. He needs to be present when we meet… This is the first meeting, it's all about trust.'

'Trust?' he yelped. 'Calm fucking down? This cunt, he locked me up for a three-stretch ten year ago!'

Tosh smiled, fondly. 'I did, didn't I, Timmy lad?' he said. 'And I'll do it again if you don't shut your neck. There's people on the other side of that door who wouldn't like to hear about our arrangement. Now grow up, and let's talk business.'

There was a bit of chuntering and posturing, but eventually Timmy sat his arse back down. He wasn't happy, but – as he saw it – he was in something of a cleft stick, even if he couldn't tell you what a cleft stick was, exactly.

'We're a three-way street here, Tim,' I said, once the atmosphere was down a notch. '*Your* job from now on is to talk to *us*, and *our* job is to look after *you*.'

It was a hard thing to say to a guy who I knew preyed on elderly ladies, and other weak and vulnerable people, but it's all about the greater good.

I'm doing *The Lord's Work,* here.

As long as it's legal, I can't let it matter to me.

I explained to Timmy that this first meeting was a test, to see how real and transparent he was being, and to see if he really meant business. After that, depending on the information he passed on, money would be agreed, favours might be forthcoming.

'That's another reason why the sarge is here,' I said. 'To look after the both of us. As an independent voice.'

'Yeah, and to make sure you don't make cunts out of my officers,' added Tosh, friendly as ever. He certainly had his way.

Timmy seemed to understand, we marched on, and he gave us a few snippets about this and that, including the whereabouts of a stolen video player from a recent burglary. By now, he had moved from 'smell' through 'stink' to 'reek', and in such a small room this wasn't okay at all.

'Have you shit yourself, Timmy?' Tosh inquired, conversationally.

'Fuck off, mush!' snapped Timmy. He looked offended. 'I have a shower every day.'

This seemed highly unlikely to me, and to Tosh. 'What, in your own shit?' the sarge said laughing.

I tapped my papers together on the desk.

'Anyway, ladies,' I said, 'let's get this signed up, eh, sarge? Then Timmy can get along home to have his daily ablutions and shower.'

As I spoke, I looked directly into the eyes of Tosh, nodding slowly.

He got the message. 'Yes, constable, we will get this signed up now,' he said, another millimetre move possibly towards some form of respect. Then he looked at Timmy. 'And if you've led us a dance on this video recorder, I'll stick every job I can find on you, do you understand?'

He jabbed his finger right at Timmy's face for emphasis.

Timmy pretended to bite his finger in fright, and raised his eyebrows. 'Aye, sarge,' he whispered, his eyes growing large and his forehead wrinkling. 'Let's be friends, eh? It's very lonely when you're on your own, isn't it?'

The threat was lost on Tosh.

But it was there.

* * *

LATER THAT DAY, five uniforms smashed in Martha Dyer's back doors (literally, not figuratively – if you saw her back then, you wouldn't have touched her with Timmy's) and, as advertised, a stolen video player was recovered and restored to its lawful owner.

As a buy-one-get-one-free, her son tried to thump one of the officers as they stormed through the door, so he met with a lock-up as well.

It was a lovely end to a lovely day.

Martha met her muffins and got a handling charge, her son 'Brutus' Dyer had an assault-police thrown at him, and later on that year fell to his death up Crabby Hill.

Apparently, he wasn't pushed.

The CID office late that evening contained only me, Tosh, and

Wolfie, in a dimly-lit, dusty corner. In the lamplight we picked over the bones of the day.

'That's a good old job there, young 'un,' Tosh said, staring at me. 'Nice 'n' sleazy does it every time.' Again those south westerly chimes accompanied by a weird arm movement.

'Cheers, sarge,' I said. 'Will you sign my overtime before we knock off?'

'Not only will I do that, young 'un, but I'll buys you a pint of that ale as well,' he said, with a demented grin. 'Wolfie, get the Bat Car.'

'Do what, sarge?' said Wolfie.

'Get the fucking beers in, big ears,' growled Tosh, his thumb once again jerking over his right shoulder. 'Me and young 'un's been out there coppering while you been in 'ere skiving. So gets the ales in, beardy.'

Wolfie looked at me and raised his eyes to the ceiling, and put on his coat.

'The beers, the beers, let's all gets the beers,' said Tosh, clapping and laughing and dancing around the office. 'Ha ha!'

Detective Sergeant Tosh was once again praising the lord of refreshment with a crazy two-step jig.

Job done, information received.

Fruity

IF OUR CITY CID was stuck in a 1970s time warp, the same could not be said for the rest of Britain.

The times they were *a-changin'*.

As 1990 drew to a close, Maggie Thatcher got the chop and was replaced by John Major. The Major era ushered in back-to-basics, the country's first Poundland store, and a mysterious new 'rave' culture, involving kids dancing all night in fields to music that sounded like a jackhammer, all off their tits on a strange new drug… Ecstasy. (For the avoidance of doubt, I think this was coincidental. I'm not saying John Major was a drug pusher. I certainly never received any intelligence in that regard.)

Anyway, with every kid in the country off their bonces on E, and thoroughly loved-up with it, attitudes were in a state of flux. Football hooligans were openly hugging each other like fashion designers at derby games, women were discovering their sexuality, and it was okay to be gay. This was the year, after all, that The World Health Organisation removed homosexuality from its list of diseases.

What was *not* okay was to be anti-gay.

Personally, I never had a problem with the 'gays', if I can call them that. I'd known a few homosexual officers, and had a number of homosexual friends, and it didn't bother me. But it *did* bother certain officers, from what you might call the dinosaur wing of the old bill. Their attitude was not dissimilar to that of the church, only they were a bit more profound and in your face about it. When I joined the 'Job', people were routinely referred to as 'poofs', or 'gay boys', and those words and phrases were used as insults. It happened in every work place, not just the cops.

I had first noticed this changing around 1987, when I was still in uniform.

We had a job on at a local 'country cottage'. (If you're not getting my drift here, stay with it.) We'd seen an increase in a pastime called 'cottaging', which is where men of a certain *bent* meet up in a public building and then utilise ingenious methods to spread their DNA about the place.

Now, some didn't see this as a a big deal, and I have no doubt it would have gone on indefinitely – had it not been stumbled upon by a local magistrate (Justice of the peace) who found himself caught short near a public convenience in the Sandfields late one night. Whilst he was mid-micturition, a dark figure had approached our JP from his right side and popped a suitably gentle kiss on his cheek.

'Hello big boy!' was muttered, or words to that effect, and said magistrate pissed all over his own trousers before running like the wind back to his Mercedes. He sped off in the direction of absolutely anywhere – and very quickly. He was also very quickly stopped by the police, mostly due to the manner of his driving, and whilst being bagged on the roadside made his displeasure known as to their colleagues' lack of activity in the local toilets.

Hence 'Operation Fruity.'

We came from far and wide for the operation, *all six of us,* equipped with a camera that saw in the dark (this was still a new-fangled item at the time, well to us), two cars and an inspector in charge of the event who was so bonkers that the next four days would be as funny as they were interesting.

Inspector Dai 'Hard' Richards was Welsh – *very* Welsh. He had a drawl of an accent (he was from Merthyr) and he would often talk about 'pride' and 'passion'.

Sadly, he spat a lot when he did so. He was at least fifty, fat, and in his final few years in the job. His briefings were the stuff of legend – 'Once more into the breach' etc…

On this day, he didn't disappoint.

In his broadest Welsh roar, like a demented Windsor Davies, he wasted no time in getting to the point. We sat expectantly on rickety steel chairs in yet another dusty room with only those little windows well above head height for light.

'Today's op, lads, is an operation relatin' to the catchin' and detainin' of queers and poofs!' He peered at us over his glasses, scanning our faces for a reaction. 'Isn' it?'

'If you say so, boss,' said someone near the back of the room.

Dai Hard exploded on the spot. 'Is it *fuck* as like!' he yelled, spittle flying everywhere. He had pure hatred in his eyes, and the veins on his head were throbbing. 'Is it fuckery-fuck-fuck as like, you fuckin', *bastard* homophobic *fuckers*!'

I was very impressed with this. An older officer actually displaying a more neutral and non-judgmental view – well, non-judgmental of anyone other than us – now this was refreshing.

He hardly stopped for breath. 'You turd-mongers had better get this straight! This isn't about hasslin' a community of people who have lost their way! *This*…' He lowered his voice, but it was still brimming with menace. '*This* is about catchin' *kiddy fiddlers*!'

Glances and looks flew around the room, and one or two sighed, and at least two lads just burst out laughing. I was a bit confused, and wondered if he was winding us up. But it soon became clear that he wasn't. Dai Hard wasn't totally unreconstructed, after all. He spent the next few minutes outlining his belief that the majority of gays were pedophiles, and dismissed us with one final pearl of wisdom. 'If you sees any trannies, boys, don't bother getting involved with them. They don't like kids!'

It took about ten minutes for the chatter and usual banter to recommence.

Three years on, and with my big hat stashed away in the loft and a grey Burton's suit hanging in my wardrobe, Dai Hard was enjoying his retirement in Thailand, 'experimenting', and things had changed.

Everywhere but in the CID office.

* * *

BY THE TIME I joined the CID we'd stopped busting cottagers, mostly, though the prevailing attitudes were still there under the surface.

'Young 'un,' said Tosh, one morning.

'Yes, sarge?' I said, looking up and away from my ever-increasing mountain of paperwork, which was fast becoming a stressy nightmare.

'Jeffrey Jizzler is once again purveying more than apples and oranges down at his fruit and veg shop,' he said, loudly, whilst tipping the kettle on. 'And you're in charge of an intrusive but covert look at his activities.'

The office was quiet, it was a Sunday.

I had three suspicious deaths in my tray, a flying baby, and two counts of anal rape (buggery in those days) on a man found in a telephone box dressed as Father Christmas. That was enough for me, back then. Oh, and various unsolved burglaries. Not forgetting a forty year old woman found in a Dorothy Perkins shop bin in the Sandfields who had complete memory loss and couldn't speak.

That was probably my easiest job. The longer she didn't speak, the less I had to do, giving me more time on the other stuff. I was praying for no medical miracle whatsoever.

But Tosh was piling it on, it was all a part of the show.

Wolfie came over to me. 'We'll handle this together, mate,' he said. 'That's a bugger of a job, if you don't mind me saying.'

'Who's Jeffrey Jizzler, Wolf?' I said.

Wolfie smiled. 'A purveyor of all sorts, youth – usually sex, often drugs, and occasionally fruit and veg. He has a shop down the High Street, next to Dixons. He has a certain way with him, if you know what I mean.'

Wolfie illustrated what he meant by mincing daintily around the desk like he had something warm up his rear end, holding his hand out with his wrist limp.

'I see,' I said. 'So what's the score?'

'I've got someone in to Jeff,' he said. 'He isn't that bad, to be honest. My man's quite close to him.' He whizzed an intelligence report across the table. 'But first,' he said, 'read this. It's all we need.'

* * *

IT WAS COLD – very cold.

Two weeks before Christmas, and I'd battled my way down the High Street past carol singers, plastic Santas and shoplifters to have a gander at Jeffrey's gaff. The basic information was a drug delivery would happen and one of the participants had informed on the occurrence to the police. In this case Wolfie. My job was to see the lay of the land and note any issues. These days it is called health and safety, back then it was 'something that had to be done'

The radio in my pocket splattered into life. 'Young 'un, what's your ETA (estimated time of arrival) back at the nick?'

It was Tosh, in what we, in radio terms, referred to as 'talk through'.

'Er... This is November Delta four, approximately seventeen hundred sarge,' I said.

'Good!' came the response. 'Fucking hurry up, and it's five o' clock this isn't the navy or whatever you were in!'

'All call signs radio discipline!' came a booming, disembodied voice from the force control room.

'Fuck off!' was the reply, in broadest Cornish.

I got myself back to the nick.

My research on The Fruit Bowl, Jeffrey's place of iniquity, apple as and bananas included had involved sussing out observation points in possible friendly buildings. My fingers had gone numb, and I was grateful to get the nod to get back in, even if it was probably just another prisoner to add to the list. The stress began to build again as I drove back up to the iconic structure we all knew as the cop shop on top of Tower Hill. That feeling would be with me for the whole of my career, managing it became an art form in itself.

As I entered the office, Tosh was on the phone.

'Listen, fuck flaps,' he was yelling, 'I don't give a flyer what you think, it's okay for you sat there in your gleaming office with your tongue up your arse, talking into a posh telephone whilst we get killed out here...'

And so it went on. And on, shouting, expletives and spitting.

I tuned back in after two more minutes of utter obscenity.

'...and your missus as well, you cunt!'

The phone was slammed down by the sarge.

'Who was that, sarge?' I enquired.

'Control room chief inspector!' he barked. 'Man's a cunt! He should take more care of his missus than moaning at me about radio procedure. More blokes have been up her than they have the station lift!'

I gasped like a goldfish. Tosh rarely failed to leave me at least partially speechless.

'Now, young 'un,' he said, moving on. 'Jeffrey's on the move this evening, so we're working late, probably very late. You ring your missus and tell her to get her boyfriend round, you're needed on the frontline.'

Tosh laughed and clapped his hands as he finished off his sentence. He came right up to me, nose to nose. I could smell his breath. It smelt of haddicks, mostly.

'Whilst you're freezing your three-incher off tonight watching for our Jeffrey, your missus will have a big black man hanging out of her before the end of *Coronation Street!*' He was cackling wildly, now, as he spat out more south-western diatribe. 'I bet she loves it too, eh, young 'un!' His bright blue eyes were piercing. 'I bet she *loves* it!'

'Fuck off, sarge,' I replied.

At times, Tosh was a menace.

And where did he get the term 'fuck flaps' from?

* * *

WOLFIE'S SNOUT HAD come across with some early and most welcome information about Jeff and his sidekick, Randy Raymond. Raymond was a bisexual burglar who had once urinated all over police officers below him when he was cornered up on top of the Co-Op over an estate called Burnside. He was also a convicted rapist, and a hard bastard to boot.

The intelligence was that Jeff would be returning to The Fruit Bowl about 11pm that night with half a kilo of cocaine, and Randy Ray would be with him. Shortly after that, two of the nastier, upper-tier drug dealers in our region would arrive for a meet, they would hand over an amount of cash, and would then leave the shop with more than passionfruit in their shopping bag.

These two guys were from the Afro gang, who needed treating with caution. There were killers in their ranks. And I do not jest.

About 7pm-ish, the strike team assembled for a quick final briefing.

The team was Tosh, Wolfie, me, and Karen, who had stopped on to help.

Karen was a good worker, though I'm afraid to say she wasn't anyone's sort at all. She was forty-five, and lived alone – as Tosh put it, *if you want gorillas you visit a zoo* – apart from a pet Labrador called *Michael*. (For the first three weeks of my attachment, I had genuinely thought this was her husband.)

It was just the cards she had been dealt.

Shame.

But on the plus side, while she wasn't the most approachable of CID officers she wasn't afraid to do a bit of work. I stamped my feet as Tosh outlined his plans. I had on a nice, thick coat, a pair of woolly gloves, and two pairs of football socks. We'd be spending an hour or two plotted up in the back of a parked-up Transit van, and it promised to be Baltic. The forecast was for temperatures as low as minus 8°C, and it was chilly even in the nick.

'Right,' he said. 'Me and Wolfie will follow the Afros in the front when they turn up, and Kaz and Barnesy can come in the back way. The door will be open, it's all sorted.'

He stood there, hands on his hips in the dimly-lit office. He was wearing a sheepskin coat from another era, and looked a bit like a cross between Ron Atkinson and Henry V just before it all kicked off at Agincourt (or Sheff Wednesday).

Tosh went on.

'I've got traffic on standby as well,' he said. 'They're on paid overtime, too, them lazy bastards in their warm cars. They can clean up anyone who does a runner.'

A few final matters were addressed, and we did a quick kit check.

Cuffs and warrant cards stowed, and the only other thing to worry about was the Maglite. This is a metal torch, about two foot long (at its largest) and full of heavy batteries, and we found them well worth carrying in the dead of night. Ostensibly, this was so you could see where you were going, but they also helped if you found yourself in an aggravating situation. The standard-issue bit of wood they gave us for protection was about as much use as a chocolate teapot if a gang of villains wanted your blood.

Problem was, if the opposition took the Maglite off you, it would almost certainly be used on you, as PC James Grey had found out when his head had been caved in the year before in Hope Street. He hadn't been back to work since, and only started talking again when his missus gave him a blow job six weeks after it happened. (Well, that was the rumour. We do love a rumour in the police.)

Tosh was wrapping up, now.

'Anyway,' he said, 'it could get a bit tasty, so let's keep what few wits we have about us.' He cackled, and ripped open the big bag of multiple portions of fish and chips which sat steaming on his desk. 'And now it's time for your last supper, young 'un! And I hopes you're insured!'

He crammed half a haddick into his gob, and started ranting about my non-existent missus (by his theory anyway) and her desire for big black men.

'What about *your* missus, Tosh?' said Karen, interrupting him mid-flow.

'What about 'er?' he replied, spraying fish in all directions.

'What about your missus? Didn't she used to keep Sergeant Murray company of an evening?'

For a moment, Tosh stopped chewing. It was the first time I'd seen him lost for words. Then he said, 'That was before we got together. Anyway, Murray's a cunt.'

He piled a fistful of chips into his mouth.

'Your missus doesn't seem to think so,' said Karen. 'He's seen her in the flesh, hasn't he? All saggy and baggy, and gagging for a Murray Mint!'

Wolfie stifled a chuckle, and Tosh looked thoughtful.

He knew when he was beaten.

Or did he?

He smiled.

He munched his fish and chips, and smiled even more.

'Wolfie,' he said.

'Yes, sarge?'

'Is your missus still living with Bent Derek?'

An excellent piece of distraction.

'No, sarge,' said Wolfie, burping glumly. 'He put her in hospital last week with a broken jaw, I always said she talked too much.'

Like I say, different times.

* * *

WHAT I'M GOING to tell you now is what happened and how it happened, word for word. There was a clear moment, 'before the breach' would be entered and anything could happen. This was the fear and the excitement building, in any format that it could. We were about to hit four nasty villains as hard as we could without ending up gripping the rail ourselves.

There were equal numbers, and that's never nice.

Okay, we did have four more on standby, but they were traffic lads – never the best in a fight, and liable to be called away at any time to catch people doing 34mph in a 30mph zone and dish out bollockings about seatbelts or lane discipline. I jest of course, but we needed distractions more than Elvis Costello at times.

I felt butterflies like never before.

This should have been a warning.

'And then we just exchanged the cash and moved off...' We were all crammed in the van by now, and Wolfie was finishing off a story of how he'd got the information for tonight's escapade. His Det Sgt wasn't Tosh for the purposes of accountability as I mentioned before.

We'd parked in the darkness between two street lights, out of their low glow. It was a good spot: already a few street urchins had pissed against the side of the vehicle and hadn't sussed us.

That was the good news.

The bad news was, it was already midnight and we had been huddled in that van for four hours, Tosh, me, Wolfie and Karen.

Waiting.

The night was pure frost.

Really cold.

We had a decent view of the side of the shop and apparently it was *not in doubt* that the Afros would pull up at the side of the road we were on. So, with it *not being in doubt* that the arrival of our targets at the shop would also coincide with it *not being in doubt* the back door of the shop would be open, we had this all boxed off.

Didn't we?

I mean what could go wrong? Bar that is - the free radical that is a human being, and of course their tendency to hardly ever do what the fuck they should, or intended to do. By one o'clock in the freezing morning, even I was getting tired, and feeling the cold a tad too. I started singing *Ice Ice Baby*, quietly.

'Fuck this,' said Tosh.

But as he leaned forwards to spark up the engine to get us back to the nick, the bright lights of a BMW turned in to the cul-de-sac at the side of The Fruit Bowl.

Four – I know, *four*, we were expecting *two* – large and intimidating-looking Afros got out. All of them in black, one had an iron bar in his left hand which he quickly put inside his jacket.

I recognised two as locals – Desmond Willets and Brian Cricket – but the other two fellas I didn't know.

And they did look menacing.

They didn't go straight in to the shop. Three of them sparked up cigarettes. Again, I was beginning to see the appeal. They were only a few yards from the back of the Transit, and I definitely heard Brummie accents.

'Right,' whispered Tosh. 'As soon as the other two get 'ere we're on 'em – OK?'

He looked round the darkened van, and could sense our reservations.

'We're outnumbered, sarge,' said Wolfie.

'I knows,' said Tosh. 'I knows.'

In the dark, I could just make out his face. It was set in a leering grin.

Today, everything – even jobs like this – has to be run with health and safety in mind. The paperwork was all signed off. Back then we didn't bother too much with health, or safety, and Tosh didn't even know what they were. Like most of us in the job, he wasn't particularly brave, or hard, but he had a certain bravado to him. You only ever found out your level of humility at times like this. The trouble was his bravado sometimes shaded into stupado. I started humming *Saviour's Day*, and I don't like Cliff Richard at the best of times. Outside, another car approached, and Jeff and Ray alighted, the latter holding something *half-kilo* sized in his left hand.

The four black males moved towards the shop to greet them.

We didn't even have time to put *Plan A* into action before *Plan D* kicked in.

The first blow to Jeffrey Jizzler's head knocked him unconscious; the second was intended to ensure that he would never open his shop again. Useful only as it depleted their numbers. Meanwhile, Ray the Rapist had tried to run but slipped over on the frosty pavement. And they were on him in a flash. The package was stripped from his hand, and then three hard blows were delivered to his head.

It all happened so quickly, that it was only as the third blow hit his skull that our doors flew open and we leapt out of the van in classic bomb-burst stylee.

I ran towards the affray, but Tosh flew past me with his Maglite held high above his head.

'Chaaaaaarge!' he shouted, his Barbour billowing behind him as he galloped straight at Big Brian Cricket.

Once more, we went in to the breach.

Brian put his hands up as Tosh delivered a blow to his side.

Down he went.

This is easy! I thought. *It's cops and robbers!*

Wolfie clashed with Dessie, and Dessie won. Two firm blows were very well-delivered, the second a cracking uppercut.

Wolfie was out cold on the floor and Dessie was on his toes.

I swung at my bloke but missed, and got a hefty punch to the head in return. Unfortunately, my bloke was the Mike Tyson of Handsworth, so I joined Wolfie in Radio Birdland. Then all I felt was the slow blows you feel to the head and body, as you're kicked, rag bag and bobbing, all over the road.

I slipped away to another place.

Karen, game as you like, chased Dessie, who stopped and turned and knocked her to the floor.

I was told this later.

Tosh crowned my attacker, but not before I was completely battered.

The traffic car was still standing by, but their radio had gone down, and they didn't know what was happening. We were saved when the driver of a passing car, er, called the police. Wolfie regained consciousness at about the same time as I did. By then, blue flashing lights were everywhere; I saw two black fellas being handcuffed and led away to a police van – though it might as well have been a fucking ice-cream van, the state I was in. Tosh still had his Maglite in his hand, a savage look was on his face, heavy breathing, cold air evident and his coat was blowing in the wind. He was restrained from hitting the prisoner. I went back to sleep.

*****

What a Bloody
Headache

THE WHOLE JOB WAS a mess.

All four of us were at fault, though at the time I blamed the boss. We were lulled in to a false sense of security, allowing ourselves to believe that the information was from inside the Afro gang. In fact it came from a mate of Jeff's who only had half the story. Still, we should have done some research; if we had done, we'd have had an armed unit with us – even back then – because our two Birmingham villains turned out to have previous for murder and kidnap. They were brutal bastards. The one who did for me had shot a policeman only four years before, and had somehow managed to gain a not guilty in court.

That stuff doesn't just happen on the tele.

I was looked over in hospital, and later that morning my wife heard all about PC Barnes being taken to hospital with head injuries. Though not from the constabulary, or a concerned senior officer – she heard it on the local radio.

Back at work the following day, yes, I know. Bathed in the glow of another old school CID evening with lunatics (on both sides), as I answered memos from the CPS asking why I hadn't submitted a file, and another threatening termination of a case, I felt exhausted. (Today, I would ring them up and tell them to do it – I couldn't give a fuck.)

My head still pounded, my heart felt heavy, and I felt entirely let down by the 'Job', and the person who was meant to look after me – my sergeant.

I could smell fish and chips.

I looked up and saw Tosh standing over my desk. His presence was as big as that of any man I knew.

'You OK, young 'un?' he said.

'Sort of, sarge,' I replied. 'My fucking head hurts, though.'

'Right,' he said. 'Gets these down ya.' He handed me a warm package. 'They be haddicks, Barnesy… Our favourite.'

I unwrapped the paper. The crispy fish looked good. My skull pounded more, though.

I shook my head. 'Fuck, it hurts, Tosh,' I said. 'I'm tired, as well.'

Tosh stared out of the window as he chomped on some chips, adding more to his mouth as he did so.

He said nothing; he just chomped and stared out of the window.

I got up and put the kettle on, two teas.

The hot tea and chips were nearly finished in silence when Tosh stood up. He put his hand on my shoulder.

'I'm sorry, son,' he said. 'I truly am sorry.'

I nodded.

In the dark glow of that night I could see beyond the mask.

His outer surface broken.

'I loves this job,' he said, 'but I loves my mates even more. I didn't mean to get any of you hurt. I'm sorry.'

'That's okay, sarge,' I said. 'We're all wise after the event, eh?'

He smiled. 'You're getting to be a proper detective Top Gun, but better you be an old one too. Now gets yerself off to that missus of yours, take a few hours on the queen, she owes ya.' His growl was returning. 'An' if you gets there double quick time, you may even find that black 'un whose been banging her all these nights!'

He was laughing now.

To the tune of *All Around My Hat* by Steely Dan, he started wheeling about the office, punching the air, and singing 'All around my cock!' He laughed so hard, he nearly choked on a piece of that haddicks. I left the office and got some clothes from my locker downstairs. The chill hitting me as I stepped out the side door.

The term is brass monkeys.

I looked back in to the CID office as I walked across the car park, no more than twenty yards away. I stopped. I walked towards the window and looked inside – I've no idea why.

DS Tosh was sitting at his desk, his head in his hands, an uneaten piece of fish still in its wrapper in front of him. The big, hard, steely-eyed detective, afraid of nobody and nothing, was crying his eyes out. Uncontrollably crying his eyes out.

I went home to my wife.

We had a debrief five days later.

Karen was still off work – Michael the pet lab was licking her better – and Wolfie and I couldn't add much, having spent most of the evening sparko.

So Tosh did most of the explaining. It transpired that he had banjoed Brian, as we know, and had then set about my attacker, leaving him requiring forty-seven stitches to his head. Then he spotted Dessie and one of the two Brummies trying to drag Karen away to an alley, for God knows what reason, so he'd steamed into them, as well. When the uniforms turned up, he was trying to bite the ear off one of them. Dessie had run off again. Tosh stated that when he next met him he would 'cut his fucking head off'. I didn't think he was joking.

Ray ended up on remand for possession of drugs with intent to supply, but Jeff didn't. In fact, his life was only saved by a uniformed officer who had carried out CPR (first aid) on him and travelled with him to the hospital.

In Crown Court the following summer, Ray got five years, as did Brian Cricket. Dessy had been nicked somewhere in the Midlands, and got three years.

Piss weak sentences, if you ask me, but the two Brummies fared better still, with an astounding eight months each for assault on police. Once again, the court believed their story that they were only out for a ride in a car as they couldn't sleep and were attacked by a gang of white people who failed to identify themselves as police officers. That much was true: as we had launched ourselves at the four desperadoes, Tosh had shouted '*Charge*!' but none of us had bothered to mention who we were.

They walked free from court as they had already served their time on remand.

Jeff Jizzler got a year, and was taken away from his sentencing in a wheelchair.

He remained in that chair until he died.

Jingle Balls

MY FIRST CHRISTMAS as a detective – albeit a temporary one, clinging on by his fingernails – rolled around.

This is a magical and mysterious time in any CID office, and in fact across the whole of the police.

Weird stuff happens in the land of the normal. Everyone is off their faces, and unpredictable. The police somehow become experts in all sorts of matrimonial incidents, and many of those officers not even in their twenties properly. Some not even married. It made you wonder why they would even consider it having witnessed so many disturbing wedded outcomes.

Domestic violence soars, pub fights go ballistic, festering scores are settled, usually with a bread knife or a lump hammer. In that sense, it's not much different to full moons, Easter, major England football games, and the first few hot days of any year – it just goes on for longer. The madness starts around December 18th and carries on until the middle of January.

So, halfway through a twenty-two-hour shift, you find yourself looking at a dead person when you should be carving up a dead turkey. Not to mention, you seem to spend your life out at office parties, with people going over the side left, right and centre. And that pretty new WPC is sitting in the corner on her own, looking bored, and glancing at her watch…

It's a heady mix which can lose you your job, enhance your chances of a disciplinary, turn you into a legend, or get you in to the best trouble ever with your other half. Tosh had experienced all of the above. He'd been sacked and reinstated, disciplined, promoted, busted down a rank, divorced twice, and arrested in Sweden (long story). It all added to the mystery of the myth of a man who was spoken about in hushed tones in every nick in the force.

There are cops like this everywhere, of course – even in today's anodyne, frightened-of-your-own-shadow times.

Our small team that first Christmas amounted to Tosh, Wolfie, Karen, Chubby Lance Legge, Andy 'Three Piece' James, Brookesy of *Jumble Sale* fame, one or two other bit part players. part-timers and hangers-on, and me.

I was just about keeping my head above water – with back-up from a very religious guy called Ian who was owned by the previous shift but usually worked the four-hour handover.

If it sounds like we were a teeny bit under-strength, you should see what it's like thirty-five years on. Back then, our force ran five CID offices, each with four shifts of between four and six jacks. (Detectives) Now we run one central unit from HQ, with half a dozen bodies in it at any given time.

But I digress.

So it's Christmas, and the decorations have been up since the DI (Detective Inspector) gave permission for '*one of the girls*' to get busy.

This left Karen and Big Gemma from down the corridor to down tools, and spend half a day sticking pink and orange paper chains, highly dangerous fairy lights, and pieces of knackered old tinsel up all over the office.

To me, it was a horror show – a pastiche of Christmas, dreamt up by a sick mind. The tree, in particular, looked like it wanted to make a complaint of GBH, festooned as it was in straggly remnants of the purchases from 1968 by officers long dead. It consisted of a box of standard red, green and yellow swirly nonsense. The receipt was still in the box – three-and-six they'd spent. The operations area of the office (i.e. the tea-making facilities) had a small subsidiary tree flashing away in the corner, making the caked-in old tea stains feel comfortable. There were more flickering lights strewn about the place, and a few decorations had already come down from the ceiling as a result of someone being stingy with old, hard and non sticky Blutack.

It was really, *really* terrible.

'That looks the bizzo, eh, Barnesy boy?' said Tosh, as he walked into the office and gazed around himself in wonderment. He was like a small boy seeing his home all done up for the festive period – a small boy, moreover, who had never heard of Christmas before, and was on psychoactive drugs.

'Really sarge?' I responded, doubtfully. 'You think?'

'Yeah, young 'un,' he said, wistfully. 'They looks the *bizzo!* It makes me feel all Christmassy, too, likes the last ghost in Scrooge, all 'appy an' warm an' that.'

'I'm not sure any of the ghosts in Scrooge were all that happy, sarge,' I said. 'I mean, I'm not an expert on Dickens…'

But he was already over the other side of the office, staring, awestruck, at a shiny plastic bell perched a foot from his nose on top of one of the filing cabinets. Wolfie tutted and rolled his eyes as he clicked on the kettle and produced a pack of Happy Shopper rich teas from the D shift' cupboard. Oh well, apparently he had unlocked with a twisted paper clip.

For a moment, though, all was calm, all was bright, round yon…

Karen broke the silence. 'Sarge!' she shouted.

'Fuck me, don't *shout*,' shouted Tosh, erupting from his festive reverie. 'Don't shout, for *fuck's* sake. Whatever it is it won't change because you *shout*, you barmy fucking mare!'

He walked quickly across the room to the not-state-of-the-art CAD screen.

The green letters reflected in the tinted office window.

Tosh's face changed colour. 'Some cunt's killed their baby,' he yelled. 'Barnesy, take Wolfie over to Burnside and see what's happening. There's uniforms all over it. Get across there, pronto, action stuff, you know all the things we need to do, and make it tidy. There's a scene to protect, Barnesy. It's your show. Wolfie – watch him like a fucking hawk. If he fucks it up, it's your fault!'

'Aye, skipper,' said Wolfie. He didn't seem phased.

We grabbed our radios and bits of stick and made our way to the car park.

Wolfie looked at me as we got in to the car. 'This, Barnesy boy, may well be what we in the CID call a defining moment, youth. It's game on.'

* * *

WE GOT TO BURNSIDE fairly quickly, and pulled up outside a scene of police cars and bungalows. It was highly incongruous. The rows of neatly-kept houses, chimneys smoking away on a cold and crisp but very sunny day, screamed normality. This was a picture of suburban calm: it wasn't where people murdered babies three days before Christmas.

'Let's have a look at things,' said Wolfie, as I started to get out of the car. He raised his eyebrows at me, and touched my arm as I was about to dismount the bat car. 'Take your time, youth, the running about has stopped. You're in the CID now.'

I must have mumbled something, and it probably didn't convince Wolfie, because he carried on.

'Look at the scene, Barnesy youth. Stand back and digest. Let's look, think, and survey, mate. Prioritise your thoughts. See that young Inspector he's here already? He'll be thinking he knows what he's doing, but he don't. All he's done is passed his exams early on, and missed out on the experience he should have got by coppering. *Our* job is to make sure *he* knows that *we* know what the fuck is going on, eh?'

Actually, I *didn't* know what was going on.

But I took my cue from Wolfie, shut the door, and sat back in my seat.

He watched and waited, so I watched and waited.

I wasn't absolutely sure what I was watching or waiting for, but I didn't let on.

After a couple of minutes, he said, 'Right, let's go.'

We went.

The front door of the house was open, so we walked in. Various uniformed officers were tramping up and down the stairs, one of them with a fistful of teas. The Inspector, Pete Grimley, was there as well. I knew Grimley from my time in uniform, where he was less than well-regarded. He'd only been in the 'Job' five minutes, and he was climbing the promotion ladder like a monkey on speed.

He started speaking in his Yorkshire tones.

'Right, chaps, glad you're here. We have the baby in the main bedroom and I have appointed officers outside the room she's in. They're doing a written log. I've got the mother in the front room. Kitty's made her some tea, and Ron's in the garden with dad. So it's all in hand.'

He nodded and looked at both of us for confirmation. 'Nothing's "in hand", boss,' said Wolfie. He looked angry.

Grimley looked quizzical.

Wolfie joined the dots for him. 'There's nothing *"in hand"* here … at all. We have officers wandering about a crime scene with a dead body in it, fucking tea and coffee being drunk willy nilly, footprints all over the shop, and no record of anything being made of any conversations, actions, exhibits, arrests or, most importantly, fucking witnesses. In hand, my fucking arse. With respect, sir, it's shit.'

As though on cue, a toilet flushed and an elderly lady came out of nowhere. Well, specifically, she came out of the room to our left – the room that would later be described in court as '*the annex*'. She was wearing a floral *pinny* over a thick, hand-knitted jumper, light brown, scrunched-up tights, and blue slippers. She started shuffling towards us.

'Who are you?' she said, peering at us through specs half-an-inch thick. 'Are you from the RSPCA?'

Inspector Grimley blinked, and did a double take.

Wolfie looked at him, he looked at Wolfie, and then Wolfie calmly walked him away. 'This is a CID job, boss,' he said. 'Don't worry, we'll recover it. All I need is four officers, one of them being female, and the prison van.'

'The prison van?' said Grimley.

'Yes, boss, the prison van. In fact, two prison vans and a secure car so we can convey three prisoners to the cells.'

'Prisoners?' said Grimley.

'The ones you should have arrested when you turned up. The ones your lads are currently making tea for, or chatting to about the romantics of fucking winter gardening. Oh, and the one you didn't even know existed till she just popped up a minute ago like a rabbit out of a fucking hat, boss. Those prisoners.'

I'll draw a breath, here. This was 1990, remember, and back then, it was a case of *Get everybody out, by any means and we'll clear it all up afterwards*. So nicking the three adults in the bungalow seemed the best idea. At the time. Nowadays, procedures in child death cases like this are dramatically different – most of the time. Nowadays a more sympathetic joint agency approach is needed. To put it mildly, only if the 'bleeding obvious is 'bleeding obvious' do we start putting on the hand cuffs.

Back there, on that crisp, cold, mid-to-late December day, Grimley just stared in to the ether, caught in the moment; it struck me then, as it had before and would again, that no matter the rank, no matter the person, it's the appointment that matters in the police. You can tick as many boxes as you like to get promoted, you can spend your career developing your portfolio, but it doesn't solve any crimes. You can fly up the ladder, skirting issues, managing your own career, standing on heads, and making yourself look good. That's a well-known fact. But if you wanted to be the person you actually joined to be, to serve and protect the public, and be a good copper, you had to leave that agenda at home, and concentrate on the reason why you joined.

Grimley was a very decent example of what not to be. His salary might well reflect a person on the move; his police brain was nothing more than a scared and stupid mish mash of bollocks. My apologies but any copper reading this worth their salt will agree. He might *wow* the regulars down his local club on a weekend, just after his ugly mug had appeared on the local TV talking about a job he had no idea about. But he was living a lie, as so many senior cops are. Getting promoted quickly takes a lot of work swotting for exams and flitting from department to department to gain what we laughingly call 'competency'. Unfortunately, it doesn't leave time for much basic grunt work, and this would ultimately be Grimley's undoing: he left the Job some years later after messing up on something big.

Right. If we've got that straight, let's get it on.

We positioned officers in the right areas and ran written logs in the correct manner. Wolfie nicked the three adults and they were whisked away to the cells to be debagged and relieved of clothing.

Well, the male and the younger female were. As a result of our initial enquiries, the old lady was de-arrested *en route* to the cells across the other side of the town. Then she was given cups of tea and made comfortable, and she became a capable and decent witness both for the coroner and the crown court later on.

Serenity retuned.

And the baby remained in the parents' bedroom as the ambulance turned up to collect the body. It took twenty minutes; there was no rush because a local doctor had already pronounced the child dead. I started to make judgments on items for seizure. I took a closer look at the body. The little tot, now doll-like and blue, was lying stiff on the double bed. No obvious marks, like cuts or bruising. Natural causes? Possibly.

My eye wandered around the room.

Reddish-brown spots on the bottom of the door.

Dried blood?

Yes. Old, dried blood.

I saw a dressing gown on the door; again, small specks on the cuff. Maybe also old. There was an *en suite* leading off the bedroom. The door had a hole in the middle – about the height it would be if a *bloke* had smashed his fist through it in anger.

'Any thoughts, Barnesy?' said Wolfie. He was standing in the doorway, chewing a matchstick, hands in his pockets, his beardy face looking directly at me. He kept glancing at the small lifeless body on the bed.

'There's bits of blood and damage, Wolf,' I said. 'But that looks old. Have you got the ambulance guys on record as attending in the log?'

'Yes, mate,' he said. 'I'm not a cunt.'

I realised my mistake, Wolfie was a veteran of these scenes of crime. Ensuring everyone who enters and leaves with exact timings was crucial though.

'SOCO (scenes of crime officers) are here, youth,' said Wolfie, looking out of the bedroom window. 'Let them know what you want.'

SOCO are generally given the title of *detective*. Some had done the hard miles, others had just done the course up north. I have to say apart from one big-time charlie, a Manc wide boy (all put on to impress - it didn't) who loved all the *Sweeney* chat about spinning drums, (and having given himself the title of Detective Inspector despite never having passed his CID attachment or course) - I always found our SOCOs excellent and very easy to deal with. Dave Monks was no different.

Monksy was a tall, gangly guy, a British Asian with a tremendous amount of experience at crime scenes. Guys like him, and I would always be led by their opinions in every case. I trust immensely. At a scene like this, they are so valuable, they detect fibres, they find blood, they see things we as normal folk don't see. And then they turn it in to evidence – this is how valuable they are. Monksy had attended thousands of crime scenes, far more than I had. Our joint knowledge and actions at this crime scene would prove pivotal to the case.

I set about noting matters and determining what I wanted from the scene of crime appraisal. Photos and video of the scene were done. The damaged and the blood-specked doors were each carefully detached and seized, as were the blood-stained garments and some sections of carpet. Baby clothing, bed clothes, the cot, toys, bottles, milk, medicines… in fact, anything and everything that we thought would prove an insight into the child's short life was taken away. I'd yet to speak to either of the parents, but they were my prime suspects, that is until anything obvious told us differently. Remember, we had a dead child in front of us and like time travellers in reverse we had to piece it all together.

This evidential collection and how we did it would rebut any defence should we go to trial. And that would be with a person who murdered their own flesh and blood. That's worth thinking about for a few minutes. For me a clear theory of what do I need ? And more importantly what do I not need, and why.

****

Two hours in, and the scene was taking shape. The body was still *in situ*, and the traditional white tent had appeared at the front door, as had the DI (Detective Inspector) who casually strolled in, whistling (as we sometimes do).

'All in hand, Kenneth?' said the DI. 'All in good order, youth?'

He took up a natural pose at the entrance to the bedroom, sucking his teeth slightly, and leaning against the door frame, hands in pockets. I can see him now, in his sharp brown suit, crisp white shirt and mustard tie. Yeah, I know, but it worked. Somehow, he could carry it off. He loved the ladies, and because he was a real detective (and if they didn't think he was he would tell them – often) they loved him right back.

He was thirty six, and had been married three times, and divorced three times. His current partner, another copper, was... It gets a bit complicated here so bare with me. I think she was an official partner for a bit, before marriage number one. She disappeared from the scene for a while as he and the first Mrs DI enjoyed their first year of wedded bliss. But then she returned as his mistress, resulting in the break-up of marriage one. Rinse and repeat for marriage two. She disappeared again while he was snaring wife number three, but when she went the way of the other two - she returned. Mistress status suited her, obviously, because she wasn't just his mistress. She came complete with a mixture of other officers' *leftovers swishing about her rarer bits*, and, if the rumours were right, she had at least five other blokes on the go.

Tasty.

'Subdural haematoma, Barnesy,' said the DI, nodding towards the dead child.

'What, boss?' I said.

'Subdural haematoma, mate. That's what's happened there. Shaking, youth. Nasty business, is shaking. It's all the rage at the minute.'

He was right. If there are fashions in homicide, then this was one of them at that time.

'Oh,' I said. 'You're saying the child has been shaken?'

'But not stirred,' came a voice from behind the DI, as Wolfie walked down the hallway.

'How's things boss, Wolfie nodded in the DI's direction.

The DI chuckled. It sounds callous, with the little baby lying there. But this is the humour that gets you through things like this. It's what keeps your head on marginally straight. It's never said in front of the family, or witnesses, or anyone else. It's just between us.

'I've had at least five of these on the books in the past year, Barnesy,' said the DI, picking something obstinate out from between his teeth with a matchstick. 'They get prolonged periods of shaking. Usually it's because they keep crying, and the parents are at the end of their tether. It pops the blood vessels in the brain, and the blood all seeps out. It kills them slowly. Brain damage. Pound to a penny, the post mortem will show spots in the eyes. It's called petechial haemorrhaging.' He looked at whatever was on the end of the matchstick and then swallowed it. 'You got a pathologist *en route*, youth?'

I looked up, and a load of butterflies took flight inside my stomach. 'Pathologist, guv?'

'No worries, boss,' said Wolfie, appearing from behind him again. 'First thing Barnesy thought of when we got here. All in hand, boss.'

He looked at me over the DI's shoulder and made a drinking gesture with his hand. 'You owe me, you bastard,' he mouthed.

He moved out of my sight.

I tend not to watch too many telly shows about the police, but I can promise you this is not like *any* of them – even the ones I've never seen. How do I know this? I know it because real-life detective work is actually extremely boring, and painstaking, and mind-numbing, and they tend not to make TV programmes that are extremely boring, and painstaking, and mind-numbing. It puts people off.

All that racing about and shouting that you see in those half-hour police specials, or those neat little murders where the DCI knows from the outset whodunnit, and it's just a matter of (not very much) time before he nails them... Nah. For uniformed cops, maybe five per cent of their working lives involves blue lights and action. (I suppose the one exception to this rule might be traffic officers, who do spend a lot of time racing up and down the road shouting into a radio and giving tickets out to averagely normal motorists. So, yes, they probably would disagree, but then they disagree with most people, what with them mostly being disagreeable.)

For us poor sods in the CID, it's more like one half of one per cent.

Now, just like the TV people, I don't want to put you off reading the rest of this book, but if I was to go deep in to the intricacies of a scene examination like this, and all the processes, you would soon be bored. Sure, there are interesting bits – the forensic trails, the lines of inquiry, and the tracking down of all the baddies. Making an arrest and then seeing some nasty piece of work go down for a decent stretch is very rewarding.

But most of it is long hours of patient investigation, many hours of training and on-the-job experience. A keen eye for detail and a tireless approach to a professional inquiry just adds to the mix. It's not for everyone – lots of people haven't got the concentration span to make a piece of toast.

What I'm trying to say is, I won't bore you with all the detail.

****

SO THERE I WAS – sat at my desk – back in the office.

'What was it like, youth?' said Ian. Our resident church basher and bible reader was sat opposite me. Colourless and plain, the proverbial grey man, he seemed totally unsuited to the job, even though he'd been on the department for three years. He didn't get the decent jobs, I could see that already and he rarely had that creativity needed to get on in the CID.

'What was what like?' I replied.

'The dead baby, it must have been horrendous.'

I didn't answer immediately. The whole scene raced through my mind.

I sat back and chewed my pen, the rain battering the window and the fans running at full pelt booming out hot air as the decorations floated down now and again to the floor. As they did so the closest officer would scurry across the room and put them back up.

I decided I wouldn't be playing that game.

I thought about the dead child, her expressionless face, her waxy smile and blue tinted lips and fingers. A small drop of blood on the corner of her mouth, the lemon baby grow and tiny fingers wrapped round a rattle and the little dummy on the bed beside her. Five months old and now life extinct. Her life more than likely ended by the impatience of a person who was meant to keep her safe and protect her, keep her close and love her.

'It didn't feel like anything Ian' I eventually replied. 'It was just a job, and one which needed to be done, I didn't feel anything and it didn't feel like anything.'

I looked down and carried on writing the death report.

'Really mate, I would have struggled with that, the whole idea of dealing with a dead child isn't for me' Ian said.

'That's because you're a bloody idiot' Tosh appeared right in my eye line. 'Barnesy here is made of sterner stuff than you Pansy lad' Tosh drew breath. 'He spends his Sundays fighting crime not ploughing they fucking fields and scattering.'

'Hang on sarge' Ian replied in his plumb voice 'That's unfair' He looked unsure.

'Whats there to be unfair milky bar kid' Tosh moved closer. 'Fancies a square go with the sarge do ya? Fancies a knuckle up round the back where's the witnesses wont see us?'

Ian gulped like Scooby Doo before the mask came off this weeks nasty character.

'No sarge' he gulped again 'I'm just saying'

He looked like he was going to cry.

Tosh screamed with laughter smacking Ian hard on the back 'Whats with e boy, does e think I would really smack e about' He danced and clapped in front of Ian like a demented fool.

Your getting it now, I know.

You can see him cant you?

'Fucking cracker, Gods apprentice here thought I would hit him then' Tosh laughed. He shouted out to the room, Karen was there as was Bilious Brian (office manager) the frequently sick and incapacitated officer who answered the phone and tidied things up. Basically he was a malingering lazy bastard with a charmed life (for now)

Ian grimaced.

I carried on writing.

The coroners file would be first, but not until I attended the 7pm dissection of a five month old baby girl at the mortuary.

* * *

I SLIPPED INTO the mortuary through the inconspicuous side door entrance. The attendants Kev and Slooth were there, dressed as usual in their knee-length green jackets. If you'd seen them out and about in the street, you'd have imagined them dispensing screws and nails at your local hardware shop – not moving dead bodies about and cleaning up all the gunge which spills out from those recently departed when their holes are opened up and bits of them placed in plastic trays. This type of mortuary as with many others were very brightly lit, very clean and came with a smell I would describe as a cross between a strong sterilisation fluid like 'formalin' and that age old house cleaner, Dettol. Remember that small brown bottled mixture ?

The mortuary at any hospital wasn't a welcoming place, and it took a specific type of person to work there. And then there is the case of a defrosted and five times frozen man who was murdered by his wife. This poor chap who for eighteen months was continuously the brunt of defence and prosecution post mortem examinations - to prove and disprove various causes of death.

Frightening, both in detail and environment.

This guy had actually spent longer in the mortuary than the officer who Tosh had told me to bring along because '*She needs to see a good PM lad*'

I'll explain.

Tracy Sparks was shitting herself. A recently joined PC, and frail to look at to boot. She didn't look too much use to me if the scene got bloody outside the Furry Duck on a Friday night. But I reserved judgment.

To an extent.

She was in fact on her last chance, her four months in the job had been catastrophic, she clearly hadn't thought through her choice of career. And this proves my point from before. If you think the police is what you see on the TV you're mad. It's nothing like it.

Tracy did, and was repenting at her leisure. She was merely hanging on by her finger tips. Why she was with me today was lost on me. It was a pointless exercise.

The mortuary was brightly lit with buzzing lights, a confined bunker set out of the way to the side of the general hospital. The staff that worked there were all male and they worked a strange but effective shift system.

Slooth and Kev always seemed to be there.

As we slipped in Kev was sat down in the rest room reading his newspaper, the headlines screaming the very job we were all there to see diagnosed. Or at least we hoped. Slooth was tidying up a body on the slab behind us,

Tracy hadn't seen that just yet.

She was clearly frightened though, she shouldn't be here

'Do you want to wait outside Tracy' I said 'This isn't going to get any better'

She looked like a frightened kid waiting to be shouted at outside the headmasters office.

'No I'm fine' she said.

She wasn't.

Mr Martin Jenkinson breezed in. A tall and slim forty year old man with a posh Scottish dialect. Not authoritative, more bright and welcoming. The type of chap who encourages attention when he walks into a room.

'Good evening, Good evening; he announced as he walked briskly by the rest room in to the slab area of the mortuary. Tracy's eyes followed him as he opened a locker door getting out various clothing to wear for the forthcoming evenings opening ceremony.

Martin Jenkinson was the local pathologist.

His job was to cut open bodies and determine the cause of death by examining bits of tissue and drawing conclusions.

He was a highly paid £1,200 per post mortem pathologist who would deliver the most concise of evidence in court far better than any bobby I knew.

He was a revered and consummate professional.

'So, who have we got here he said looking at us all'

We introduced ourselves in turn, I shook his hand, this was only my second PM but I felt oddly the senior pilot here. Not wearing a uniform - and as I have often found since, my plain clothes earned me a certain degree of reverence as well.

'So your the OIC then?' (officer in the case) said the pathologist.

'Er … (here were go again) yes, yes I am the OIC Martin' I said somewhat cautiously. 'It's a bit of a rough job I am afraid'

Martin patted my shoulder 'Ive seen many and loads more to boot. This is just a part of the road we all have to tread to determine who did this – if anyone did'

He slipped his gloves on.

Slooth got a small body out of the mortuary drawer, wrapped in a white blanket, tubes in her nose. Waxy, doll like and dead.

He handed the small child to Kev who smiled, and walked towards the small slab in front of us. He placed the baby on the cold surface just as Tracy fell to the floor knocking two of her front teeth out. The games had indeed begun.

Suffice to say this inquiry could easily become a book on its own, reacting more than investigating and discovering we had a real problem.

Mutual Aid

MURDERS AND SUSPICIOUS deaths sometimes happened on county and force boundaries, and the lines were always drawn between forces very specifically. They had to be, it's a costly thing.

I learned this early on.

The boss came in one Saturday afternoon, not long after Christmas.

I wasn't in the best of moods. I had an absolute shitload of work on, and I didn't seem to be getting anywhere with it. Partly this was because I was still getting to grips with the magnitude and repetition of the crime file system. This was on its way to developing into today's astonishingly complex, mindless and largely pointless MG file system, and which appeared to have been devised by a pedantic, police-hating sadist with shares in a biro factory. It was meant to decrease the time it took to build a file for prosecution.

I had my headphones in, listening to the football, and was basically writing my name and the date over and over again on lots of sheets of paper. I was also praying for a clear shift, with no phones ringing or radio messages or heads popped round doors; I needed to make some inroads in the many and varied files and jobs I had been given, and which were becoming a pain. I don't like officers who half do a job, or cuff an inquiry, but I can also understand why this sometimes happens. It's generally down to workload, and the copper in question being overworked and over cooked. Though I suppose there are some who are just lazy – they're hiding and sloping off in all walks of life remember.

So anyway, the boss came in, just as Tony Gubba was getting excited about something, and I reluctantly took my earphones out.

'I've just had a call from the DI over the boundary,' the boss said.

I knew what was coming; the guvnor rarely spoke unless it was to deploy us somewhere, or to send us on what he thought was the important job of the day.

'Are you busy, Tosh?'

Tosh looked up from his *Daily Mirror*. 'Always busy, boss,' he said. 'The boys be busy on all the work ye give us.' He sniffed, rubbed his nose and closed his eyes. A moment or two went by. 'The boys are always busy, boss,' he said. Then he opened his eyes quickly, and looked surprised that the boss was still there. Clearly, it wasn't going to work.

'Come on then, sir,' he said. 'What's the news? What's the story?'

'Well, sergeant,' said the DI. 'Step in to my office.' He beckoned Tosh towards his little, plant-filled utopia of serious crime.

I put my earphones back in.

I'd missed a goal.

Tosh was back in seven minutes.

'Boys, we has a job on!' he said, somehow managing to smile and growl at the same time, and rubbing his hands together dementedly. 'We be the mutual aiders!'

Wolfie looked up from his paperwork; Karen said, 'Oh, no.'

Tosh already had his Barbour on. 'Come on, young 'un,' he said. 'And you, Karen. 'We're off over to Sunny Town CID, where they seem to have a difficulty reading a fucking map.'

From this I gathered that we had a dispute with our neighbouring force as to the location of an offence, and that the sarge and us were being deployed as a show of strength to sort it out.

What I had failed to appreciate was that as we were going to Sunny Town, and not they to us, they had the whip hand. We were off our patch and open to abuse, and – given the merest sniff of a chance – they would abuse us with glee. It's always the way.

* * *

TOSH FILLED US IN on the way, in between sucking on a Hamlet.

Me driving, Tosh as co-pilot, Karen leant forwards in the middle in the back.

'They've found some fucker in a field right on the cusp,' he said, as we roared down the A road joining our two towns. 'He's had his head cut off. They haven't found it yet by all accounts. My bet is it's in a fox hole.' He laughed and slapped his leg.

Karen pulled a face.

I hadn't seen a headless corpse before.

'He's been there a while as well, lads,' said Tosh. He had no time for gender specifics. 'Maggits, no doubt, and lovely fungus. Then Tosh screams 'Watch this fucker… He's going to pull out! Oi, you blind bastard, watch where you're going, we're the police!'

'Fungus?' I said.

'Yeah', Tosh replied, with a chortle. 'Mushrooms growing out of his fucking big nose, I expect.'

He was, at times, shocking.

Karen sat back, and I grimaced. 'Whats you got that face on for, young 'un?' he said. 'These jobs are alright. You play it right, you can have some overtime on it, and you won't need to have your name all over it.'

Maybe he had a point. This was an art form; yes, I'd be expected to put in the hours and the graft, but if the DS looked after me in the right way it could well be a breeze. A little bit of locate and trace, and a little bit more of this and that, and it could be a well-earned rest from all my specific, high intensity jobs back home. All I had to worry about really was the files; they'd still be sat there waiting for me when I got back.

SunnyTown CID was bigger than our office, and it had everyone in, they had three major inquiries on, all dead body related, and this was their fourth, I quickly saw the reason why they too wanted to cuff the investigation on to us. Not dissimilar to the officer wanting to do the same with their paperwork the force didn't mind doing it either. They had too much on.

They had a drinks machine in the office and a TV, which was on silent but had Grandstand on for the football updates. I recall vividly Helen Rollason at the helm as the interference changed the context of the picture now and again. They had more pictures than I had ever seen before on the walls, all prime criminal targets if the headings were to be believed.

Operation Zinc - identity sought

Operation Pie Catcher – Intelligence required

Stop, check and record details, sightings to this person, info to that person.

It seemed a full-on operation at SunnyTown CID.

But that was just the illusion.

On behalf of the Government the police do illusion very well indeed.

They were no different to us, we shared training accommodation, and for some courses we shared trainers for specialist crime training like surveillance. The busy office was enhanced because they had combined a burglary unit into the CID office making it look like the pinnacle of operational achievement.

Take away the burglary unit and the intense prostitute murder (three DC's) and they had four on – just like us.

So like us they needed all the help they could get.

A loud noise echoed round the office.

The DI came in, he was a huge, fat and blustering type with a thick Scottish accent 'Aye, I ken, I ken' He was talking to nobody.

He walked over to the kettle and the large pies cooking in the microwave.

I must admit I thought he was talking about me !

'Aye I ken ' he said again

'Fucking sweaty; Tosh mumbled.

The DI looked over, his sweating arm pits in a green shirt and beige 'slacks' the best I can remember. Oh, and his huge floppy belly swinging about under his shirt. He was followed everywhere by a lapdog, a thin spectacled pasty faced spotty boy who I would say was about nine. Everywhere the DI went this little puppy like human followed. He was carrying a bundle of papers all huddled in to his chest and looked like some form of cartoon caricature from Scooby Doo.

The DI looked over.

'Ah, boys, boys boys, you must be the hired help ?' he said.

He blustered over as the lapdog ran alongside him, dropping things and looking stupid. In reality he was about twenty, wearing a white t-shirt and blue jeans, surely he wasn't in the cops ?

Tosh couldn't keep his eyes off him.

'Im Inspector Warren ' he said holding his hand out to Karen.

'Im not ' she said and jumped up, kissed him and smiled 'You were on my CID course ten years ago Nigel '

Jesus by fuck and Christ it is, Karen dear – how the devil are you ?'

'Oh you know' she replied

'Ah, still unemployed in the marriage stakes then ?' he smiled.

'Of course' came the smiling reply.

I had this vision that Karen was actually a bit more to DI Warren than an ex CID course colleague, but surely not at that weight, he must have been twenty five stone, and I do not jest. His backside didn't look like it had done much up and down work for a long, long while.

But we cops love a bit of scandal at work.

The lapdog spoke.

'Sir, Sir these are DS Tosh, DC Ken something and her, Karen' – he pointed. If you want a comparison, think the character 'Derek' played by Ricky Gervais.

I looked at Tosh who was still transfixed and staring at the lapdog.

'Yes thank you Peter 'And this is Peter the DI sighed – he is in the specials and aspires one day to be a regular, don't you Peter ?'

Yes Sir, yes Sir, indeed ' Peter replied. He had a ridiculous high pitched voice, and was frail and skinny, I just couldn't see it happening.

'He calls in and does my admin on weekends' The DI said. He raised his eyebrows. He looked frustrated.

'What?' our DS blurted out.

We all looked at Tosh.

'What?' …….. 'The'

'You must be DS Tosh' DI Warren took a hold of his hand and shook it, he didn't get much of a response. Tosh continued to stare at Peter the lapdog over his shoulder. Tosh looked so quizzically at him he looked like a monkey from planet of the apes.

'What the fuck is that?' Tosh said pointing at Peter.

'Ive told you Sergeant, that's Peter, the Scottish dialect in the DI becoming a bit firmer.

He stared at Tosh intently.

Tosh looked at DI Warren, then at me, and then at Karen, returning his gaze to the big Scotsman.

Tosh wasn't loud, he wasn't quiet, his voice was just audible.

'I wants one' Tosh said 'Gets me one of those Barnesy boy, and that's an order'

Tosh walked away with a vacant stare in his eyes, looking back at Peter.

'I wants one of those puppies to do me works I do'

Tosh clicked the kettle on and stared at Peter.

I thought he was in love ……………..

The DI walked over to the kettle as well.

'Ah, so you're the DS in charge, DS Tosh – Ive heard a lot about you'

It didn't surprise me that the DI had heard of him, in fact it wouldn't surprise me if an officer from Australia had heard of him. One who works alone in the middle of wherever the middle is over there. That's that then, the inquiry had started.

Probably the easiest inquiry I had been on in months.

*****

THE INSPECTOR WAS A COMPETENT LEADER. I could see that immediately. A huge man as I have said, he ate a tremendous amount of saturated fats and consumed I would say in the region of a thousand calories an hour.

Easily.

He ate pie after pie after pie, steaming steak pies, cheese and onion pies or Cornish pasties, pure cholesterol driven, buttery loveliness I know, but so many …

It was an incredible feat.

The microwave was a constant dinging as the next pie was consumed and the next one put in. He knew his pies.

The irony on Operation Pie Catcher dawned on me then as well.

Two hours later we were all personally aware of the current state of affairs and ready for the formal gathering.

The assembled briefing had seven officers and Peter present.

We were huddled together in a side room next to the Inspectors office.

'Desmond Arthur Reid' The DI cleared his throat.

He even sounded Scottish when he coughed.

'PM is this afty, the belief is he has had his life taken from him, I say this as I have yet to see a way of killing yourself by cutting your own head off and then placing it in a bag, but I remain open'

'Er the head has been found?' Tosh interjected.

'Okay, for the benefit of our out of force colleagues this was my strategy to announce the head hadn't been found, and to be honest now the more I think of it the more I wonder why' He smiled and looked around the room, he didn't get a response.

Tosh looked at me in a very bemused way.

'A contact in the Met suggested it' Warren said.

'And you took him for real?' Tosh said.

'Well yes sergeant, I did, there is a method behind this, my thoughts were it may attract the attention of the killer or killers, throw them off the scent as such, and I stand by it, and there is an evidential reason for doing this as well'

Tosh shook his head.

unless any of you have any other bright ideas that will help (he looked at Tosh) report to A/DS Quinn, he is the action allocator'

The action allocator is the officer (usually a DS) who allocated actions during an inquiry, little has changed over the years, sometimes the process is run via a database called HOLMES, (Home Office Large Major Enquiry System) we had that system in 1992, I recall it came in when I joined up in the mid eighties, and we still have HOLMES today, but this inquiry it seems had been kicked off using paper. A nightmare if this was to be transposed on to a piece of technical kit like HOLMES.

'Your in my seat' Tosh growled at a thin and rather frightened looking plain clothed officer in a brown suit.

I could hear him across the room.

The officer who was being growled at was A/DS Quinn.

'Your in my seat see Quinny boy, Im the DS here, you're an actor, and not a very good one….. fucking move'

Tosh had arrived.

The DI came in and carefully managed the confrontation, I wont go in to it too much, suffice to say Tosh was quickly placed in charge of the allocations alongside A/DS Quinn. I could see he was a very frightened man by this point but he was to remain the allocator.

However, he did lose his chair.

DI Warren looked very red in the face, he had twenty years service and I have to say I couldn't see him collecting much if any at all of his pension. But round one in the 'managing Tosh' stakes was down to him.

We were to stay for three days then bail out our colleagues each day by way of reviewing the actions already allocated. Apparently we could offer some guidance and advice from a neutral perspective. A pair of fresh eyes as such.

True to form the PM came back that there was no way that Desmond had cut his own head off and put it in a Co-Op bag, but that was the key, and a clever one too. The reason for its exclusion in press releases.

Impressive move number one by DI Warren.

The Co-Op bag.

For some reason the bag that contained the head also contained a receipt.

I know, it sounds magnificently convenient, and it was. Sometimes this is how these things kick themselves off, but the mistakes of others under pressure to kill, dispose of a body and remain undetected whilst doing so can be their downfall. You see I refuse to accept the belief that there is a perfect crime. The person who put the head in the bag may well have been the person who killed Desmond, it could be they did not, and the receipt was a red herring, you just never know sometimes.

I have to say at this point I hadn't met that many top tier criminals, even those hardened ones who were this clever. It could well be that it was us that were being fitted up and sent off the trail of the killers. However, it seemed to us all that the bag, the receipt and the head would lead us to conclude a fairly quick inquiry.

Would it be that easy?

Yes, It was that easy.

The bag and receipt were traced back to Ilford in Essex in a matter of hours by Karen, and then we had to plan to approach the store and secure evidence. This was underway sharpish.

Luckily led by the Scottish DI.

Tosh's idea was to smash the door down at 5am the next day and start from there. DI Warren decided to send a team over (including me) to sit up and watch the store and any activity around it for eight hours and see what came up.

This would be impressive move number two.

And luckily we did it his way too.

Three doors down from the CO-Op store was a detached house in its own grounds, the activity there from four black males distracted us to the extent we recorded the vehicle details at the address whilst mooching round the area.

Initially this was for intel purposes for the local boys, but it soon transpired to be much more than that. One check came back as the ex brother in law of our Desmond and I have to say had we 'put the doors in' at the shop this information would have been a few days in getting to us. The intel check on the persons meant we could well have people present who knew how Desmond died, or maybe the culprits?

In any event we at least had witnesses.

This is detective work at its best.

It doesn't always happen as a result of due diligence and graft, sometimes these inquiries go so swimmingly they were almost meant to be. Things click in to place as a matter of fact. The last thing we needed to do was alert those involved to that fact that we knew where the bag came from, evidence would have been moved that much quicker that's for sure, it would have spooked them majorly.

I knew as did most of the team that once an offence of this nature had been committed that those involved, if there were more than one would be spooked at the slightest change in their daily detail. They were also going to be self protecting too, and this is where the worm can often turn in a inquiry. Do you know that in a lot of cases the offenders will almost certainly break ranks at some point and start talking. Not because they cared about the poor sod they had killed or disposed of but because they wanted to protect themselves.

Self preservation if you like.

I have learned much as a detective, and to start each inquiry off in the minds of those who you suspect of doing it, or in the event of having no suspects, imaging the character your looking for can help hugely. At the end of that Sunday we had sufficient officers with local help to hit the address three doors down and ask the owner of the Co-Op to open up and let us search the premises with his permission. Basically all we really expected from the search was some accounting and any video evidence, we knew the receipt was dated the Wednesday before. Get that boxed off and anything else would be a bonus.

'Carrots, Beans, Spuds, Meat, Frozen chips, polish, Rizlas's and Old Holborn Boss' I was reading from the till receipt on the telephone kindly supplied to me by Asraf the manager of the Co-Op.

'Excellent work lad' The DI responded. It wasn't but he knew how to inspire his officers, that much I had experienced already. This could well be impressive move number three.

Keep your officers chirpy. I could have been anybody, but it worked.

Plan A was to execute a warrant at the premises three doors down (the dodgy house) and not to hang about worrying about the formalities of the situation. Once we had collected the video from the store ten of us marched down and covered the front and rear. Four went in the front.

The house was stinking, sticky carpets and the sweet smell of cannabis was over powering. It possibly was last decorated or 'developed' in the fifties. Everything was tobacco stained or kitchen chip covered. The smell along with the cannabis had a ripe sewerage odour with a distinct taste (yes you could taste it) of heavy tarmac. I braced my self for a good old dust up.

It never came.

I had a feeling that this was indeed one of those jobs that no matter what we did the clues would mount up quickly and the perpetrators of the crime would be rounded up just as quick.

We walked straight in to the house and secured three men in the kitchen all smoking a bit of ganja and cuffed them all.

No resistance, no complaining.

I told them ' You are all under arrest for the murder of Desmond Reid between January 14th and January 18th 1991 ' I cautioned them..

The look on their faces was a picture.

No struggle, no shouting, no fuss, it was easy.

The search team turned up and we assisted them with the formalities, this was a case of search and see what you can find. A/DS Quinn, not being the greatest of leaders left it open to the rest of us to organise ourselves. I have to say it maybe wouldn't happen so fluidly these days, there would be a lot more supervisory interference. Protection of ones status overtaking the good will and detective work of a major inquiry.

Karen quickly took the mantle of leader.

Together we spoke about the shopping list and how the items could well still be in the house, then a phone call from Tosh to the address asking for me or Karen.

'Have a guess what Barnesy boy' the voice of the west blared down the telephone lines.

'Go on Tosh, make me happy' I said

'Desmond had they Rizla's and Old Holbers in his pockets when he was found'

It wasn't a clincher but it made our shopping list that much more important.

Carrot and spuds may well not be unique to this house, but the specific polish brand they purchased was. The store had sold four since last Tuesday.

Already the officers left behind were on their way to find out when they were purchased, and to make an attempt to track down the purchasers. The polish was found in the front room, it was 'unopened. It was a beeswax type, a circular tin, not a spray.

The three arrested were taken away and one more was later arrested at a local ale house. Little else was found linking Desmond to the address, a pair of underpants later examined and found to contain his DNA (he didn't have any underpants on when he was found) and all those interviewed stated they hadn't seen him for three years.

Back in those days telephone analysis wasn't used that much, well, it wasn't that much of a factor lets say, but it was in this inquiry, it was clear that much telephoning was done on the run up to Desmond's demise. And the calls stopped at 7.25pm on the day the PM decided Desmond had died.

The polish was carefully bagged up, the smooth surface telling me that if there were any fingerprints to be found it would be on that item. Tins of beans were also seized, and one used tin from the bin.

You may be asking yourself why ? Well, these smooth surfaces won't just contain the potential fingerprints of our offenders, or the person purchasing them. They could also contain the prints from the shop staff, even beyond that the distribution centres staff or even the delivery driver. It would all provide us with a trail come any clever arguing by an offenders barrister. And trust me where this case was going was direct to Crown Court.

The beauty of this inquiry was as I expected, it was over quite quickly for those brought in to help out. (that's us) For the officer in the case and file team it wouldn't be that quick a conclusion, but the truth of my feelings at the start of all this were borne out. I only found out the result of the investigation by seeing it on the local news some seven months later. All three were found guilty, yes, all those that were arrested in the house. One for the actual murder of Desmond, and the other two for concealment offences and perverting the course of justice. The one arrested in the ale house was cleared on appeal for the same.

I didn't even have to give evidence in court, my evidence including the seizure of the tin of polish was agreed, I never heard from the Sunny Town CID again on the matter. These type of endings rarely work so smoothly, they are remembered fondly though.

The sight of Tosh as we returned like union soldiers from Ilford, bags in hands as we walked towards each other in the driving rain at Sunny Town CID was like a scene from 'I need a hero' Tosh was smiling as the rain ran down my face like a giants tears, Karen walking towards the car as we shook hands and met midway across the car park.

It could have all been in slow motion.

'Nice one Young 'un, you did good' Tosh said

Desmond's fingerprints were found on the tin I recovered, sealing the fate of the defence of those arrested, which meant that we celebrated long in to the night at our local drinking house. Wolfie danced as Tosh sang and Karen screamed with laughter at fellow detective Shakespeare's poetry quotes and one liners. I once again felt that warm glow of belonging as we cheered and shouted with everyone else who had turned up from the station to join in the festivities. And no, it wasn't because we had solved a problem or cared about any of the investigations we were involved in. Why would we celebrate that? It was because we could, and it was a time before we had other agenda's thrust upon us.

It was a time that the honour of the job looked after you – and a good sarge of course. Something which has been slowly taken away and eroded for whatever reason over the past twenty years or so, but something that brought teams together for the better good. And got results time after time.

I suppose I would call them the good old days, but of course, they weren't that bad, so why not ?

The Exploding Cigar Man

WAS EARLY ONE morning, an early turn about seven, and the quiet in the office was interrupted by the ringing of the grey phone on Tosh's desk.

He picked it up.

'Tosh?' he said. Pause. Then, 'Yes, of course I knows him. Right. Yes. No. Yes. Okay. I dunno. Yes, a bit. Okay. Ta-ra.'

The phone went down. Tosh stood up.

'Ere,' he said. 'We're getting that Hamlet (Shakey or Shakespeare to you and I) on the shift, lads.'

He was particularly bright-eyed, and he looked like a country squire in his brown checked shirt and green corduroy trousers.

At least, I think he looked like a country squire; I could hardly see him for the dazzling sunlight – split into brilliant daggers of dusty, smokey light by the old grey blinds – which was bursting into the room. He drew on his cigarette and pointed to the spare desk next to me. 'I've no doubt he will want to sit next to young 'un,' he said. 'Yes, he'll like sitting next to young 'un. He can be his Othello!'

He laughed at that, and as usually happened when he set himself off it took him a while to stop. The saliva ran down his chin. He sucked it up.

'I likes that Hamlet' he said to himself, as he whirled away.

Wolfie stood up, stretched his arms, and yawned. 'Boss,' he said, 'are we having a slower one today? Only I've got a lot on and two files to juggle for the CPS.'

He looked at the sarge, who nodded in agreement. 'We needs a *few* days of quiet, not just the one Wolf,' said Tosh. 'You crack on and I'll keep the bastards at bay.'

I was pleased to hear this news. I had a coroners' file from the ongoing child death to review and submit, along with an in-depth report on a local handler of purloined goods, Greasy Gilbert.

He loved a TV, did Gilbert, especially if it was yours. He also loved a video recorder, a CD player, a microwave… in fact, if it was shiny and made in China, he wanted it. He could easily win the *Generation Game.*

We knew he was at it, but the trouble was that he knew we knew.

He was clever and quick-thinking, and he always seemed to be one step ahead of us.

How many times had we done warrants at his house and left potless? Plenty.

Recently, though, we'd come across intelligence which suggested that he'd stepped up a gear, to the point where he was now moving masses of property, enough to furnish a good-sized three-bed house, on a reasonably regular basis. Apparently he'd teamed up with a gang in Holland; twenty-four hours after it had been pinched from your living room, it was being loaded into a container bound for Felixtowe. That meant more reward, but it also meant more risk. What we didn't know is where he was stashing the gear before moving it on. Find that, catch him with it, and we were in business.

It was as though Tosh had read my mind. He was strolling towards the kettle, hands in his pockets, when he stopped and turned to look at me. 'Ere young 'un,' he shouted. 'I need you to get that intel on Greasy. I want to start moving towards giving him a cracking late New Year's party. I hates that little fucker.'

What the sarge actually meant by 'I need you to get that intel' was: 'I need you to develop a decent job, Barnesy. I need you to get the paperwork done, turn a few informants, and get a warrant, and arrange for a decent number of uniforms to be available. Once you've got all that sorted, I'll jump in a car with you and we'll race down there and I'll watch you kick his door in. Once we're inside his gaff, you nick him and whoever else is there and start seizing exhibits and building the case. That is while I wander about pointing at things because I'm the sarge. Eventually it'll go to court, but I'll be on a rest day so I'll leave that to you as well.

But I knew that anyway, my education was complete when it came to this scenario. And I have to say, it didn't really bother me. It goes with the territory of being a junior fish in a big pond.

'I'm doing it, Tosh,' I said. 'I'm rattling the bars, but it takes a little time, you know. Intelligence doesn't grow on trees.'

'Then you'd better be getting your little network of talking elves into gear, sunshine,' he said, walking towards me in a faintly menacing manner. 'Because I be the type of bloke that gets all impatient when things don't go as quick as they should.' He stood there, glowering at me, and slung his thumb over his left shoulder. 'Gets ye to work, boy,' he growled. 'And shakes some o' them trees.'

'Don't worry, sarge,' I said, with a sigh. 'I'm on it.'

He could be a right little fucker himself, at times.

'You'd better be,' he said. 'Wolfie boy, where's they rich teas?'

A few hours of relative calm passed as Tosh dunked his biscuits and read the paper, and the rest of us busied ourselves duplicating things we had already written and then, as is common in the police, duplicated it all again, just so someone else didn't have to.

In my case that meant writing the name of the dead child thirty-two times at the header of each of the forms I needed to fill in, and then another eight times on the coroner's report.

I really enjoyed the new file system we were pioneering, it made so much sense. Who needs computers with a cut-and-paste function?

Tosh drifted out – Ladbrokes no doubt – and the clock ticked away in the quiet office.

For ages, all you could hear was the scratching of biros.

Then a clatter, as Tosh flew in through the fire doors behind me.

He looked flustered – hot, red-faced and dishevelled, and he shouted, in a whispering type of way, 'Here! Quick, Barnesy boy! Hamlet's arrived! We need to booby-trap the cunt!'

He was all arms and legs and wide-eyed excitement.

He handed me some drawing pins and pointed at Hamlet's chair, and turned to Wolfie.

'Quick, Wolfie!' he hissed suppressing a manic giggle. 'Make him explode, or blow up or something! Like that thing you did at Walters' fortieth birthday! I loves that!'

He looked like he would wet himself.

'I'll sidetrack the cunt,' Tosh said, looking like a huge light had switched on in his head. He ran back out of the fire doors, leaving them slamming in the wind.

I closed them.

There followed five minutes of frantic activity as we carried out our detective sergeant's orders. You know when you're doing something that you shouldn't, such as booby-trapping a detective, and time is of the essence? You're all fingers and thumbs, and you keep breaking off to giggle, and it all gets worse the closer you get to finishing? It was just like that: two grown men, feverishly sniggering and shushing each other as we went about our work. I'd just located the drawing pins when Karen came in from a visit to the tape store. 'What the hell are you two doing?' she said.

'Booby-trapping Shakespeare's desk,' said Wolfie.

'Shakespeare?' I said, stopping mid-sprinkle.

'Yeah,' said Wolfie, who was bent over the drawer, fiddling with something. 'It's only Tosh that calls him Hamlet. He's known as Shakespeare. Always has been.' At that, he stood up. 'There,' he said, with a satisfied grin. 'Mission accomplished.' He closed the desk drawer slowly, with some precision, and sat down.

Karen tutted and dropped about thirty tapes on Tosh's desk. 'These are all yours, Barnesy,' she said.

'Mine?' I said. 'How come?'

'Tosh asked for them. The DI wants you scrutinised a bit to see how your interviewing style is getting on. There's a course coming up at the big house in April for new CID folk. Looks like they're deciding if you need to go or not.'

'What, if I'm no good at interviewing?' I said.

'Maybe,' she said. 'Or maybe if you *are* good at it. I find it hard to work out what this job wants most days.'

The childish excitement of a moment or two earlier had vanished, and suddenly I felt like I was on the brink. I'd only been in the office for a short while, but I was beginning to feel a part of the place. The thought of not being there filled me with dread.

I put it behind me, and turned to Wolfie. 'Why's he called Shakespeare, then?' I said.

Wolfie sat back and chewed the end of his pen.

Karen sniggered.

'You don't know, Barnesy?' said Wolfie.

'No,' I said. 'That's why I fucking asked.'

'Well,' he said, sucking in some air. 'It's because he's three hundred and fifty years old and he writes boring books.'

Wolfie laughed out loud, Karen too.

Was I missing something?

Two minutes later Tosh burst back into the office, this time with a country gent in tow. Chequered tweed jacket, mustard cords, brown brogues, all topped off with a gunmetal rain cape. He was tapping a posh, silver-tipped walking stick on the office lino.

'Young 'un,' shouted Tosh, pointing to the tea corner as he strode across the room. 'Put the fucking kettle on. Get the biscuits out and crack open the kegs, splice the main brace, and raise the flags. Fucking Hamlet and his cigars are here.'

His eyes positively shone as he spoke.

'Hamlet' stopped in the doorway. Then he nodded and walked towards a desk at the far end of the room.

'Where the fuck are you off to?' growled Tosh.

'I like it over here,' came the reply. 'I've always worked here. There's no sunlight in your eyes.'

Tosh bounded across the room after him.

'Hamlet?' he said.

'Yes, Tosh.'

'I'm the sarge.'

'I know.'

Tosh pointed at himself. 'Sarge.' Then he pointed at Shakespeare. 'Constable.'

Then again. 'Sarge. Constable.'

As he spoke, he crept forwards like a warrior in *Zulu*. The only thing missing was the drum beat. His Cornish dialect thickened with each step. 'Sarge,' he said. 'Constable!'

'I know Tosh, for fuck's sake,' replied Shakespeare, eventually. There was a hint of exasperation in his voice.

'Then don't you fucking forget it, Hamlet,' yelled Tosh, 'or I'll shove yer quill up yer hooter. Now gets yourself back over there with the lads!'

Hamlet quickly about-turned and joined us in our little corner. Tosh followed him, a smile creeping across his face. The closer he got to us, the broader the smile grew, until he was almost jumping with glee, hands between his legs and making a high pitched noise, suppressing his laughter.

A scowling Hamlet sat down.

Then he stood back up even quicker.

'Aaaaaaaagh,' he screamed as twenty drawing pins greeted his backside.

Tosh whooped with delight; Shakey held his backside and made a noise like a howler monkey as tacks sprung out of the seat of his pants and hit the floor.

Tosh, laughing fit to bust, collapsed. Wolfie and Karen were both doubled up.

'That's really fucking funny, you bastards,' screamed Hamlet, wincing and still feeling his arse. He looked accusingly at me.

I put my hands up. 'Not me, mate,' I lied.

At length, after much wincing and moaning, Shakey composed himself and brushed the final few pins away.

'That really hurt,' he said. 'That's taking the fucking piss, that is.'

The laughter died down to just the odd splutter. Still glowering at us all, he took some items from his pockets and opened the drawer to the desk.

Boooooom!!!!

The bang was absolutely deafening, and it was accompanied by a large white cloud which covered Hamlet from tip to toe.

Tosh had remained on the floor, seated like a small boy at a birthday party, staring intently at his victim. Now rolled backwards, crying with laughter, his legs in the air.

Wolfie staggered forwards, laughing so hard that he bounced out of the room and spilled into the corridor.

Hamlet just sat there, completely white apart from his startled eyes. His hands were raised in shock, and they stayed there, immobile. He looked a bit like a Hindu god, or one of those mime artists in Leicester Square.

As for his face, shocked doesn't really cover it. He looked somewhere between stunned and disbelieving, with hints of angry and terrified.

The giant dust cloud started to settle, and I smelled the unmistakeable aroma of Johnson's Baby Powder.

'Hamlet's exploded!' was all Tosh could say. I think he actually had wet himself a little bit.

Wolfie stumbled back into the office, bent over, creased up with laughter. Tears fell from his face. Then he fell on the floor.

I can honestly say I had never seen anything like this before.

Shakey licked his lips, nervously.

'That's fucking gunpowder,' he said, eventually. 'You bastards booby-trapped my desk with fucking gunpowder.'

'Only a little bit, mate,' said Wolfie, snorting.

'I don't believe this fucking job,' spluttered Hamlet. 'What type of people do we employ? Seriously, what type of people? You blew me up. You fucking blew me up!' His voice was on top of the scale.

He finally moved his hands, wiping some of the talc away from his face.

Tosh produced a hanky to dry his own eyes, and Karen – who had made the brews for me – plopped four mugs down on the desk. 'Boys will be boys,' she said, with a tut. 'Even when they're old men. You should know better, Barnesy.'

We gathered ourselves as the noise died down.

'That was fucking glorious,' said Wolfie.

Just as the DI appeared at the door.

'Stand by your beds,' shouted Tosh, standing up and saluting the guvnor.

'Nice one, Tosh,' said DI Pearson, suspiciously. 'What the fuck's all the noise?' His eyes travelled across to us, seated at our desks. 'And what the fuck have you come as, DC Hill?'

'They ffff… ff... they fucking blew me up, sir!' stammered Hamlet.

'Who did? The Germans?'

No, the… these fff… these fuckers.'

The boss walked further into the room, a grave expression on his face. 'What *has* happened here, DS Tosh?' he said, standing with his hands on his hips.

This, I thought, *could go wrong.*

He stared at Tosh, who stared back at him.

Nowadays, I don't think blowing someone up with an improvised explosive device using a matchbox and the gunpowder from a shotgun cartridge would be considered an acceptable practical joke in the police. In fact, I'm sure it's not. Even back then, it was problematic.

'Well, boss,' said Tosh. He looked resigned to whatever was coming. Then.

'Fell over,' shouted Shakey, loudly, interrupting the sarge.

'You what?' said the DI, looking straight at him.

'I just fell over, sir. Just fell over.'

He looked at the boss with a pleading look in his eyes – his cravat blown sideways like Biggles' scarf.

The boss tried to look stern, but eventually his lip twicthed upwards. He tried valiantly, but he couldn't hold it.

'You fell over, did you Hill?' he said his face almost crumbling. 'You genuinely fell over?'

'Yes, sir. Walked in, tripped up, er, fell over. Into some... talcum powder.'

The DI tried and partially succeeded in suppressing a giggle. 'Is this right, Barnes?' he said, looking at me.

'Er...' I said. 'Well, er...'

'He didn't see it,' said Hamlet. 'I fell over... outside.'

The boss rubbed his chin and studied him 'So when you say someone blew you up, that was wrong, then?'

'Yes, sir. Nobody blew me up. That was just my imagination, sir.'

The DI looked about the room.

I looked down at imaginary papers.

Wolfie was under the table at the other side of the room (yes, he was hiding).

Karen had her head down washing some tea mugs.

It was like a standoff: everyone weighing up the situation, mentally counting the cost.

The DI smiled. Then he smiled some more.

He walked away smiling, and stopped at the door.

'Well I suppose you ain't called Shakespeare for nothing, youth,' he said. 'But try and come up with a better story next time DC Hill. That wasn't nowhere near what I would call of a bard's quality. Oh, and if you're all going to have a day on the Queen, at least do it quietly. Wolfie, come out from under his hiding place. The boss exclaimed 'You look like a twat.'

He closed the door.

We all looked at each other.

The police will devour your soul if you let it. DS Tosh knew it, the DI knew it, we all knew it. So there comes a time when the hair has to be let down, and the desperate people who bring with them desperate jobs have to be placed on hold. If we didn't, I doubt very many of us would last thirty months – let alone thirty years. If you commit yourselves to the job twenty-four hours a day, you'll burn out. That's when you lose your mojo, and start making mistakes. And when that happens, you can end up losing your job, your liberty, and your loved ones. If you're really unlucky, you can even lose your life.

It happens, I have seen it many times.

We'd just released that pressure valve for a while.

Hamlet got up, dusted himself down, and walked across to Wolfie. Jutting out his chin, he calmly said, 'If you blow me up again, or even think about it, I'll have your head on a fucking plate.'

'I don't know what you're talking about youth,' said Wolfie. 'But you do look the part in all that country gent gear. Maybe a bit of gunpowder fell out of your pocket?'

Wolfie patted his back and picked up his mug of tea.

He slurped, and we all smiled – even Hamlet,

Tosh was jubilant for the rest of the day. Greasy Gilbert was removed from his mind, we spoke about the job, our days off, family, and the police and laughed as we chomped on biscuits and cakes and chatted the afternoon away.

DC Pete Hill (Hamlet) looked on, and eventually joined the throng. He wasn't that bad a bloke, he was a decent detective that's for sure.

We laughed and chatted, smoked and coughed.

We swore a lot and made tea.

Me, Wolfie, Karen Tosh and Shakespeare, all cosy and happy, feet up on our desks.

The cold bright day outside turned to a dark and freezing night as the wind picked up and sailed round the building. This made that haunting wailing noise that signals a storm brewing. Dark by 4pm.

The rattling of the boards above us dividing the lower floor and the admin offices banged and clattered. Then, just before we were about to call it a day, the phone rang.

The phone on my desk.

'DC Barnes?' The caller sounded excited – and very, very Welsh. 'It's me, Billy Boo.'

Billy was an informant I'd recently inherited from another detective who'd left the force, and whom I'd not yet got round to meeting. Obviously, his real name wasn't Billy Boo; we give all our informants different handles to ensure that they are protected, to an extent – and they needed protection trust me, regardless of the kind of people they are.

'Oh, okay Bill?' I said. 'What's up?'

There was a silence. Then he said, 'You wanted information on Gilbert, din yow? Well, I got some. But I needs to see you, look see.'

I put the telephone down and looked at Tosh.

'Looks like we may be in for a long night, sarge,' I said. 'Gilbert's on the radar.'

Tosh smiled and looked quite wicked. 'It's time for an equaliser then Barnesy,' he said. 'Overtime it is.'

He rubbed his hands and looked out of the window at the cold and dark night that was looming.

In police terms, we were on the bounty trail.

Greasy Gilbert

SO WHAT I SHOULD HAVE been doing was eating my supper with my missus.

What I was actually doing was lurking in the shadows of the Windy Way estate, on the grassy 'play area' opposite the little shopping parade. I was waiting for an informant called Billy Boo to turn up so that he could give me some information on Greasy Gilbert. In return he would get some money (eventually), and we would be a little bit closer to closing down Gilbert's considerable criminal empire.

In the darkness, only dimly lit by an orange street light some fifty yards away, Tosh and I had somehow got separated, and now a familiar voice came out of the darkness. 'Oi, young 'un, where the fuck ye be?'

I could hear him cursing and chuntering as he stumbled round the uneven, boggy waste ground. The wet now inside our shoes, the slippery surface deadly.

'I'm here, Tosh,' I hissed. 'And, for fuck's sake, keep it down!'

As I spoke, I saw my breath in the distant orange glow: it looked like I was expelling smoke from a thousand fags.

'This better be good, Barnesy,' spat Tosh, as he rolled over to me, 'or else we be having a punch up in the quieter hours. Fucking Greasy Gilbert isn't worth this temperature. It's fucking freezing I be.'

Old Tosh had on a thin cotton farmer's shirt, covered only by his elderly wax jacket, and he'd left his gloves in the car. His feet were clearly sodden from staggering through the undergrowth, and he was shivering like a petrified dog. I dare say, in a funny sort of way, he was enjoying himself. He did like a good moan, after all. He carried on, hopping from foot to foot, shivering, cursing, then shivering some more…

And then a tall and muscular character rounded a nearby fence, loomed up out of the gloom, and literally bumped into Tosh.

Even in the dark, it was unmistakably Brian Damage – with his curly hair and perm, he looked not dissimilar to a cockney Terry McDermott, and on this occasion, he'd gone the whole hog and was wearing shorts and a t-shirt. Despite the Baltic weather, Damage was a well-handled local hard-nut with a hatred of the police in general, and the CID in particular. He seemed to view our insistence in interfering in his career of petty theft, low-level drug dealing and drunken violence as some sort of affront. The previous year he'd stabbed a uniformed bobby, though he'd got off with it, and he was emphatically not the sort of bloke you want to meet unless you're nicking him with a bit of back up.

So when a nasty thug like that surprised Tosh in that manner… well, Tosh was only going to react in one way, and that was in panic coupled with extreme violence.

One minute Damage was strolling along, minding his own business; the next he was sailing through the air on the end of a stiff right cross.

'Oof,' he yelped, as he sprawled in the mud. 'What the fack…?'

'Run, Barnesy!' yelled Tosh, and he was on his toes like a headless chicken on speed.

I watched him disappearing, Barbour flowing behind him, in any direction but that of our car. This was fucking crazy. We hadn't even disturbed an hour's overtime yet.

But, yes, I joined in and ran away.

As I did so, I dropped the car keys. I slid to a halt, picked them up, and turned round just in time to see Tosh slip over – his leather-soled country brogues not being ideal for this kind of caper. Slowly, very slowly, like he was on a conveyor belt going backwards, he slid down a grassy slope and disappeared from view.

The darkness, and his ridiculous ungainly manner, had beaten him.

'Oh, fuck,' I said.

I ran towards where I'd last seen him, and stopped. He'd slipped into a steep ditch – almost a ravine – and was now floundering in a stream. At least, I assumed that was what was going on, from all the splashing and cursing – I could see absolutely fuck all.

'You all right, Tosh?' I shouted.

There might have been a slight echo.

Other than that, nothing.

'Fer fuck's sake Tosh, are you okay?' I said.

This time I was met with some general growling.

Feeling much like the star attraction in Fred Carno's police circus, and uttering a few oaths of my own, I started to scramble down the slope.

I'd made it a foot or two down when I was hit from the side by what felt like a Morris Minor, but was actually Brian Facking' Damage. The wind blew out of me. I genuinely saw stars.

We rolled down the slope, right into Tosh.

I was completely winded and defenceless, which was unfortunate because Damage was intent on revenge.

'You facking copper scum!' he screamed, in his dulcet Whitechapel tones, as he started to rain blows on to the top of my head. 'I just wanted to talk to ya, ya pair of cants!'

Then he hit me some more.

I came to my senses and started grappling with him, as Tosh lolled about getting all mixed up in the commotion but doing nothing.

Until…

Suddenly, he sprang into action. Soaking wet and angry.

First he bounced a random piece of four-by-two off Damage's skull.

Then he grabbed his leg and bit it. All the while he was screaming Cornish swear words like a lunatic Banshee – a wailing sound that, I have to say, haunts me to this day.

I am not even going to begin to try and convert it into English.

But my goodness it was haunting.

More furious splashing ensued accompanied by swearing, falling over and pain.I head-butted Damage – who was understandably distracted by having a grown man chewing his leg – and then I did it again.

He held up his hands.

'Jeeeeesus fack boys!' he yelled. 'Stop, stop, stop!'

The pain must have been immense.

Inside one minute he had been twatted by a lump of wood, bitten most frantically by the world's maddest copper, and head-butted very hard indeed.

Twice. I grabbed him as hard as I could round his head – we called it a scarf hold in the police back then, it's banned now, it kills people – and dragged him up on to his feet.

I then knocked him down again with the hardest left hook I had delivered for some time. Damage fell on to his back into a pool of ravine water (probably Windy Way sewerage). Deep panting and gasping for breath all round, massive billows of cold breath and much hands on our knees followed.

'Enough, boys,' he gulped. 'That's e-facking-nough, fer fack's sake.'

He was panting wildly, his breath rising from him like a sportsman's body after a solid workout. Like the back of a rugby number eight at the rear of the pack on a frosty January night up north somewhere.

He was propped up against an outlet pipe.

Tosh was bent forwards both hands on his knees, spitting, and gurgling.

I was panting, too – my chest hurt madly.

What a fucking night this was turning out to be.

'Boys, boys, listen,' gasped Damage, pushing himself up from the floor holding his hand out in a stop motion, sodden wet through and slipping backwards.

He looked bloody daft in shorts and a t-shirt, covered in mud.

'I'm genuine, you facking morons,' he said. 'Just listen.'

He gulped down air, sat back down in the water and put his hands up in surrender again.

'You really need to know this,' he said.

Pant, pant, pant. More steam and gathering of breath.

'I'm here to talk to you about Greasy Facking Gilbert, ain' I?'

I looked at Tosh. Tosh looked at me.

'How d'you mean?' I said.

I could be slow on the uptake in those days.

'I'm facking Billy Boo, ain' I?' he said. 'I'm your facking informant, you dozey cant!'

I blinked at him. 'Eh?' I said. 'Billy Boo's Welsh, and you're a cockney.'

'Am I, boyo?' said Damage, and in that moment he'd gone from the sound of Bow Bells to the deepest, further valleys dialect – far from civilisation. 'No, I'm not, look see. When I talks like this, I'm Billy Boo, see?'

I looked at Tosh, Tosh looked at me, and we both looked at Damage.

'I'll say this for you, Brian,' said Tosh. 'You do a good sheepshagger.'

'My mum was from the Rhondda,' said Damage. 'It's second facking nature to me.' He wiped blood from a fat lip and coughed. 'I'm serious, boys' he said. 'This is facking massive for you. I can give you the works on Gilbert… who he gets his gear from, how he gets it to Europe, who his contacts are there. He uses lorries from Davis's Removals, so if they get stopped it don't look suspicious. That's run by a copper's brother-in-law, as it goes.' He grinned and stood up. 'You may even make the rank of double twat between you with this job,' he said, spitting and laughing in to the water.

He held his hand out to Tosh

'Cracking punch, chief,' he said.

'That was me,' I said.

'Okay then boys… cracking punches. But I bet you wouldn't have got anywhere near me if the odds was even and there was two of me.'

He had a point.

I will go as far to say that this meeting with an informant was one of the more livelier events of my CID attachment.

But not as lively as what was coming next.

*****

BACK IN THE OFFICE.

It was three o'clock in the morning.

The slow ticking of the clock, only noticeable at night.

Warm, heating on, clothes changed.

Round two.

I analysed the information Damage had given us – we'd parted company as very good friends! – and I started to put together the triplicate informant forms for Tosh to sign up.

Wolfie was making a brew and Karen had fallen asleep in her chair. Hamlet was filing his nails (I know).

We had been on duty now for over twenty hours.

But that was the scene. The buzzing lights and the deadly asbestos hidden in the office walls were our company.

'Whatcha reckon then, sarge' I said, looking at Tosh.

'Seems we have a dilemma, boys,' he said. 'Seems the dilemma is down to me to think out, an all. I needs a brew and some quiet.'

He walked out of the office.

According to Damage, Greasy Gilbert was moving a large amount of gear that very morning. By all accounts, it was the accumulated stash from burglaries going back half a year, maybe more, and it was being stored in a furniture warehouse on the Ponds industrial estate. Three lorries would be arriving at 5am to load up and take it all over to Brussels and then on to The Hague. If they were stopped at any point – well, the paperwork would reflect household goods, the lorries were removal trucks, so it would all appear to be above board.

Clever.

It seemed bullet proof. It's not like customs get notified as to your stolen telly, is it? Once they were out of our immediate area they were home and dry, pretty much.

Tosh's issue was what to do about it.

We could invade the industrial estate and flood it with cops and retrieve the goods. That would mean tea and medals on a local level.

We could let them roll and follow them with surveillance, and maybe catch others in the network. That would mean tea and medals on a regional level.

Or we could do nothing, put the details in and go home. That meant no tea and medals, but really, who cares?

Tosh returned, his mind made up.

'We'll call in the morning's duty team early and hit 'em hard in the industrial estate boys,' he said. 'That's my shout. Let's get it rolling, Barnesy.' He kicked Karen's chair. 'Wake up, you mare, it's time to go to work. Gets that kettle on, sleepy.'

He growled and stalked around the office, muttering and whispering to himself, 'We means business, we do.'

Growling.

And muttering.

Prowling.

We needed an army, and pretty quickly.

The co-ordination was easy enough. The office manager (sounds grand, it wasn't, it was usually a detective on light duties) came in straight away. This week it was Davey Spencer, and he busied himself making calls and sorting vehicles.

The night uniform Inspector came in to the office. She was immediately made to feel incredibly unwelcome by Tosh, and left quicker than she'd come in.

But gradually our wheels were put in to motion.

Of course, Damage wasn't doing this out of the goodness of his heart, not least because there was no goodness in his heart. He had an agenda, which was his own gain. If he got rid of Greasy he could move in on his territory. I made a vow to myself that I'd make sure he didn't get away with it.

Revenge amongst criminals, that was his prime motivator.

'There will be a briefing, but not till I'm ready,' Tosh shouted in to the phone.

I guessed that was the Inspector again.

'Fucking women!' he shouted.

The frenzy was definitely building.

Wolfie wandered over. 'Tosh,' he said, putting an arm on his shoulder. 'It's all a game, youth. Chill out, mate.'

'I knows, Wolfs,' said the DS, quietly. 'But this could be a biggun.'

He leaned forward, sleeves rolled up, both hands on his desk, staring in to the still dark abyss of the car park. From where I was sitting, I could see a sparkle of light in his eyes. And those eyes were dark – very black and dark. Like a shark ready to strike.

The memory of the Jeffrey Jizzler stakeout – and the violence which had ensued – swam back into my head, and I felt faint for a moment. The toughest of men are allowed to be nervous. It happens.

The briefing started fifteen minutes or so later.

It was simple enough – a quick-fire map, blown up on the overhead projector as Tosh pointed to the key covering points and selected his teams.

Traffic were there too, and a motorcyclist.

The early turn uniform added to our numbers.

We had gathered the troops well, and in quick time too.

Twenty eight officers, all crewed up and tooled up, all briefed. And with surveillance ready to follow if the need arose.

All this on the say-so of one criminal lunatic, Brian Damage.

Actually, that's not fair. We had other intelligence – we knew Gilbert was bang at it, for starters. But still, the quality of the information was not the best, we used a five-by-five system to grade intel tittle tattle. Imagine a graph with A to E on one axis and 1 to 5 on the other. You plot your info on this matrix according to various factors – reliability of the informant, results of surveillance, whether Pisces is in Leo, that sort of thing.

Grade A and 1 was prime grade stuff, the sort you only get in films. Grade B and 2 was about as good as it got. What we had here was more like E and 5. That said, I'd acted on information like this before – a hell of a call, but it had come off. We all had, otherwise we wouldn't be doing it now. And that's what you, the public, expect, isn't it? You want a quick thinking and firm response to public reporting of crime?

Of course you do.

So do I.

Even when that member of the public is Brian Damage, and he is a signed up agent of the crown for a few grand. Oh, I forgot that: Tosh agreed two grand if it all came off, and a kicking followed by a hell on earth if he was lying.

Radio silence was the plan. No warrant – we would be entering after arresting one of the occupants on section 32 of the PACE codes, which allowed for a building to be entered and searched if it was the location at which an arrested person was present before that arrest. Equally, if we suspected others who were wanted and at large were within the building we had section 17 to fall back on.

It was a decent coverall, back then.

It saved an inspector or above pontificating about signing up paperwork. As I've already said, career before duty the higher you went. You could never mount an operation like this now. Too many health and safety beaks would need to be poked in, for a start. But at the time it was all normal. As I looked round the briefing room, at all those grim-faced bobbies, I felt my nerves settle. The station emptied quietly, as it does on occasions like this. The odd slamming door, the odd voice and quiet laughter, lockers slamming shut.

Echoes.

The battalion formed with hard sticks and metal bars of all sizes (for wrenching open doors, obviously), truncheons, batons (we'd just started piloting batons), and heavily weighed down belts containing torches and accessories.

Tosh led us across a quiet car park to our vehicles.

'He be a cunt, that Damage,' he whispered to me. 'He be one *hell* of a cunt, that boy, but by fuck can he fight.'

I gingerly rubbed a bruise or two and nodded in agreement. If there'd been two of him…

I slid into the driver's seat, Tosh next to me. Wolfie, Karen, and Shakespeare were jammed into the back, bickering about budging up and not having enough room.

'I'm freezing,' said Shaky, shivering.

'Shut the fuck up, Hamlet,' said Tosh, over his shoulder. 'Or shall we drop you off home on the way?'

Shaky said nothing; like all of us, he knew when to quit with Tosh.

It only took us four minutes to get to the industrial estate, which was a bottleneck of small factory outlets, dodgy garages and larger storage units.

We crawled past the pub at the opening to the estate. I knew it well: it was mostly frequented by the people who plied their trade on the industrial estate, and more often than not they were criminals, and trust me, more often than not is what they mostly were. Most of the lads parked up there, ready to roll on Tosh's order. Two – armed with a video camera – split off with a big ladder to get on the roof of a building which overlooked the warehouse and gave them a good look at proceedings. Meanwhile our car rolled in to the darker areas, all concrete and asbestos, and big fences. We plotted up round the side of the funky chicken factory, a small stinking mess of cooked chicken bones and fatty waste in bins that were once rumoured to contain the remains of 'Flexi Les', the drugs pilot. They probably didn't, but then 'Flexi Les' had at that point been missing for five years and has yet to be found. He must be somewhere; maybe he's swapping war stories with Buddy Holly, Glen Campbell, and other shit pilots in another place.

Fifteen minutes before it was all supposed to go down. We were cutting it fine.

We had a clear view of the furniture gaff in the grey early dawn. Our engines and lights were off, but our brains were on. Alert for any movement. I was getting the adrenal buzz we all get before a strike on a premises; no matter how tired you are, this is a drug which keeps you flying.

Right on cue, the sound of a lorry. Diesel engine, the bleeping of a reversing warning. Then another.

Two fat blokes driving, each with a passenger.

The beep, beep, beep reversing noise continued.

Dimly lit, sodium lights and dark doorways watched.

Shadows.

Another truck pulled up and waited.

That was six bodies already.

They moved slowly in to position and backed towards the metal rolling doors of the furniture warehouse building. The passengers jumped out and spoke into radios, the metal doors rolled open slowly, making that metal-on-metal screeching sound.

This looked very organised. I mean, radios …?

We have radios, too, and now Tosh spoke into his. 'All units stand by, stand by. Radio silence.'

No sooner had he said that than a car appeared. It was Greasy, with four of his oppos! This was a turn up, and a massive bonus. We'd been expecting a lengthy post-raid investigation to tie him in to it all, but here he was, actually at the helm, and at the scene of the crime. He must be confident.

We now had eleven bodies and counting.

Three more appeared on foot, shaking hands and lighting up fags and talking.

Fourteen. Then another car arrived. I gulped as I recognised a local celebrity boxer, Brighty, and his mate, Muller. Muller was a karate kickboxing lunatic who had once consumed three fingers off a man's hand for queue-jumping (and, yes, he swallowed them, too). Muller wouldn't come quietly if you offered him a Caribbean island to live on. At this point I feared we would all be killed. But, to my delight, Brighty got out of the car, handed Greasy a package, got back in his car, and left.

'Phew!' said Wolfie, reading my mind. 'Thank fuck for that. I'm not insured enough for those boys.'

We continued to watch, analysing, taking it all in assessing our own safety for sure. The lorries were in place now, and the doors were opened. Blokes were starting to carry stuff out to them – boxes and boxes of it. I counted twenty plus TVs. Then fridges, freezers, furniture and more furniture. Antiques, probably, though I wasn't an expert.

It took half an hour to load everything up, and we watched and waited.

The videos recorded.

Then one of the fat drivers smacked the back of his mate's lorry, to signal that loading had finished. The engine started and revved, a cloud of blue smoke belching out of the exhaust.

'Strike! Strike! Strike! All units strike!!!!' yelled Tosh into his radio.

'Fuck me!' I shouted, my ears ringing.

We hadn't given any notice or pre-strike assessment on the radio, so we were now in the lap of the gods.

Cheers Tosh.

Turning the engine on, I gunned it and screamed into the loading bay.

Where I jammed on the anchors and slammed straight into the side of lorry number one.

Typical!

(In my defence, it was very frosty.)

Shaky was first out, leaping on top of a youth in a green pullover, and I grabbed a fat youth in an oily, dirty-red boiler suit.

He spat at me and head-butted me – it was a cracker.

We were off again – dancing with the criminal elements.

Slipping and sliding, this was just a fight now, a freestyle battle, only best will win, and it couldn't be them. That would be disastrous.

More screeches and slams were heard as more of our team entered the fray. The opposition met us head-on, sticks were produced from nowhere, and more faces entered the mass brawl.

The thuds and smacks of fists on flesh, sticks on heads, and massed bodies colliding was unbelievable. If you haven't been in a situation like that it's really loud, trust me. I had a strange moment of clarity, where I felt like I was living a folk memory from Agincourt, or maybe Poitiers. But who were the French? People we hadn't seen before were appearing, in full fight. Unknown quantities, and big quantities too.

We were in danger of being overwhelmed.

Out of the corner of my eye, I saw one of the traffic PCs fending off a big lad with a bin lid. Another was lying unconscious on the frozen tarmac, being kicked by Brian Damage's younger brother, Rudy. And just when I was starting to think it might not be able to get much worse, Brighty and Muller screeched to a halt, leapt out of their car and started karate-kicking their way through the crowd like Battling Tops (IDEAL®) from days of yore. Bodies were skittled out of the way – some were cops, some were villains – and I realised that Muller was jabbing and boxing and dancing to my left, and getting closer.

'Come on yuse all,' he was yelling, in his horrible traveller tones.

'C'mon boys!'

For a moment, the whole thing was in the balance, but then another van load of bobbies arrived. I'd got the red boiler suit chap on the ground and cuffed him to a metal post and re-entered the battle to my right.

A fat lorry driver was being dragged down from his cab by Wolfie, who was punching him in a frenzy. Both fell a good ten feet to the floor, but Wolfie clearly had the bloke's measure, spinning him round to land on top of him. Karen was holding her head and bleeding from her nose, and some geezer took the opportunity to kick her in the face. Her head flew backwards, and she hit the floor with a thud, sparko. Some bastard jumped on my back and started biting the top of my head; I threw him over my shoulder, and recall being relatively impressed. Then I delivered a punch to the side of his head.

Textbook officer safety – I had no cuffs, and he was still dangerous.

My old mate Duffy appeared to my left, striking and hitting, moving and dancing, grinning and cackling as he stepped in and out of the fray and put various people to sleep.

In this mood, you were going to have it.

A grey-haired lad produced a baseball bat and swung it at Tosh. Tosh ducked, grabbed the bat at the apex of the swing, nutted grey hair and took away the bat. Then he set about anyone who wanted a taste of his new toy.

About then, I saw Micky Lewis, the patrol sergeant from our local community nick, have it away on his toes. I followed him to see who he was chasing – then I realised he wasn't chasing anyone. His bottle had gone, and he was running away, writing a resignation letter from the Old Bill with his own feet.

Then a white flash, a crack and I was down.

Brighty had got me.

Again, I felt the kicks and the punches as I drowned in to

unconsciousness – this was becoming a habit, it really was.

Then I was up. Dragged to my feet by Tosh, who was roaring and screaming like a drug-infested monster.

'Fucking come on, ya bastards!' he roared. 'I'll kill fucking ye all!'

He whirled the bat around his head and held me up with his left hand. Custers last stand stuff. He ran with me towards the lorry, me stumbling and trying to focus as he backed us against the side of the vehicle.

Two hands on his bat, he despatched Muller to the outer echelons of his life.

Then Tosh was off, raised bat crashing down on every head he could reach, smashing into the skulls of every villain he could find.

Wolfie joined me and propped me up half unconscious against the lorry and others joined us, too – nine or ten of us, backs against the wall, breathless, panting and angry.

At our feet, seven or eight villains, two unconscious the rest handcuffed.

And then the rest of them staring at us.

They looked afraid.

This was a brief stand-off.

Then Tosh raised his bat once again, his coat wide open and blowing in the wind, and shouted 'CHAAAARGE!' They scattered, and we polished them up in quick time. Five got away, and sixteen arrested. Seven of them went to hospital – that's what happens when you don't come quietly. On our side we had four in the hospital, including me. Nothing too serious – one fractured jaw, a few black eyes, and Karen had lost a tooth. She still moans about it now.

There was a debrief, but I can't remember it; in fact, I could barely remember how to make a cup of tea and had five days off sick afterwards with concussion.

I knew that my recuperation was complete when I got a call from the Complaints and Discipline team three days into my brief convalescence. When the missus told me the Inspector was on the phone, I genuinely thought he was ringing up to see how I was, but he wasn't.

'We've had a complaint of people fighting at two-fifteen in the morning on Windy Way, PC Barnes,' he said. I could almost hear the sneer. 'You, another officer and one Brian Damage. We'd like to interview you about it, and you *will* need representation. When can you come in? Tomorrow?'

Was this guy for fucking real?

'I won't be in tomorrow,' I said, flatly.

'Well, this is serious, PC Barnes,' said the guiltier on the other end of the phone. 'Offences may have been committed. Don't make it difficult.'

'Fuck off,' I replied, 'You twat.'

I put the phone down, and went in to the kitchen, unsure as to whether to laugh or cry. In the end I did neither. I just had a drink of water and reflected on the conversation I'd had with my tutor when I'd joined the job.

'The more you do in the police, Barnesy,' he told me, gravely, 'the more shit you'll get.'

I laughed at the time. He was a highly respected PC of twenty eight years' service, but obviously I thought I knew better.

'You just see,' he said.'You just see'

And now I'd seen.

I was eventually cleared of fighting a random member of the public in a ditch in Windy Way back in 1990, but I learned an important lesson. Never go the extra mile unless the people involved are deserving of it. Never trust Complaints and Discipline, and for fuck's sake steer clear of mad sergeants in charge of baseball bats at any time of the day or night. Their definition of the minimum amount of force necessary may well be different to yours.

Sergeant Micky Lewis I never saw again.

Last anyone saw of him, he was on the A390 heading towards the ironworks, still at full pelt.

One In Four

I WAS JUST THINKING of wandering off to the canteen for an egg and chip lunch when Linda Thomas wandered in, followed by a cloud of Givenchy, holding a letter for me.

It was a court warning – often delivered by hand by Linda or one of her heavily-perfumed colleagues from the Criminal Justice Office (CJO), our administration department. These ladies came not only with court warnings but warnings of their own, largely based on gossip about promiscuity.

Linda dropped the letter on my desk and exited stage left, smiling at everyone, waving to nobody in particular, and wiggling her behind as she went. She had all the fragrance and all the make-up you could ask for: she fitted the bill perfectly for a police rumour.

I smiled to myself and picked up the letter.

'She's filth, Barnesy,' said chubby Lance Legge, from his seat a desk or two away. He sounded exactly like 'Boycey' from *Only Fools and Horses*. He even had the laugh.

I looked over. Lance was smoking his twentieth fag of the day, and the blue fug he was emitting obscured a good fifty per cent of him. But I could still make out his brown suit, yellow shirt and red tie combo, and that broad grin. I glanced down, where the air was clearer, and saw that he was wearing grey slip-ons and white socks. Truly incredible. He dressed like a blind man who stole his clothes from Oxfam.

'I guarantee you, bruv,' he said, before going into a coughing fit.

I waited, patiently. More coughing. Once he'd recovered, he said, 'I guarantee you, she is definitely filth.'

'I'm not sure what you mean, Lance?' I said.

I knew where we were heading, of course.

'I would put *money* on it, Barnesy. She fits the criteria spot on. You can tell, you know.'

I looked at him. Was this some sort of test? Had Lance been put up to it by Complaints and Discipline, to test my tolerance of sexist banter? Back then we spoke a lot more freely than we do now, but still. I decided to err on the side of caution. 'What the hell are you on about, Lance?' I said. 'Is it just fags you toke on all day?'

Lance leaned in to me and whispered. 'I may not be the best detective in the world, youth,' he said. 'But I know the ladies, mush, and that one is no stranger to the spam spear. That is a dead cert.'

Sure that I was being stitched up, I said, 'So when do I complain to the sarge then, Lance?'

He looked confused.

I laughed and stood up. Papers fell to the floor, a few colleagues looked round.

'What?' said Lance.

'When do I complain to Tosh?' I said. 'This is a test isn't it? To see if I tolerate certain behaviour. Is is a professional standards thing?'

He goggled at me. 'I have no idea what you're talking about, sunshine,' he said.

He got up and walked off in a cloud of smoke, shaking his head in mystification.

I looked at Wolfie. He grinned at me. 'It's not a test, mate,' he said. 'Lance is a sex machine, remember, a real ladies' man. Or or so he thinks. He's just passing the time of day. We may be a lot of things in this office, but we don't stitch each other up for that, not here, not ever. The day that happens, I'm off.'

I glanced down at the letter Linda had brought in. I'd been lost in the moment, and now I read it. It took a short few seconds to sink in.

'Fuck!' I said. 'Fuck! Fuck!'

'What's up, youth?' Wolfie stood up.

'I'm in court at two o'clock today,' I said, looking at my watch. 'That's in an hour, for fuck's sake.'

I made towards the office door.

'Oi, youth,' shouted Wolfie. 'Stop. Slow down and focus. First of all, what's the trial?'

I stopped okay, but I was struggling with the focus bit.

'I don't know,' I gibbered.

'So how the hell do you know what it's about, and what to take?'

He had a point.

'Just slow down Barnesy, you won't make it any better for rushing now'

I walked over to my desk.

I read the warning again.

Regina v Jizzler

Possession of class A with intent to supply.

'I don't understand,' I said. 'It says here it's in the case of Jeffrey the fruit shop bloke... you know the guy who had the big pile of coke a while back. But I'm not even the officer in the case Wolf. What's that all about?'

'Not sure, youth,' said Wolfie. 'It's an odd 'un, that's for sure. If I were you I'd get myself off down the court and find out.'

'I will,' I said. 'Maybe it's a mistake, eh?'

He looked dubious. 'Probably not,' he said. 'Probably not.'

His reply didn't fill me with confidence.

I started for the door again.

'Youth,' Wolfie shouted.

'Yes?' I said. 'What now?'

'Which court are you going to?'

'Crown in the town centre mate.' I responded.

'What does your court warning say?'

I glanced down again at the piece of paper. 'Er... Oh shit, it says the crown court !' I gulped. 'Am I in the shit, Wolfie?' I had visions of all sorts of complications buzzing around my head.

Wolfie smiled. 'Don't worry youth,' he said. 'It can't be that bad, or complaints and discipline would have arrested you by now.' He was laughing, I wasn't.

I moved to leave.

'Youth' Wolfie shouted.

Where's your pocket note book, CID diary and associated papers?

I stopped, and gathered up what I could, I needed to calm down.

I left the building in a foggy mess, a bit like Lance had blown one of his fags all over my face.

* * *

I'D ONLY BEEN IN THE crown court twice before, and only on one occasion had I given evidence. That's the difference between CID and uniform. The bigger the job, the more time in court.

It wasn't too difficult on that occasion, to be honest. All I had to do was read an interview I'd done at the roadside for a breath test. It took five minutes and was painless.

Court appearances are generally painless – until livelihoods and long jail terms are at stake. Violent incidents involving top gangs of regional lunatics who deal in cocaine and beat the fuck out of the police... that was definitely a step up to Mr Smith on the roadside after three pints of Pig's Ear.

The crown court building I was attending was a structure that could talk. A grand old affair, a domed, grey stone building with echoing floors and distant laughter, over the previous two hundred years it had seen the incarceration of thousands and the putting to death of sixty-three men and two women in the days when it was trendy to hang murderers within its forbidding walls.

The sunshine broke through the coloured glass and shed bright light and dust on to the musty stone floors as I made my way up the fifty-two steps to the main hall and reception area.

Smooth floors, that clacked and scuffed as you walked.

Authoritative floors.

Many a cloaked barrister walked briskly about carrying large bundles of papers and talking awfully properly.

Truly an intimidating place for a young cop.

I went to the front desk.

The lady on the desk had worked there for years. She was about ninety three.

She looked at me.

'Yerssss,' she said poshly, looking me up and down over Dame Edna Everage's spectacles. Her perfume was overpowering.

'Er,' I said. 'Er, I'm Ken Barnes. I'm due here for two... Er...'

She perused her papers and smiled.

'Oh yes, Mrs Champion (a barrister) wants me to notify her as soon as you arrive,' Don't talk to anyone, Barnes, and sit there.' She pointed at a wooden bench; like a disciplined schoolboy, I did exactly as I was told.

The bench was hard and cold. The light was white and dazzling. I blinked. *Gah!* I'd left my diary and notebook in the car. Would I need them?

She went away and spoke to an usher, a decrepit and grumpy-looking man who glanced over at me and shook his head.

Hammer House of Horror, I thought.

This felt weird.

I heard tutting and indecipherable talk, as the usher walked off and opened a door that stated 'Barristers Only'.

The butterflies started, my stomach churned and as I drifted away trying to work out why I would be required at the crown court at short notice for a job I had no idea about. I couldn't work it out, and as usually happens in these situations you settle yourself down by reassuring yourself that it's something and nothing - and nothing to worry about. This is the first lesson in not dropping your guard in any court situation because as soon as you reassure yourself that it's 'nothing' it quickly becomes a nightmare when it becomes 'something'.

If that makes sense?

This was a free form situation, an ever changing free radical in motion.

People suffered here, dreadfully, and more.

And I felt like I was next.

If this doesn't make sense yet you will soon grasp what I am on about.

I was deep in thought.

A smiling face appeared about a yard away from mine.

The first thing I noticed was a big boil on her nose, and then the usual dress of a barrister, with one difference, she had a badge on her lapel, a yellow and purple badge with a horse on it.

'Hello Barnes' she said very plumy in a very posh and highly trained dialect.

She had the perfect voice for the BBC circa 1956.

'Er … Hi, PC Barnes from Er, … the CID'

'Yes I'm sure' she replied.

Her perfume remained, but she was gone.

People do wear fragrance and it always leaves an impression on me.

She walked briskly away.

'Follow me Barnes' she said as she walked quickly away, she was waving her hand in the air and was holding a gold pen.

'Now have you spoken to anyone about this case Barnes' she said as she opened a door which led to a room with two chairs in it and no table.

Stuffy, dusty, enclosed and an overbearing smell of lavender.

'Sit' she said and proffered a hand to indicate I had no choice.

Gold pen still evident.

I didn't have a choice, I sat down, very nervously.

'Did you hear me?' the barrister said. 'Do you have any defects, hearing senses, sight?'

Now I realise she was asking me in a rather posh way if I was stupid.

'Er … no ma'am' I said.

I sucked in some air.

I was quite queasy.

'Why am I here?'

She drew breath and pointed her boil ridden face right at me.

'I said, have you spoken to anyone about this case since it was mentioned for trial?' That was firm enough.

'No' I replied. 'I didn't even know it was going for trial'

I may have sounded a bit angry too.

'Right, now answer things in turn, and compose yourself, lives are at risk here, and long prison terms are going to be dealt out if this case gets a guilty finding, so think, okay Barnes ?'

That didn't help.

Er … 'Yes'

'So you have no idea why you are here then?'

'As I said ma'am, no'

'Don't call me ma'am, I am Cynthia Champion' she said very firmly yet again.

She stared intently at me, eyebrows scrunched, she seemed curiously mad.

Her voice was penetrating, very highly pitched and made me feel rather ill.

'Champion' I repeated as I stared at her.

She was all fuzzy round the edges, I could hear seagulls and light music.

Violins?

My head lolled forwards.

Oh dear, rock n' roll Barnesy, I felt all honky.

The world was a blur, the light continued to shine on me like gods own sun ray, picking me out for punishment - and I am sure I heard a choir singing, the violins had gone.

Then the room went black and I fell off my chair.

Another Ken Barnes spectacular was unfolding.

The water hit my face. And I am sure I heard the words 'Blithering idiot' as I came round with the grumpy usher and the champion Barrister staring at me.

I lay there trying to focus, and quite wet as well.

'Officer, are you okay?' Champion said.

She was still being hoity toity and sharp.

'Er … What?'

Everything was a haze.

'I said Officer, Officer, Officer' her voice just faded away.

And so did I yet again.

Goodnight, I'm not ready yet.

The next thing I recall is me shouting '*Fuck off Wolfie you twat*' whilst staring at the same two people. I would imagine now from me falling off the chair to being watered down to coming round and fainting again was probably about twenty seconds, to me it could have been a lifetime.

'Officer, now come on, there is no need for this' Miss (she had to be a Miss) Champion shouted.

I almost winced expecting a slap round the face.

I was still lying on the floor.

Most embarrassing.

A thought occurred to me that I had wet myself, this was going from bad to worse, and then I remembered the water.

Slight relief, but I was still fucking wet!

'Just hang on a sec will you' I said. 'You're doing my fucking head in'

The old Barnesy was back.

Maybe I needed the short rest?

I saw Mr Grumpy smile and Miss Champion stood back somewhat aghast.

For the first time in a while she said nothing.

They continued to stare at me as I tried to get myself off the floor, I slipped back down.

'Okay' I said as I sat up, this time successfully. 'Just give me five will you, I'm getting there'.

If I was watching this, I would be laughing.

I recall having my head in my hands as I collected my thoughts, then I stood up shakily. Miss Champion helped me up, and behind the hard exterior I almost sensed compassion.

'Are you sure you're okay Barnes' she said.

'My name is Ken' I said.

'Detective Barnes then' she said, reinstating her place in our relationship.

I still felt shaky, and sat down drinking some water Mr Grumpy offered me.

'That was weird' I said.

I looked at them both and Grumpy left the room. Clearly a man of few, if any words.

'Okay Miss Champion, what is this all about?' I said again.

'Are you sure you're okay?' she replied.

'Well, I could do with a sandwich, I was about to have my lunch before I got here, and I didn't have time for breakfast this morning' I replied.

I assessed then I hadn't eaten for some twenty four hours, a late finish yesterday and then bed absolutely knackered. I then quickly realised this would only end in further bouts of falling over if I did not get something to eat soon.

The police do this a lot, and too much, then they become diabetic.

The door opened again 'PC Barnes, court three please'

It was Mr Grumpy, and he was smiling again.

'What?' I said

'Court Three now please officer' the usher said.

'Follow me'

Miss Champion left the room via a different door, fuck me this was like a very bad dream that constantly changed, and the characters were all ghosts. Doors opening then closing, disappearing characters, it was a bit overwhelming. These people were on roller blades constantly moving in and out of my sight, giving me one hell on earth after another.

It was surreal.

I walked out in to the corridor, again the echoes of feet on stone, I noticed the usher had clicky things on his shoes to impact further his walking on anyone who cared to listen.

Odd.

I was now floating.

I entered in to the arena of conflict very nervously, but also when you consider my recent events of fainting, in fairly decent order, I was still floaty but ready to face my tormentors. I mean, after all I only had to tell the truth.

Anyone who has done this walk will know that it is a blurry mess, and you take very little in if anything at all as you take the short walk twixt court door and witness box.

I took the affirmation (not the oath, I take an affirmation telling everyone I am here to tell the truth) and introduced myself to the court.

It was then that I noticed there was no jury.

It was explained to me that this closed session had come about as a result of information that had come to light during that morning's court, and this information was something I no doubt could help the court with. A closed court will convene when everyone is cleared from the proceedings, this includes the jury and all. Then a matter or point of law will be discussed between the judge, counsel and in this case the police.

I was still none the wiser as to what was going on here and prepared myself for a long afternoon. The court room was oak panelled and old, dark and imposing.

It was quiet and claustrophobic too.

Wigged and gowned men were seated looking away from me. These will be barristers in waiting or advocates on the cusp of their chosen trade, even secondary barristers to aid the defence.

Then Miss Champion walked in, bowing towards the crown as she did so (I didn't do that) mental note for next time. She took her place confidently to the right of the judge as he peered out above his glasses, between myself and the defence counsel.

'Your honour, before we start may I make it known to you that Detective Barnes was taken ill just prior to coming in to court, although he assures me, he is okay to proceed'.

Miss Champion had struck first.

But I didn't recall any words of reassurance between us, luckily, she wasn't on oath! The judge looked over towards me, he was an elderly man and well known for many years as the presiding judge on many a well-known case.

'Officer, is this right, you're unwell?'

He peered more intently at me over those glasses.

'Er … yes your honour, I'm feeling fine now'

He smiled 'Well don't go curling your toes up in my court laddie, that would be one for the club'

He laughed out loud as did both defence and prosecution as the judge looked round for confirmation, it was indeed funny. He peered round over those glasses like a children's TV character, his mouth larger than his face and glasses slightly above his nose, being held on with nothing.

His red robe singling him out as better than I.

Oh lord, don't flake out again mate, I thought.

He had a gentle but firm voice that echoed his authority around the empty court room. As it was a cleared court, that made it far easier for me. Less prying eyes. There were actually only eight people in the court.

What could go wrong?

'As you have gamely soldiered on officer I will ask the defence to take it easy on you' the judge smiled again above his glasses – his red robe and wig (slightly off kilter) seemingly moving with him as he spoke.

'I don't intend to keep the officer long your honour' came a response from the defence, a young man, bright in presentation and sharp voiced too, creating the belief he had a precise ability to communicate.

He spoke as he rose from his hard seat.

'In fact I have only one question to ask the officer'

'Oh as brief as that then' replied the judge

'Go on'

The defence barrister paused and poured a small amount of water from a glass jug into his clear glass. The judge waved a hand towards me prompting the clearing of a throat and a pointing of the papers he held in his hand.

'Proceed' He said.

The defence counsel steadied himself and looked round slightly, then placed his hands on his waste he stared directly at me, he took a sip, and then picked up his papers.

Very dramatic.

This was obviously going to be a thrilling few seconds.

'Officer, have you at any time managed an informant in relation to this trial who gave you information that led to the direct arrest of the accused in this matter?'

'No' I replied.

'Thank you, officer,' came the response.

The judge looked at me and said 'You may leave officer'

I left.

The whole thing took eleven seconds.

I motioned immediately towards the doors.

As I walked out of the court into the bright sun but cold day I breathed the sweet fresh air of winter, I could smell oranges and pears, and stopped to pause for breath.

Did that really all just happen to me?

Well, it did and for all the fuss I created prior to giving evidence it went rather well. I looked up and saw Mr Grumpy, he smiled and walked away shaking his head and tutting. I walked over to the chippy, bought some sausage and chips, walked back to my car and drove back to the nick.

From the time I had received the court warning from Linda (The Lovelace) Thomas to this moment only seventy-three minutes had passed.

Quite remarkable.

I walked back in to the office as a cheer went up.

You know you are gaining popularity when people cheer your arrival in to a room.

'How did it go Youth' Wolfie was in first.

I decided to play this cool, like an old sweat.

'Oh, same as ever Wolf, like you said nothing to worry about mate' I said

'Oh, I see' Wolfie said 'No dramas then?'

Karen and Lance were getting closer, obviously wanting to know what brought about the emergency court warning.

Then Tosh walked in.

'Barnesy boy' he said in true pirate fashion.

'They judges didn't hang ye then' he laughed and drooled.

He almost bounced in front of me, his coat was open. His tie loosely fitted round his neck, thin and imperfect. 'Did they ask ye all those hard questions about your dodgy policing methods' he laughed.

Tosh punched my arm and laughed again, he was building up to one of his office jigs again.

'Hey Sarge, leave him alone' Karen said. 'Let him speak, how did it go love, take no notice of these animals'

Shakespeare walked in, then stopped, looking over and immediately joined in the throng all watching me.

'You all right Ken' he said.

'Seems there was a bit of fuss down the court I heard'

'Shhhhhhh lad' Tosh said. 'Let Barnesy tell us how it went'

'Yeah, go on Barnesy' Shakey agreed.

They all watched me, all leaning in, it was quite scary.

The Barnesy inquisition, the faces sitting in judgement.

'What the fuck are you all on?' I said.

I was sat back leaning away from them, they all looked bloody spooky to me.

'Well' said Tosh,' When you goes up to that big court it's always a drama isn't it, we are just checking you is all right and that'.

He walked away slightly.

'But if you're okay Barnesy, then I suggests we all get back to work' he added and waved his arms about.

He was chuckling, 'I'm sure the mystery of Barnesy in court isn't as we understand'

More laughter.

Then there was a knock on the office door.

It was Miss Champion, Barrister, and once again she rolled in to my life, but this time smiling and looking far friendlier.

'Cynthia, what do we owe the pleasure for this visit?' Tosh smiled and walked over to her.

He pecked her cheek.

He clearly knew her. Watch the boil!

'Oh, I thought I would just check in on Detective Barnes after this afternoons events in court' she responded.

A Barrister checking on a Detective in the police station after a court appearance?

Odd.

'And of course, I have to pick my husband up too, I saw you all gathered in the office from the car park, how are you Detective Barnes?'

'Detective Eh?, that's a long shot Cynthia' Tosh laughed.

'Oh, he did fine today, once he was brought round he did very well'

She smiled again and looked at me sympathetically, her voice very caring now and motherly'

'Brought round?' Wolfie said. He stood up!

A bit of a cheer from others, and you can sense a whole room looking at you, even if you can't see them.

Oh no - He wouldn't let this go.

'Please tell us more' bellowed Wolfie.

Cynthia Champion smiled, and revealed to them all of my fainting experience in court just an hour or so earlier.

Wolfie's face cracked first, then Tosh, then bloody Shakey.

Karen looked at me sympathetically.

Lance was slapping his leg in a complete melt down.

'Thanks' I said staring right at her.

'Cheers for that' I added.

Some people, may well be clever and well educated but they should also have a caveat that should be drawn underneath them – *'Not the brightest when it comes to real life'*

'Oh, if you can't share these stories with friends, then who can you share them with?' she said dismissively. She clearly had no idea of the banter and haranguing I would receive as a result of this latest drama.

This would no doubt go on for about seven years, if not longer!

The wurring of hamster wheels inside the brains of Tosh and Wolfie could be heard as she spoke.

Tosh could hardly contain himself.

'One question, one bloody question Barnesy'

He was almost jumping up and down with glee.

He laughed and laughed and laughed.

He then went down on one knee.

It was entertainment time.

'Oh please Mr Judge, don't let them be naaaaasty to me, I'm not well Mr Judge, I'm fainting because I'm scared Mr Judge' Tosh was loving this.

'Oh fuck off Sarge' I said and walked away.

It was amusing though.

'Oh please Mr Judge, don't shout at me, I'm all fainty, I'm fainty Barnesy the weak little Detective from the town centre CID, don't hurt me, I'm meek and mild' Tosh was now laughing so much he was crying. His West Country drawl getting more pronounced (as ever) as he prayed on both knees to his pretend judge. I looked at the barrister 'See what I mean?'

She looked surprised.

'See what you've done' I smiled.

'This will be legend in twenty years' time, but like all legends it will change focus, and names (thankfully) and probably end up with me sleeping with the judge just prior to rubbing melted cheese on to his bits in his chambers'.

'Oh please Mr Judge, pleeeeeeeeease' Tosh went on and on.

Our Barrister was indeed waiting for her husband, he was Superintendent Champion who walked in to our noisy office as Tosh was about to set about pleading for more mercy on his knees.

Tosh stood up quickly.

'Afternoon sir' he said, clearing his throat and saluting in his suit!

Tosh was still smiling.

'I seem to have broken up a party Cynthia' he said

She was laughing too.

'I think maybe we should go'

Supt Champion was a good man, a solid bloke in my eyes and a kind chap too.

Approachable and easy to talk to would sum him up.

Lance spoke. Or blubbed in his silly way.

'I mean what are the chances of that happening Barnesy, you go to court and just before you give evidence you bowl over, faint and then abuse the barrister and usher in a fit of fainting madness when you come round?'

It was almost as if Lance wanted the Super to know what had happened.

Tosser.

'It's a brilliant story Barnesy' Lance added.

The barrister walked towards him smiling.

'What are the chances indeed Lance' Cynthia said.

She became a Barrister again and spoke like one as she talked to Lance.

'You, a young man of extreme wit and wisdom - and you don't know the odds in this case? I mean a man as educated as you Lance surely would know the odds?

Cynthia nodded and looked at him for a few seconds, awaiting a response.

She got none. Lance shrugged his shoulders and looked around as Cynthia and her husband walked from the room.

She stopped as she left and patted Lance on the shoulder.

'I would say young Lance that the chances are just and right, in your terms I would say they are about one in four Detective. Yes, I would say they are exactly one in four'

'What do you think?'

Lance blushed and went bright red.

She walked from the room smiling with the Super, and as they disappeared from view into the corridor I heard them both laugh.

I looked at Lance and then at Tosh.

Tosh had a beaming smile on his face, reddened now from his pantomime exertion, but beaming.

'I likes them odds young 'un' Tosh said. 'I likes them odds a lot'

Quiet descended on the office once more, and a semblance of normality returned.

If normality is the right word ....

A Very Major Inquiry

'THERE MIGHT BE a bit of mileage in this report, young 'un', said Tosh, sliding across a signal from the control room.

I had a quick scan. It was a MISPER – police slang for a missing person enquiry. Most of our missing persons turn out quite quickly not to be missing after all, and so the enquiry doesn't go much further than the production of an Intel report. This helps with finding them the next time they go missing. These reports are eventually weeded on some arbitrary date decided by whoever decides the dates upon which MISPER intel reports get weeded.

Not the sort of thing that usually makes it to CID, even to the desk of a lowly wannabe like me.

The MISPER on this occasion was a gent called Raymond Baxter. He'd not been seen for three days, but he wasn't the sort of chap to disappear. It was most out of character, and his wife and two lovely daughters were most concerned. (I didn't know it yet, but in time the eldest daughter would find her life seriously affected by this disappearance. More on her later.)

'What do you want me to do with this, sarge?' I said.

I can't say his reply was unexpected. 'I don't care!' he snapped. 'Do with it what ee likes, sunshine! You're the investigator! I've told ee before – investigate it! And put that head into gear before you speaks!'

He grabbed his Barbour and marched off out somewhere, tutting and shaking his head. He hadn't been right for a few days. Karen wandered over to have a look at the signal – she'd been on the new computer access course so that she could 'access' information held on the computer by our local Intel office, the LIO.

'I'll see what I can dig up,' she said. 'What's got his goat, Wolfie?' she said asking the question on Tosh's current attitude. Wolfie was deep in concentration and fiddling with a drugs bag. These new bags had just been rolled out: they sealed at the top and were apparently going to be the catalyst in storage of drugs for years to come. Only problem was, most of us couldn't work out how to open them. They were sort of tamper proof, so any attempts to break the seal would be noticed, especially since our drug store DC has been caught selling his wares to our local criminal class.

We like catalysts in the police; they often become nemeses.

'Gah, these are fucking useless,' said Wolfie, throwing his new drugs bag onto his desk in disgust. 'Who's got *what*?' Wolfie said agitated.

'The sarge,' said Karen. 'What's got into him?'

'Ah, he's got a few home-based issues at the moment,' said Wolfie. 'Best leave him be.'

'Well,' huffed Karen. 'He doesn't need to bring his bad manners to work, does he?' She strutted off to put the kettle on, that great British resolution to most problems. 'Tea, Barnesy?' she said.

I nodded.

'Yup,' replied Wolfie, with a wink. 'If you're asking.'

He winked a lot.

The silence returned. For a minute or two, all I could hear was the quiet roar of the kettle, the odd curse from Wolfie, and the rustling of polythene bags.

I scrutinised the brief details on the MISPER, and then I was interrupted by a voice.

'Er, hello mate,' said the voice. 'Can you help me?'

I looked up. In front of me was a tall, skinny officer in uniform, holding a hamster cage which appeared to contain a sleeping hamster.

He went by the name of Delhi.

I knew him, vaguely – he'd joined my uniform shift not long before I departed it and was one of two officers of Indian extraction on our force's strength back in those antediluvian days. The other lad having joined earlier, Delhi was our new Indian.

Hence his nickname.

Delhi.

Because he was *new*.

It took me ages to get it as well.

'Alright, Delhi?' I said, grabbing my biscuits as Karen placed a mug of tea in front of me. 'What can I do you for, youth?'

He stared at me – all dark eyes, big hooter and confusion. 'Sorry bud,' he said. 'Only, I'm just looking for some help. Can you be arrested for killing a hamster?'

I paused, chocolate digestive in hand. 'Eh?' I said.

'Can you be arrested for killing a hamster?' he said, again. 'Only, the shift hamster has died, and we suspect foul play.'

He held up the cage and I peered at the hamster. Perhaps it wasn't asleep after all.

'Er…' I said, playing for time and searching the room for smirks and grins. There were none. Karen had gone to the ladies', Tosh was at the bookies, and Wolfie was fully engaged in swearing at plastic bags. The only other person there was our new office manager, Billy Hoover. He'd replaced the previous one a day or two earlier – these guys came and went dependent on disability, mental well-being or recovery from busted bones – and Billy had nothing that you might describe as a sense of humour. The only time I saw him even smile was when a young WPC fell down the stairs at the front of the nick and showed the world her pants.

I looked back at Delhi.

'What are you on about, mate,' I said. 'Are you winding me up?'

He looked very uncertain.

Then, over his shoulder, I saw a face at the door.

It belonged to his sarge, Dave Benson, and he was simultaneously shushing me and giving me the thumbs up.

Okay, this was a wind-up, I thought, alright – just not mine.

That's fine, I'm game.

Benson grinned, stifled a cackle, and legged it.

'The sarge said I should come and see you,' said Delhi, uncertainly. 'He says you lads have the brief on animal deaths.'

By now, Wolfie had given up on the plastic bags totally and had quickly cottoned on. Unfortunately, he wasn't in the mood.

'So we do,' he said, standing up and placing his arm round the hapless Delhi's shoulder. 'That's what we are all about in here, youth. Death and mayhem, distress and harm, it's part of our daily bread.' He steered the bewildered PC towards the door and helped him out into the corridor. For a moment, Delhi stood there, forlornly, holding his hamster cage. Then Wolfie quickly turned round and locked the office door.

'Barnesy,' he said, sternly. 'We can't keep amusing your old pals in here when they want to send someone on a wind-up. We have work to do.'

This from a man who had just a few weeks back had blown up Shakespeare.

He sat down with a deep sigh and returned to fiddling with his drugs bags.

Never one to be beaten clearly..

One minute we're blowing each other up and it's the funniest thing ever… I thought, bitterly.

'This one's broken an' all, ' shouted Wolfie, slamming his latest plastic bag down on his desk and picking up another.

'They're all iffy, Wolf,' said Shakey, who'd wandered in from somewhere. 'I reckon they are a bad batch.'

It was obvious from six feet away that Wolfie was trying to open the wrong end.

Fuck it, I wasn't going to tell him.

Silence.

'Raymond Baxter,' said Karen, suddenly. She was peering at the new office computer, looking through the LIO Intel reports.

My ears pricked up. 'What have you got, Karen?'

'Not much, just a telephone number which they found when they turned over that brothel at Sandgates a few years back. The number was written in the receptionist's notepad when the warrant was executed. Subscriber check on the number came back to a Raymond Baxter. It was stamped *Nothing followed up* on the signal. Let's see… forty-nine years old, works at the engineering place down the road, seems like Mr Average.'

'That's it, is it?' I said.

'Well, not all the records have been inputed on the system, Barnesy,' she said, 'so I'll have to check the paper records, too.' Being the newly qualified LIO hack she was best to do this.

The police are past masters at introducing new technology and using it to duplicate processes. She wandered off to the LIO, with a resigned air.

I looked out of the now one-way office window.

It was breezy and chilly out there.

In the car park, Delhi was winding police tape round the duty Inspector's car.

****

I PUSHED AHEAD WITH the basics of the MISPER investigation by talking to Mrs Baxter on the telephone and asking for her phone bills over the recent past. She sounded very worried, and kept saying, tearfully, 'I just want him home, please find him.'

I could hear the kids crying in the background, and I did my best to reassure her that we'd track him down. I didn't convince her (or myself) and I was actually quite distressed as I replaced the receiver. Clearly out of character and obviously not a run of the mill situation.

I hoped to goodness he was just taking a few days out.

Karen wandered back in. 'Nothing in The Killing Room, Barnesy,' she said, hands on hips. That was our pet name for the LIO – it had been since the day that 'Bill' Wyman, the LIO sarge, went wild and started threatening to murder everyone; he was restrained and led away crying. Most of the staff were there because they had messed up, or were on light duties, or were stressed to the eyeballs by the long hours, pressure and family disasters that affect approximately fifty per cent of all cops at some time or another. Back then, being stressed wasn't manly, and very few talked about it. You soldiered on, you got on with it, and remained one of the boys – until it all went pear shaped. Barry Spencer was another – he loved the job, but took everything to heart, that and the drink turned him into a monster. He had two sieges and finally threw a fridge at the Superintendent negotiator before they sacked him. He eventually got better and apologised to the Super by sending him a bottle of piss in the post. He stayed sacked. Those that could handle it bottled it up (scuse the pun) for so long they exploded, like Bill Wyman.

But I digress.

'Nothing?' I said.

'Just the telephone number, I've printed off the report for you, it is in the control room'

Back then we had one printer, and the Inspector looked after it in the control room. Later on in my service we would have loads of printers, either unplugged, out of ink or not connected to your terminal. When all else fails I still print my stuff to the control room printer. The five minute walk across the road quicker than a long call to IT or three of us wiggling leads about and getting our heads stuck in dusty places underneath desks.

The last time I did that I found a hundred year old sandwich, an apple core and a three bob bit. I will also know immediately when it comes out of the printer because the control room Inspector will radio me angrily telling me my paperwork was clogging up his life.

It's like having your own voice-activated print receipt.

The early nineties had no internet, email system, telecoms access, mobile phones as such or databases full of info. We had the police national computer (PNC) and a sort of command and control system that crashed regularly. This command and control system could only be accessed by a nominated Sarge or a duty Sarge. These poor souls were often seen pouring over a screen in the corner of a room with a manual on their knee tutting angrily, and on one occasion I saw one old sweat punch the big glass screen so hard he bust his knuckle.

Investigation, especially the types we were dealing with was based on case theories, but a Misper to some extent were different. For a start the human life form is a free radical, it acts on emotional impulse. Tick boxes and manuals don't reflect the human Misper's state of mind, free radicals as I said. Nothing that electrical or run by hardware is in the mix. Investigative pathways are just that, they are inanimate solutions to theories.

People are not.

Nowadays we have strict timeframes and guidance on a Misper. Young people and vulnerability taking precedence, and actions that must be done and performed in goodly time too. Back then it wasn't taken too serious until a few days had gone by, and probably by then the Misper as well.

In some cases forever.

A lot of evidence could be lost, so I always moved quickly on these inquires, especially when my name was all over them. That was another problem back then, at times we investigated these cases, so we didn't get in to trouble, which sort of clouds the actual reason for doing it in the first place in my opinion. Investigating because you don't want to get in to bother should never be the driver, but it is for many reasons.

Even today.

I had his car details, and put a marker on PNC, this would alert any other officer or force of the possibility that Raymond could be the driver, and he was missing. He wasn't suicidal, and didn't offer any concerns regards this. I got his medical records quickly via his wife, and noted a dose of STD, a sexually transmitted disease, (crabs) three years before. That was it, he was given a vapour rub and he was good to go.

No criminal past and no reason to go missing.

Then I linked the STD with the brothel – I put two and two together and got seven.

'Barnesy it means nothing' Tosh said, hands on his waist as he looked at me laughing.

'He has gone off and will be back tomorrow – you see'

Tosh went on to talk about crabs, the pox and a chap's right to spend a few quid on the quiet.

He went on.

And on.

'She isn't coming across with all the info, she's embarrassed Young 'un', don't you worry, he will be back'. Tosh was prowling about looking at of the new drugs bags. I noted that the discovery of the telephone number at the Sandgates brothel coincided with his dose of crabs, maybe something and nothing but I had nothing other than that.

'Sarge, maybe he was being blackmailed, we don't know do we? Maybe he was under pressure, nobody knows what is going on in the mind at times. If he is visiting brothels he has marital problems – yes?'

Tosh wouldn't have it, Wolfie didn't help either, so after a few hours work I was left with a few inquiries done, and not much else.

I decided to slow burn it and do as I was told, and went home.

I got back in to work at 6am the next day to be told that Raymond Baxter was dead.

Police had found his car just off the M42 near Birmingham, more than a fair way from home and at that point hadn't noted any suspicious circumstances, problem was his wife didn't know.

Oh jeez, it wasn't even time for our first cup of tea.

'Take Karen and go and tell her' Tosh said. 'Death messages are best delivered by those who the family trust' he added.

'I spoke to her for ten minutes on the phone yesterday Sarge, that's it '

'So she trusts you then' Tosh replied.

He clattered the spoons about in the draw and fumbled with his tea mug. 'Now go on before she hears about it on the bloody radio'

It was one of those chilly but sunny mornings, everything moving steady, people locked in their cars and going to work.

A forgettable day for most.

I went to the address with Karen, the door was opened by the youngest child Mary (aged six) she was just ready for school. Mrs Baxter, slim, casual clothes, brown hair, glasses – about 40 years I would say, attractive to a point as well. Mrs Baxter was there in the kitchen, coffee being made and the eldest daughter Philippa (she was ten) was eating her breakfast.

The house was in lovely condition, it was in the most salubrious part of town I would say, a big old building, town house in design with plenty of room all round, on four floors a superb family home.

Traditional black door and big knocker too.

These people were not our usual clientele.

The kitchen was open plan, breakfast bar and had a TV on in the corner. I asked Mrs Baxter if we could have a moment of her time in a different room. I am not sure how that affected her, I didn't give any insight in to what was coming next, but she went in to melt down.

It's hard to describe melt down.

But it's serious.

'No. No.No.No.No.No' She ran towards me screaming 'Tell me he's not dead, Tell me he's not dead' She went on and on holding on to me and screaming, she was crying and out of control. Punching my chest.

Her mascara immediately ran, her face distorted.

The kids started as well, screaming and wailing, and the eldest started throwing things at the window. It went bang! as plates, cutlery and most bizarrely a soft cloth were thrown at the walls and windows. She ran from the room screaming and I could hear her running up the stairs, the youngest was in a star shape on the floor screaming and kicking.

Then it upped a level.

There would be a lot of upping levels over the next half an hour.

Mrs Baxter punched Karen, not hard, but in a side of her fist sort of way, she did this a number of times and as I said by doing this, she raised the tempo.

'Why didn't you stop him, why didn't you stop him' she wailed.

I tried to hold on to her.

I can now let you know reader, nobody can deal with this scenario, not even one of those Sergeants promotion exam part two scenarios in training can deal with this.

The smashing of glass upstairs was deafening.

Philippa was smashing the windows in to the street. I let go of Raymond's wife and ran upstairs.

Philippa was covered in blood punching out the windows in a bedroom with a small cricket bat.

This took some doing.

This wasn't getting any better.

Blood spurted all over the place.

Hammer House Of Horror time again.

I went in to *save a life* mode, quickly getting bedding to stem the blood flow, applying direct pressure as I tried to get to my Motorola radio to summon an ambulance. I could hear crashing and banging downstairs too and Karen shouting 'Barnesy help'

It was pure and utter fucking chaos.

Philippa wasn't hard to subdue, she was ten, but she continually screamed, tried to bite me and then spat continuously in my face.

'You bastard, you cunt, you filthy whore' she shouted.

Kids know these words, and closed doors don't reveal as much as we would like.

Her legs kicked out, her arms a blur of movement.

Then a bloke appeared in his dressing gown in the doorway of the room we were in and attacked me.

 Just as I was stemming Philippa's blood flow and gaining some control I had a bloke round my neck.

When I say attacked he grabbed me by the head and shouted 'Get off her you pervert' and somewhat limply slapped my head.

'I'm a fucking police officer you cunt' were the *exact* words I used.

I screamed them too.

He immediately stopped.

He started to ask questions, as I held the girl down firmly, I interrupted him.

Very firmly.

'Listen, if you want to help call an ambulance and help my colleague downstairs, this is serious'

He seemed to come to his senses and ran downstairs like a freaky Kenny Everett shouting 'Shirley are you okay?'

Mrs Shirley Baxter was anything but okay.

This was madness.

Again.

I know swearing at members of the public is not the done thing, but at times you have to gauge the situation as it is, and then look at where you want it to be. In such a highly charged situation the whole scenario can be diluted by a well-placed 'cunt' I make no apologies for this, it's all a part of my training…

My on the job training experience that is.

And as we can see now, it worked perfectly.

Philippa was sobbing as I calmed her and I could hear the sound of sirens in the distance.

'It's okay 'I said as I stroked her head, the injuries as ever not as bad as the blood that was everywhere. The flow had subsided somewhat from three major cuts.

I was out of breath.

I picked her up, the blood oozing through the bed sheet as I carried her downstairs. I got her to hold her injured arm up high and stemmed the flow again in the kitchen. Mrs Baxter was lying on the sofa sobbing quietly and Karen was comforting the youngest daughter on the kitchen floor.

There could have been no more than two minutes passed since we walked into that house and totally destroyed their lives.

I have met people who don't like the police, and generally that is because we stop them being criminals, however there are people out there who don't like the police for different reasons, and this was one.

No matter how well we managed this from here on in, they would never see the police in any light other than negative from this day onwards. All three were taken to hospital and as the ambulance drove off Tosh arrived.

'Fuck me Barnesy' he said 'You looks likes you have just come home from the fucking Somme'

My suit was covered in blood, as was Karen, but on inspection in the hall mirror revealed I looked like 'Freddie's fucking Nightmares' Smeared blood on the floor, smashed crockery and a fish tank completely empty of water and many a dead fish on the floor.

Two I noticed flipped slowly.

This would take some cleaning up.

In amongst all this the male in the dressing gown (paisley pattern and silk I noted) came in with a tray full of tea's. He definitely walked with a slight suggestion - and was most effeminate.

In fact he was the epitome of what is male and effeminate.

Tosh's eyes followed him across the kitchen floor.

Mouth open.

'Thanks mate' I said, interrupting before Tosh could get anything out.

'Most appreciated' I said again.

I drew a breath.

'That was a crazy five minutes eh?'

I walked across to the big kitchen table and the male (who I still know today as Karl, a quality guy) placed the teas carefully down.

I slapped his back lightly.

'Thanks for your help bud' I said.

Karl said nothing but looked thoughtful.

His star of David necklace shining and his slight slim frame was leaning left.

He had a glint in his eye and looked a bit like a young David Niven.

Hands on hips.

He beckoned me close in to him so he could whisper in to my ear.

I leant in.

He had small beads of sweat on his forehead.

In a very camp but controlled way he whispered 'I may be many things officer, but I can assure you I am not, and never will be a… cunt'

A few seconds silence.

'Sorry mate' I said.

Karl smiled 'Your apology is very welcome and very much appreciated' he smiled.

He went on.

'If I can be of help I'm next door in the annexe' He gently tapped my shoulder back and gave me a second a glance as he winked and walked away.

Tosh and Karen watched him as he left.

Tosh was about to say something.

'Not a fucking word Sarge, please, not a fucking word' I interrupted.

I returned to the nick after a wash and change of clothes at home. I saw that the duty Inspector's car was still cordoned off with blue and white police tape blowing in a sharp wind. Stood alongside it was Delhi, very alert, legs apart, standing at ease but looking very official. Pen poised etc. ....

I walked over.

'What's all this then youth?' I said.

'I'm looking after the crime scene mate' he replied.

'The Sarge said I was to make sure nobody enters this area'

'That's good' I said, and you're running a log too I see, that's excellent'

'Yes, and now I am going to have to ask you for your details as you are in conversation with me at the crime scene and I have to record it in my log' He did know me, but I chanced it.

'Oh well, of course that's only right and proper' I said. 'Er, I'm DC Shakespeare, for the record, but you can call me Hamlet'

I didn't wait for a reaction.

I walked away.

I heard him say 'DC Shakespeare' and I glanced back.

Delhi had assumed the natural position of 'at ease'.

Most impressive.

I engaged with Dave Benson when I got back inside, Delhi's sergeant.

'How much longer are you going to run this one for Dave?' I said.

'Oh for a few hours yet' he replied.

He smiled.

'It's all about his development anyway, nobody can call us on this one'

'Development?' I replied.

'Yes youth, he has some deficiencies in certain areas, and we are addressing them in turn, today its log keeping at crime scenes, we haven't got a crime scene on the go, so we have manufactured one. It's like training but on the job.

I immediately thought about the scenario I had just left at the Baxter's abode, and then quickly dismissed it as a non-starter as I didn't want any of them anywhere near it.

Development or not.

Benno smiled.

'So you're not wasting public money then?' I said.

'How can we be mate, Delhi is in training still, he is a probationer, at the end of all this he will have another tick in the box and be more of an asset at crime scenes than he is now. It's a win - win bud'

Tick box, I had to smile.

But he had a point.

Even if Delhi was convinced that this was all linked to the death of the shift hamster.

'Oh, by the way Benno' I said.

'What's this with the shift hamster?'

He smiled again 'Oh, that's from property youth, the hamster isn't even real'

I walked away smiling, but I have to confess I was very worried that Delhi actually believed all this, but then he had come to us after failing his probation elsewhere in another force.

So we were taking a punt on him.

A bit like a free transfer.

Some more cynical officers would talk about ethnicity and cultural numbers, maybe even bullying on hearing about Delhi's experiences. But this would have happened to anyone regardless of who they were.

So, I would like to think not.

****

Over the next few days I gathered a lot of information on Raymond Baxter. I saw that he had a lot of money going out, and with help from our financial bods 'upstairs' much more was going out than coming in. Baxter was a company director whose annual turnover was in the region of two million. After costs and all other side issues he had a very nice self-paid income of £125,000 a year.

At the time a nice wedge.

His business was a successful one, so why do yourself in?

We were back in the office.

'The Inspector agrees that you can guide this one Barnesy' Tosh looked over his glasses at me as Shakespeare clumsily dropped his spoon again on the floor.

'Not sure if I should thank you or not Sarge' I replied.

'This guy seems to be a bit of a mystery, big incomes always seem to bring with them a problem'

'And that's why thee will never be a problem as long as you is in the police Barnesy boy' Tosh was scowling as he smiled 'Thee be a copper, and there ain't no rich coppers, just divorced ones'.

Tosh was a divorced one.

He knew.

'Oi Barnesy, Baxter had an offshore company set up with five grand a month going into it' Wolfie walked further in and across the room as he spoke, he was holding some paperwork that he had managed to get earlier from the financial team.

'Baxter had been under investigation by the Dooley's upstairs, they know a little bit about him too' Wolfie walked away from me as quickly as he came.

'Come on Youth – time is of the essence.

Tosh nodded at me indicating I should follow Wolfie upstairs.

I shook my head, one minute nobody wants to know, the next it's the next big thing! I followed suit and looked outside as I walked out of the office door.

I saw Shakey through the window walking across the car park and then he completely disappeared.

I also heard a shout.

His weird suit and plus four type arrangement on his trousers turning upside down was my last view. The last I saw him his legs were akimbo as he disappeared from view.

It was almost as if he had been flipped upwards by the invisible man.

Then a large bang, like corrugated sheets falling.

'Fucking hell Barnesy' Tosh said as he stood up quickly.

Then another crash was heard as Tosh's mug hit the floor as he stood up from his desk, not breaking it, but dispersing tea everywhere.

That won't ever be cleaned up I thought.

Tosh shouted.

'Hamlet has fallen in to that big hole'

He pointed towards the missing Hamlet and ran outside.

I ran outside with him and saw Tosh's Hamlet at least eight feet below me in a recently dug hole in the car park, he was half covered in corrugated sheets and was completely unconscious. I jumped down and checked him quickly, pulse first and then for any real signs of broken bones or blood injury.

Nothing.

I looked up and a large crowd was peering in to the hole, it was so dark because there were so many gobs peering at me.

'Any chance we could have some day light' I said to no one in particular.

They stepped back a bit.

Hamlet moaned and briefly opened his eyes.

'Barnesy, Barnesy' he said. 'Fucking big hole'

And slipped back to sleep.

Then a clatter from two floors above.

It was Wolfie.

He was looking out the admin office window.

'Oi youth, what you doing down there, get yourself up here, we have work to do'

I think I can safely say at times I didn't think there was any caring in our caring, sharing police service.

A Very Major Trial

AS SOME OF YOU READING THIS WILL KNOW that police investigations move swiftly once you are on to a line of inquiry, especially when you're on the right line of that inquiry. This generally leads you to some serious answers to even more serious questions.

'We could have our very own live *Whodunit'* Wolfie said as we poured over the paperwork given to us by the Dooley brothers, two very bright geeky types in the financial building. I mentioned them before, but to clarify.

Neither of them were police officers, however they were the type of person I have always found invaluable in the police. Professional, intelligent and trustworthy. In some cases people become members of police staff because they are looking for a new life, that's okay I suppose, we all need a job, and others because they haven't got anything else better to do. Then there are those dedicated few who stay with the team for year after year, enjoying the life and loving the mix.

This was The Dooley's.

So we quickly had information regards an offshore bank account and then various bank accounts connected to this offshore trail.

All in the name of Raymond Baxter.

It was a decent break through.

'What would you do now Wolfie?' I said.

Roughly translated as, *What the fuck do I do now Wolfie!*

I was slightly out of my depth here.

We decided that the best approach was to identify the benefiting bank accounts through the Dooley's network of helpers. Back then the paperwork wasn't too bad to do to get the right replies from banks, and in fact the briefest of phone calls could put you on the right track. Nowadays it's a specialism on its own, and the responding companies charge hundreds and sometimes thousands for the information. And their attitude at times too is questionable. The delays can affect crime investigations badly.

The Dooley's quickly got on the case as we twiddled our thumbs, and within an hour we had two lots of bank details connected to Baxter, one was to a man called Martin Drinkwater, a man who owned a few night clubs over the motorway from us towards the country, and the other – Shirley Baxter.

Wife of the now deceased Raymond.

Chin rubby time.

I walked back in to the office triumphantly holding the paperwork.

I was feeling pleased that police investigation, for once, was so easy.

The bump that brings you down at these points had three stripes on his non uniform shoulder.

Then Tosh said 'The post mortem is at two o' clock kid, get yourself along and speak with the pathologist pronto'

Tosh looked at me intently.

'It's on in half hour Barnesy, get yer skates on' He was bellowing again.

He yanked his thumb over his shoulder but wasn't looking at me as he did this, the Racing Post was sprawled out over his desk. His sandwiches now being spat over the two thirty from Kempton.

'Move it Barnesy and take Wolfie as well'.

We both looked at each other, the prospect of watching a pathologist dissect an older man on the slab of the mortuary didn't fill us with much glee. But it was a part of the job, so we had to get on with the show. We made our way over to the newly opened mortuary at the hospital.

It always had that smell.

I can't describe it too well, like a mouldy, disinfectant, dried hot blood aroma.

I saw Martin Jenkinson before he saw me.

He was singing loudly.

'Onward Christian Soldiers' ......

He was unloading bits from his car in the car park near the rear doors of the mortuary, just close enough for the smell to be ready to hit you.

'Oh, its him again' I said to Wolfie.

Wolfie looked a bit pale, and like Tosh wasn't a huge fan of these deadly processes. As I walked towards Jenkinson I saw a plain black coloured vehicle open up its back doors to my right. A large (clearly a dead person) black bagged body was wheeled in through the back doors of the mortuary.

The body wobbled under a green covering.

It was so obvious who this was and what he was about to participate in.

'Jeez' said Wolfie, 'He must be twenty stone. This is going to be messy'

'Hello, Hello, Hello officer, we meet again' Martin held out his hand to greet me as he strode up to us.

He looked pleased to see me.

I couldn't say the same, some people you just associate with bad things, and Mr Jenkinson was one of those people on my list. Remember how Mrs Baxter and her kids must feel when they see the police?

It isn't much different.

'Hello DC Wolf' he said smiling, how are we both today, this one is a big lad by all accounts, a lot of blubber to get through'

Jenkinson looked pleased he had such a hard job to do.

He walked ahead of us and Wolfie said quietly 'The amount of money this lot get paid for posh butchery youth, I suppose he has every right to be happy'

Jenkinson was the only one who was happy, I hated these processes too.

The PM took over six hours. Much was removed for analysis later, and at the end Jenkinson revealed that Baxter had possibly died of a heart attack.

'Possibly' is what our Pathologists do best.

The tissue and other related bits from the heart were placed on blue trays and covered in the cling film, then in to a cooler box, yes, the picnic was ready.

Usual stuff now.

'Straight forwards gents' he said. 'Not a hard one to diagnose, of course there will be more work to do at the lab, but this lad died of myocardial infarction.

'Eh?' Wolfie said.

Jenkinson smiled 'His ticker stopped working as a result of heart failure DC Wolf'

'Will we get that in writing boss' Wolfie said.

'Of course, I will make sure DC Barnes here gets all the detail. And don't forget the coroner will want a file too' he said this as he climbed in to his sports car.

Jenkinson roared off in his premium sports vehicle and Wolfie said 'Hundreds of pounds earned for cutting up dead people, it ain't right Barnesy, it just ain't right'

Wolfie tutted and shook his head.

I just stared at the road.

I tended to disagree, for me, anyone who could do that job on a daily basis deserved every penny.

We were back in the office by nine that night.

'No foul play then?' Tosh said, hands on hips.

There was a hint of fried fish in the room.

The usual Detective stance, questioning and prompting you to agree.

'Seemingly not Sarge' I replied 'A heart attack is the diagnosis'

I was feeling good about our work.

And also pleased that the possibility of no foul play was favourite.

'Brought on by what?' Tosh asked.

He peered closer at me.

I could smell drunken tea. A musty concoction of bad breath and a bad diet.

'What brought it on Detective, this heart attack you speaks of, what brought it on now you have all the answers?'

I wasn't feeling so good.

I fell silent. That wasn't a bad question.

'Er …. Well' (yes, you guessed it)

'Well, we won't know that Tosh till the PM report gets through to us will we?' Wolfie walked over to our desks.. 'We can't give an exact cause until we get all the details Sarge. You know that'

Tosh smiled, Wolfie had saved me.

The police had this way of punching you in the face. Just when you think you have cracked it something comes along that whacks you hard.

In this case the bloody Sarge.

'Young 'un, never drop your guard on this investigation, not for a second'

Tosh patted my back as he walked out of the office.

His fag already lit, his echoing footsteps in the corridor may as well be saying *'Going down the pub, going down the pub'*

Never a truer word has been spoken, dropping your guard for a second can cause weeks of misery. What Tosh was doing was letting me loose slowly in to the investigative ether, yes under the guidance of Wolfie, but I was slowly being released in to the wild. I was liaising with pathologists and working out case theories based on what we knew, and *Tosh's gut instinct* at times.

And I was being allowed to have an opinion on the job in hand as well.

Sometimes.

Tosh said to me once 'I remembers that time Barnesy boy, I remembers it well, you were like one of they little terrapins on the beach, with thousands of other little terrapins, getting let loose on the sand. I Let's ye lose Barnesy boy hoping no bugger will eat ya, there's plenty of they sharks out there Barnesy, but you swerved the hungriest of em, and took on the rest like I knew you would'

This is what investigating is all about.

Being able to see clearly, fight when necessary and protect your own.

Apparently I had the ability to see through the clouds in the sky, and swerve the sharks in the sea.

Or, that's what I thought he was saying …..

We gather the information, present it as evidence, assume lines of inquiry and theorise what we believe to have happened from the content we retrieve.

After all, at the end of this inquiry, the investigation in to the death and life of Raymond Baxter - I would be expected to put in not only in (possibly) a criminal file but a coroners file as well. That is if we ventured towards wrongdoing of course.

The first one, the crime file would may well be placed before a criminal court and need a burden of proof called *'beyond all reasonable doubt'*

The latter a file that would go before the coroners court which acted upon the *'balance of probability'*

Two very different burdens of proof.

I had to get it right because nobody else would be in court as the *officer in the case.* That of course would be me. It's no good blaming the Sarge in crown court when he is putting a tenner on a gee gee at Aintree, smoking a fag and drinking his winnings. The court do not understand the police when blaming things on others, they never have, and you are the Detective son, so take the responsibility.

I had a dead body from the M42 in the mortuary, all cut up and sad.

And what made it come in to our office were his home based activities which made Raymond Baxter interesting. It may well lead to a joint inquiry, but for now we had it in our back pocket, and that's where it was staying. And Tosh's desire to see if I could decipher the rubbish from the real rubbish continued.

I also had a wife all emotionally cut up and unhappy in a house in town with two very fragile kids. Then I couldn't forget the Dooley's side of things, two bank accounts, one in the name of the wife and the other in the name of a Martin Drinkwater.

Something told me that this would be my next line of inquiry.

*****

The next day Wolfie and I both cleared up some loose ends and set about looking at Drinkwater. He had been arrested before, but only drink drive and a domestic assault five years ago. We did have a bit of Intel on him, late drinking and the odd bit of finger pointing from ex employee's that he dabbled in class A. (drugs) That could be put down to revenge for getting the boot from their jobs, and then I noticed a piece of Intel about money.

'Wolfie, what do you think about this?' I showed him a short report from two years before from a so called business colleague of Drinkwater's regards money laundering in Jersey and some Swiss involvement. There was nothing specific but it showed a degree of planning in to his criminality.

'Seems he likes to hide his cash' Wolfie said.

'It isn't surprising youth, men who make lots of money want to make more, and they often hide things, money included' Wolfie went on 'Nothing unusual there, he seems to earn a wedge or two, but this is useful, we need to corroborate it though.'

'What about this?' I said.

A footnote to the report stated that the person offering the Intelligence had more information on prostitution and gambling.

'That's more like it' Wolfie said rubbing his hands.

'It's Al Capone time Barnesy'

Wolfie laughed.

On the CID we do have some mundane and pretty straight forward stuff to investigate, we also have really interesting inquiries too, and then we have slow burners that take off!

'I do like an investigation that moves from lust to money to death youth' Wolfie said. 'Makes me think some of those Sunday night Detective dramas have got a bit of reality to them'

Sometimes you have to take stock. We had a variety of low (ish) grade intel from upstairs, a Pathologist who albeit thought it was a heart attack had to do a lot more work to prove or disprove it, this meant that we had to continue this as a criminal inquiry for now. In fact we did continue because we wanted to. We tracked down the scribe of the report, an old DC who was now housed in our serious crime unit.

He was biding his time and counting off the days before he retired. He told us of certain issues with Drinkwater, seemingly on the face of it a lovely chap, lots of money and a good old raiser of funds for local charities. On the other hand he made huge amounts of cash on top of his two night clubs by selling drugs via third, fourth and fifth parties and had a string of ladies queuing up to nestle their lips on his trumpet most evenings.

Drugs of a Class A nature tend to have this accompaniment.

We all make our beds.

The main thing with approaches to men like Drinkwater is how he perceives things, not how we perceive things, or how we want to be perceived as people. It's all about the police and what we can do to him long term that he needs to be scared of, not us as individuals. If that was the case he would just ring up a few of his heavies and do away with us, no, lets sit back a moment, this needs planning.

Let me explain.

Drinkwater needs to be on the back foot from the off with this inquiry. At no time must he at all think we don't know stuff.

And by stuff I mean quite simply – stuff.

Anything.

If we must - we should give the impression we know more than we do, and from there on create an aura not dissimilar to those Sunday night TV drama's Wolfie referred to. After all, nobody really knows how the police works, and their only reference is programmes like this. We had to retain the upper hand, and give Drinkwater the *impression* we were just a step away from *'bringing him in'* (not that we had anything to indicate we could, just give him a few thoughts along those lines)and use this confusion to further our best interests.

All above the law you understand.

Perception is a wonderful thing. How you think and understand a situation is only going to be based on what you perceive that situation to be, which brings me round three sixty to my original point.

The first ten seconds with Drinkwater may well be crucial. If he is put off and unbalanced by us he may well make a move that isn't within his character. From that we will gain the upper hand, then he will become quite cautious of us, he will know we aren't fresh out of the box, and he will do things (if he is in anyway involved) as a result of our meeting.

If that's what we need to create to get the result, then so be it.

Of course he could be completely innocent and nothing to do with the death of Raymond Baxter, again there are no real suspicious circumstances as to why he died, just a heart attack on the M42.

But the side issues were expanding already.

Remember we haven't got our blinkers on, we are open not only to Raymond Baxter's death, but other offences too. Thing is, these reports etc … are just that - intelligence stored for inquiries just like this, it can be evidential but without an *officer in the case* allocated they will generally just remain there until needed. If ever. Unless of course the information is such that it requires immediate attention. We put our heads together and went to Drinkwater's office in the the town.

It went to plan, he wasn't in.

On our way to the office we got a warrant to enter and search the premises based on the money aspect of the recent death, the intelligence and the bank account link from the Dooley's. We could mention favourably in conversation our other less qualified info. The information we lay before the magistrate was basic, we had a dead body, we had indications of some odd bank account movements - and that was linked to a shady character who dabbled in drugs and ancillary matters. It took half an hour of our time at Mrs Magistrate's house in the new development of million pound plus houses which attracted the odd big burglary. She made us a lovely bone china cuppa with homemade cake as well.

Getting warrants at a magistrate's home address is far more acceptable than a quizzical gaze from the bench in a cleared court. It's far less formal. This would enable us to lever ourselves in to Drinkwater's life conveniently. It's always nice to have a little bit of serenity in your back pocket, especially if it ensures access to where we want to go.

I parked out of the way, two minutes from the High Street.

I didn't even break the glass on his office door as I kicked it in, it was a flimsy lock that flew off in to the far wall.

Bang, and a ping.

The door bounced back slightly from the door / wall stopper fitted to the floor.

Dull lighting flickered in the corridor. A flight of stairs below us.

I could smell perfume and mints.

Then we walked in to his first floor office above Boots.

Drinkwater did have a secretary downstairs whom we managed to bypass easily, she was talking in loud terms to a friend about make-up and her boyfriend.

Her voice still sailed upstairs when the lock broke.

A table was placed diagonally across the far wall, a computer on the desk which to me made it look like it was all a bit space age. One of those big grey computers that cropped up here and there in those days. I am not entirely sure anyone knew how to use them.

Various framed film posters on the dark mauve walls gave an arty and gracious feel to the room, and made me feel (albeit momentarily) awkward. He also had many, many framed photographs of him with celebrities or actors wishing him all the very best.

Yes, he was one of those.

Combining the dark mauve wall with the rest of the room was a lush green wall, fixed to it were lots of tropical fish tanks that bubbled away peacefully. These contained many expensive tropical fish. I knew this as I had kept the odd guppy myself. The smell was clean and the whole office set up was clinical.

But I could definitely smell lemons.

Wolfie set about opening up various drawers and I sat down at Drinkwater's desk. I fiddled with the computer and it lit up all green and black before going off again.

I also opened up drawers.

Ah, lemons, and some tonic water and a bottle of Gin too.

Classy.

The CID are not renowned for their search ability, we just went with a gut feeling back then, and these events were at times pretty much unplanned.

Much has changed today I may add. This style of searching went on for about five minutes, me perusing, and Wolfie banging about behind the door.

Then we both heard footsteps on the stairs and a deep Scottish voice boomed from below.

Two coffee's Connie dear' as the footsteps trotted upwards.

Within seconds he was there.

I froze, Drinkwater stood in the doorway.

'Who the fuck are you?' He shouted and walked towards me.

He was a big lad, 52 years I would say, more overweight than worrying, I could smell his after shave before he got too close, good god it was strong, his large winter grey coat and crisp black suit, white shirt finished off with a green tie were perfection.

Very nice.

Drinkwater stopped a few feet away and said again 'Who the fuck are you?'

'Who the fuck is who?' I said.

I stood up.

He stopped.

'You' he said.

He pointed at me.

Me?' I replied.

I pointed at myself.

'Yes' he said.

'Well, I'm not a burglar' I said.

I looked around.

'And I'm not repairing your computer' I added, pointing to the big glass screen.

'So who am I indeed?'

I leaned forwards, hands astride his desk, staring at him as the evening was descending outside. Voices, traffic and the odd vehicle horn interrupted this moment. I switched the desk light on, a green topped desk light much seen at the time. I didn't raise my voice, but then I didn't shout, looking back now I would say it was slightly menacing when I said – ' I wouldn't be too worried if I was you Mr Drinkwater, I would be more worried about why I am here'

Then a voice boomed behind him which made him turn round dramatically and yelp slightly.

Drinkwater leapt backwards.

'And Mr Drinkwater, may I ask just what you are doing in possession of a Browning pistol, and may I also ask …. Is it loaded?'

Wolfie had appeared from the shadows behind and him he was pointing a gun right at him.

Drinkwater put his hands up.

If Wolfie had one of those 1930's gangster hats on and there was a little bit of dramatic music to boot I have no doubt we would be recreating a scene from an American gangster movie of old, James Cagney et al.

The street lights and darkness cut across Wolfie's frame.

He had a white / grey diagonal line of light across his face.

Shadowed. It was perfect. The traffic buzz continued.

Drinkwater walked backwards slowly towards the window, arms raised, and kept flicking his gaze between us both.

Wolfie was still holding the gun, walking towards him.

It was brilliant.

Wolfie spoke.

'Now Mr Drinkwater, Let's not be silly, sit down and do it slowly, and after my colleague has searched you properly (Wolfie looked at me and gestured) you can tell us all about why Raymond Baxter is dead'

I searched Drinkwater relieving him of his wallet and a small flick / pen knife.

As I did so my face was as close as it could be to his.

'Nice and easy Drinkwater' I said.

We were so close I could have kissed him, or indeed punched him.

'No silly business, and well, you never know, we may well all get home tonight in one piece eh?'

He was sweating and nodding.

His breath was intermittent, deep and he was panicking.

He didn't say a word.

'Good' I said quietly.

I patted him down, and pushed him back slightly towards the chair behind him.

I winked.

'Sit down Mr Drinkwater, and keep it very quiet'

He sat.

The dust in the room was lit up against the air con heater which had just kicked in circulating particles by the false lighting next to the window.

Sodium yellow was breaking through the chinks in the blinds.

Hopefully, now I have told you what happened that evening you understand perfectly. Coppering comes in many forms.

On the hoof at times, with a bit of luck, and of course we owe a big thanks to the mystery created by the press, the people who read the press, and of course at times people like you. Because without you all Mr Drinkwater wouldn't have literally shit himself when he met Barnesy and Wolfie for the first time.

Perception see.

*****

The finding of a Browning pistol by Wolfie was what we call 'an added bonus' in Detective terms, and the moment that Martin Drinkwater met Barnesy and Wolfie, *'Crime Detectives'* would have stayed with him to his dying day. That much I am sure. The scene as it unfurled before him was a ping pong discussion in the twilight of that winters evening, and it could not have been scripted better.

He simply fell apart.

The dialogue was simple and easy to understand, Wolfie started off the chat.

In situations like these in those TV dramas the question that would be asked of Drinkwater would be *'How do you know Raymond Baxter?'*

Wolfie was made of better stuff than that.

'We know about you and Raymond Baxter, Mr Drinkwater, the bank accounts the money, the link to Shirley, and now he is dead on the motorway. You have plenty to talk about. But don't think there is anything we don't already know. If you're not involved criminally and want to be a good witness, trust me Mr Gangster man it's time to talk'

Very clever.

When I passed on from the police in less than perfect circumstances (no leaving is really accompanied by any sweet sorrow) the cops were beginning to be too concerned with not upsetting people, back then it was a chess game. The best part in any chess game is getting your opponent on the back foot from the off and keeping them there.

It seemed at that point that Drinkwater knew that we were the cops. Introductions at this time were not forthcoming. He seemed slightly relieved too, at least he wouldn't get a hiding or worse, unless of course he believed the nonsense sometimes seen in the press. And if he did, maybe that would help. Remember this is about perception of what could happen, not about the people involved and what will happen.

Drinkwater didn't strike me as this felonious villain who helped himself to who he wanted - when he wanted. He looked petrified and when he tried to gain some control he was immediately brought back in to focus.

He wasn't going to get away with anything, not with the two of us seated in front of him.

Cigarettes were lit (I had slowly started the habit of old again more routinely) as we spent the next three hours recording details, searching under the terms of the warrant, and now having found evidence with more search criteria we had plenty to go on. We were being offered letters and papers, drinking coffee and slowly understanding the world of Drinkwater.

He was being a very helpful witness.

He was properly cautioned, and a contemporaneous note kept.

He was one of those blokes who preyed on the weak, or took advantage of those who saw his wealth as important and a powerful thing.

None of these things interested me or Wolfie.

Fifteen Love.

His lifestyle of snorting powders and top class restaurants, chilled beers and top hotels may appeal to some, but good coppers don't take advantage of this either.

Thirty Love.

Criminally obtained cars, noisy night clubs and all night party people may appeal when certain folk are young and gaining maturity, but they don't appeal to the steely eyed investigator with the bit between their teeth.

Forty Love.

And when all else fails, when it is evident that your local coppers are not for turning, and that your wealth means nothing to them, and indeed throwing some it their way won't work.

Its game, Set and Match.

And if you are in the cops and any of you disagree at any point then hand your badge in now, or go to a mirror and have a good hard look.

PS – I hate fucking tennis too.

Drinkwater told us about Raymond Baxter and his insatiable appetite for sex as a result of blue pills and cocaine. Nowadays it's seen as a mental health issue, and it is to an extent, back then it was just a sordid side to a sordid character. He told us that Baxter was forever pestering him for cocaine and loved the ladies. He said he gave him cocaine every other day. Well, the toxicology would tell us if that was true in time. He insisted that Baxter would 'take' at least four women a week and he was being sent far and wide to quench his thirst for this pastime.

Hence the M42 possibly. That indeed was far and very wide, Drinkwater had arranged two girls over two days, miles away from home. He admitted that he was having an affair with his wife Shirley, purely for personal reasons, she was available and happy to oblige. And admittedly there is no rule broken here of a criminal nature. There was no future in it, but her availability whenever he wanted her was fine by him.

He knew too when Baxter was away from home, almost very convenient.

I wanted to know why Baxter was friendly with Drinkwater and why Drinkwater continued the friendship. He told us Shirley was the reason, and of course Drinkwater liked to be in control of people. He didn't tell us that last bit, but it was clear to me. The main reason though was that Baxter paid in to an off shore account five grand a month for the constant supply of women, drugs and hotels. Basically Drinkwater was earning two to three grand a month from this arrangement.

See, it always comes down to money.

There was no link between the two accounts of Drinkwater and Shirley Baxter, the payments by Baxter to his wife would have been made as a result I suppose of his guilty conscience to hundreds of partners and loads of drugs.

Little did he know she was benefiting in kind as well.

I had no choice but to interview Drinkwater for the supply of drugs which he wasn't aware was an offence if you gave them away, just goes to show how daft people can be.

He had admitted this already.

The prostitution side of things was also charged in time as well.

Once I had reasonable grounds to suspect Drinkwater had committed offences I arrested him for supplying class A drugs - and the rest of the night and the next day was spent in the custody area of our lovely cells complex. At no time did he ask for a lawyer or any legal advice, he seemed accepting of his fate, even relieved. In fact at times I reminded him of his right to free legal advice, he just held his hands up and said he wasn't interested.

He was bailed pending the PM report.

As a catch up, the bail given was being concerned in supplying a class A drug. If the post mortem revealed the drugs contributed to Baxter's death, it would get very sticky for him. I liaised with Shirley a few times, she was embarrassed, and I will say this now I was totally truthful with her about Raymond's lifestyle, and insisted she must be truthful too. It was going to be an embarrassing time for her and her family. I even got a family liaison officer (they were very much in their infancy then) to be the go between. Basically I didn't trust her at all, nor her mad kids!

It wasn't their fault; they were raised how they were raised.

However, the eldest daughter would later become the victim of more sexual offences than I have ever dealt with in twenty seven years of detective work. She would find herself in more compromising positions with other married men than the age old 'hot dinner theory'.

What happened next in this saga though was quite bizarre.

It was three weeks later, after the death of Raymond Baxter that I received Mr Jenkinson's PM report, and yes the amount of cocaine in Baxter's blood was immense and caused a huge heart attack (systolic dysfunction) He had hardened arteries, heart muscle walls twice as thick as they should have been and incredibly high blood pressure when he died. I will add to that he was three times over the drink drive limit too for good measure.

He was a ticking time bomb.

His hugeness alone wasn't going to keep him alive for too much longer either.

The only noticeable thing was that a fair bit of sperm was recovered from his stomach skin and penis, possibly as a result of dying when he ejaculated.

So he may well have been in the company of someone when he died.

For some this is not a bad way to go I suppose, rock stars do it all the time.

This second person took a bit of finding, but after a bit of phone work, and a few calls country wide she was found in Edgbaston in Birmingham and became a witness. She was a nineteen year old street worker who was with Baxter for twenty minutes before he died.

She panicked and ran away.

Honest, if not a tad unhelpful.

The coroner wouldn't conclude any findings until the criminal trial was over. Now we had the factual information it would be held in Birmingham, the place of Baxter's demise. We were happy there was no major impact of a criminal nature on Baxter's death, and the corner put him in the pending tray.

Then the bizarre bit.

First of all I had a complaint from Drinkwater via our professional standards team that his confession was made under duress, he mentioned a police gun being used to threaten him. Well, I'll let you in to a secret, we don't have guns on the CID in our desks, that's for the Sweeney on the TV.

The gun found by Wolfie was later proved as an imitation firearm, and not a good one, Drinkwater stated that it was planted by us. But the worse thing he reported was the beating he said he took when he met us, quite bizarre, and of course untrue.

The working parts of the gun had Drinkwater's fingerprints on them (the inside of the gun) as did the magazine, none were mine and Wolfie had a partial finger mark on the barrel. I'm not sure how that happened, he had gloves on. Poor handling by Wolfie when seizing the item for assessment from our firearms department ?

The custody records did not reflect any injury he said he sustained when we first met, in fact he signed the custody record to say he was happy with everything, no injury and no medical conditions mentioned. If he was as badly injured as he said, and his description was very dramatic, cuts, grazes, bruising, it would have been immediately picked up on entering custody.

What a liar!

He never produced any pictures of any injuries either.

Surprisingly.

I had to laugh though, I was asked in time why I didn't take any photo's of him when he came in to custody?

And that from professional standards who are also allegedly police officers.

I replied' You are asking me why I didn't take photographs of injuries that were not evident or caused by anyone, that are fabricated and made up?' I went on 'How the hell can I take photographs of things I am not aware of or that do not exist?'

However, complaints of this nature do fit in nicely with the public perception of the police at times. Or should I say those members of the public who have good reason to deflect their misdemeanours from the public gaze.

Now when I say perception I mean of us, the police, as an organisation and not as individuals. This idiot was trying to get me and Wolfie sacked, and I was furious.

This made him game on for me, there's a saying in the police *they will come again.* Not once had I at any time done anything that wasn't approved or unlawful. The internal inquiry wouldn't take place until after the criminal trial either, and boy did I push for that.

Enter – Cynthia Champion.

She would be our barrister for the crown court trial.

Drinkwater had been charged with imitation firearms offences, drugs offences and various procuring offences under the 1956 sexual offences act. His laundering of money in Switzerland was also charged under four counts. The Inland Revenue got involved (someone must have told them) and served him with a bill for £88,000. Yes, his complaint had certainly annoyed me. My determination to destroy this person for his disgusting way of life was let's say determined. The Dooley's were brilliant with their assistance, and on the financial front, Dave Iron in the Financial Investigations Unit polished things off lovely. Our hard work had also seen four hundred grand seized as a proceed of crime. We didn't have the legislation back then, but did it by other means, it was possible, it just took graft.

The more Drinkwater made allegations, the harder I went out of my way to seize his assets, freeze his money, get court orders, close his night clubs, and generally cause him bloody grief.

For every ball he bowled I hit him for six.

I was on fire.

In my quieter moments I got a bit angry, but I was never really under suspicion of any wrongdoing, if I was, I would have had my house turned over and I would have been suspended. All I was, and all he was up against was a young Detective well up for pursuing a particularly nasty criminal.

Drinkwater was at his best when he wasn't in contact with people, this is why he did what he did after the event – he was best when he was getting people to do his dirty work for him.

Hence this tactic to defend himself.

It wasn't that clever, but it was all he had left.

I seized his cars, froze his assets, closed his businesses and smiled in his face at court hearings. If he was going to try and ruin my life, I was going to go a step further and do it for real.

I do love a war.

Our first meeting with Cynthia was a few weeks before the trial. It wasn't to be held in our town or at the bigger house up the road, but at a crown court three hundred miles away. Drinkwater's defence team had managed to take the local limelight away and get a trial far, far away.

It didn't bother me at all, I was dealing in the truth, what could go wrong?

The legal arguments that take place at the start of these type of trials can go on for some time before a jury is sworn in.

And for this trial there was a lot of legal argument.

The defence wanted all our investigation at the start of the inquiry, that is the warrant and information gained at the office of Drinkwater thrown out and they didn't want the fact that Baxter was dead mentioned as it would 'influence' the jury. The statements of Shirley Baxter they wanted dismissed as hearsay and the link between her and Drinkwater should also go ignored.

Basically, they wanted all the crucial bits left out so the judge would direct a finding of not guilty during the morning of day one.

Nice try.

I was asked to leave the court at times, even though I was the *officer in the case.* They do this because they don't want you to hear certain mentions. Tosh came along now and again, and Wolfie was there throughout. He had managed to move all the harder bits of the inquiry in my direction, all for development purposes you understand. If I experienced the hard bits I would understand them better next time was his theory.

He was of course right.

Baptism of fire I call it.

When I would later tutor officers on the department I would also employ this method with those who needed the experience. None of what the defence wanted happened, all the evidence was admissible, and on day three of the process, day one of the trial started. The jury, after much debate were sworn in, twenty three faces whittled down to twelve. Nine men, three women, all over twenty five, all white. The first defence tactic had worked, they had the profile of the jury they wanted. They may well have failed in getting evidence removed but they at least had a collection of people who they could carefully manage throughout the trial.

It was fixed for two weeks.

I was ready for anything, and Cynthia after debate with the *'other side'* made it clear much was going to be alleged, but nothing evidentially could be provided to back up their claims. The opening of the trial sets the scene, the jury are often attentive at this point, their newly assumed positions of jury members weighing heavy upon them. I have heard some talk of their 'legal' responsibility during trials. Basically, no jury has a legal responsibility, all the responsibility they need is regards to their own personal ability to listen, understand and not be scared of the defendants. They are not legal experts, and from many trial outcomes, clearly don't fucking listen or understand either. Let alone have any responsibility for their verdicts.

I would be cross examined on day three or thereabouts, and should expect a rough old time. Wolfie was in to court before me and I wasn't allowed to be in court when he was spoken to.

He was in for ten minutes.

Now this wasn't going to be as bad as I thought.

I was wrong.

I was in for three hours on day three and the whole of day four.

Basically, anything they could think of from my personal conduct with witnesses to fabricated rubbish. They partially alleged Shirley and I had got it on at one point stating she was a woman of ill repute. In the end I just answered by saying 'Have you any proof I did that?'

They didn't.

At these points it is advised to answer the question to the barrister, then turn your gaze to the judge and then the jury. But the allegations were there for the jury to convert into any theory they liked. At one point I was asked 'Did you and Shirley Baxter develop the type of relationship that would be considered unprofessional?' It was a decent question because it had no fabric to it.

I replied 'What is unprofessional?'

The barrister responded by saying 'We are visiting an area you don't like are we not?

He went on. 'Does the question confuse you?'

I in turn said, 'No, but I think it's fair that the jury understand what you are inferring fully'

The reply was unbelievable, he said 'This court doesn't need to hear what I am saying regards your conduct officer, because it was so unprofessional it shouldn't be recorded here'

The judge went berserk and shouted at the defence 'What poppycock are you talking about now?' He then turned to the jury and asked them to disregard the last off hand remark. But of course, it had been made, and would be very hard to disregard, they were looking at me sternly now, too daft to see through the defence tactic?

And yes, believing the tabloid press theory more and more.

I was so dismayed.

Cynthia wasn't that useful when the allegations were flying about either, later saying that if she interrupted the jury would think there was something wrong. I recall saying 'There was something wrong Cynthia, you didn't support me at all in there'.

The professional standards department were there, the press were there, and reported the facts gracefully.

'Cops accused of gun, sex cover up'

The Police Federation got in touch and offered support and advice *'In case it goes wrong'* What they meant by that I will never know. The only saving grace at the time was Peter Thomas, another barrister I knew. 'Barnesy' he said 'They need to go to these lengths because they have nothing at all to go on. They have to attack you and your colleagues, it's because there is so much evidence against them. And remember, the hardest witness to cross examine is one who tells the truth.

I remember that every time I go to court today and have done so ever since.

The trial lasted for nine days, and much went on. After my cross examination had finished, I began to enjoy the experience. Working with counsel, offering information in written form over the shoulder of the CPS lady when a spurious moment occurred. The topping and tailing were a joy to watch, and the jury got bored as well. One fell asleep and was shouted at by the judge, the juror adopted a most unpleasant attitude and was shown around the cells at the end of that day's work.

He looked very pale when he came out.

The police officer who showed him round offered him a sewing kit if the judge does send him down for a few weeks. The sewing kit being useful should he need to stitch few holes up when he met with a prisoner who takes a fancy to him. Well, that was the rumour.

This juror later became the jury foreman and didn't even blink for the next four days, let alone yawn! After all was said and done, Raymond's life was battered in the court room and the press, I was pilloried and courted as some evil Detective genius (I added the last bit) well, everyone else was having their heads muddled.

Wolfie was called the mentor of a horrendous police cover up,

Martin Drinkwater was found guilty on all counts and given 6 years inside. The press then reported a brilliant police investigation that had stopped a predator in his tracks!

Was this the same trial?

I heard from professional standards three weeks later, they told me their investigation was over and I wasn't to be further interviewed but the reports would be kept on file. I later got this changed, but it took some very good work from the police federation solicitor. The coroners court verdict was natural causes with a narrative regards the drug levels in Baxter's blood. It also concluded the impact of his long term addictions were the cause of death, not solely Drinkwater.

I gave evidence there as well, but it wasn't in any way difficult, and the coroner thanked us on a thorough and most professional investigation. I later received a chief constable's certificate for being a good bloke.

I left it in my garage and the mice consumed most of it.

Tosh was indeed right when he said that I was not to drop my guard for a second during this inquiry. It was indeed most valuable advice, and to this day I never drop my guard, nor did I take anything for granted when in the evidential arena again.

Never.

Drinkwater wasn't a nasty man, he was a greedy, controlling man, Baxter was the same, and it was just that he found himself at the customer end of the arrangement, Drinkwater was the blue chip company provider.

In 1996 I saw Drinkwater again, he was scruffy, old and down on his luck after his prison term was served. He saw me too, we were outside Boots, yes, that Boots in town. He looked surprised, I smiled and asked how he had been doing since he came out of prison.

'Oh not bad 'he said.

'Really?' I replied.

'Well, things could be better officer' he said.

He shuffled away.

There was not much more to say, he was on the bones of his backside.

Martin Drinkwater died a year later in a small council paid bedsit in a drug pit of a street., He died of a drugs overdose that resulted in a heart attack.

For some there may be something fitting in his demise, for me it just tells me that he too should not have dropped his guard for a second.

Because there will always be someone waiting in the wings to take your last order.

And indeed - take your place.

Messing About On the River!

THERE COMES A TIME IN EVERY POLICE OFFICERS LIFE when they have to unwind and relax.

Most of the 'thin blue line' will find that time with the family and away from the station as sufficient time enough to recharge their batteries. Others may well find themselves in one of the *'Privately Funded'* police rehab centres, where they can *'privately'* recharge their minds and recover from all manner of injuries. These can be from work related stress to life changing issues. I went there once, it was full of very anxious people. Some as an example were either recovering from some form of trauma as a result of a member of the public getting a bit excited with a gun to the very thing I mention

– stress. This was a laughed about illness back in the days of my early CID service. Stress was something that the malingerer got involved in, and those diagnosed with it were viewed sceptically. As I have already mentioned, there were departments that catered for this type of officer, and I mean catered, they didn't assist, or mend or treat the person. They basically hid them away from the public and waited for the inevitable explosion from within. One of these explosions resulted in the same Superintendent I have mentioned before, remember the guy who had the fridge incident thrust upon him?

Well he was involved in another kitchen appliance incident.

This time involving a microwave.

I know this happened near as damn it because the Super told me personally.

It occurred from within a police house on Greens Estate, and involved Constable Kevin Mantle.

Kev was running about in the house with all the doors locked, he had set fire to parts of the kitchen already, and thrown a large tin of Dulux paint over the next door neighbour's apple tree.

'You're a cunt' he screamed.

'Now come on Kevin, we can talk about this man to man' added the Superintendent. The Super was outside the house looking up to the bedroom window.

Kevin was furious and very angry.

He screamed at the gathering crowd below.

'Fuck off you Norwegian cunt'

I have no idea why he shouted that. The Superintendent was from Gateshead.

The end of the nonsense came about after our man let his much loved birds out of the top window of the house, various foreign birds, traditional cockatiels etc, all flying in many numbers out of the window.

The crying and distress heard from the house was enough for the officer's close by to force an entry and find Kev in pieces on the living room floor. He was partially dressed, sitting cross legged on the floor with his head in his hands. He was led from the house in his underpants and white string vest balling his eyes out.

Another one bites the dust.

I too had a police house on the salacious Greens Estate. A decent three bedroom house that became the target of local villains, as did I and my family. I won't go to deep into it but suffice to say they didn't get away with it lightly. I had bricks through the window and my daughter's school visited (that was when war was declared)

And of course threats a plenty.

It took over my life for a while, until I stopped it.

All so I could copper my community and keep it safe, well I suppose in a way when you think about it. Whilst they were planning their next sortie' on Chez Barnes, at least your house was left relatively untouched. But I didn't put in an overtime claim to sort the matter - don't worry.

I'm not sure how many other jobs carries with it this invasion of your private life, I suppose there are quite a few jobs that come with lots of *moolah* which compensates for varying degrees of private life invasion. But do these jobs carry with them the threat of your kids being attacked or injured? Your wife being threatened with rape and general damage at any time of the day or night.

And usually when I wasn't there.

We had alarms fitted, special patrols were done and none of it worked.

Then the battle was taken to the offenders, and it stopped.

Luckily for them, and possibly me I suppose when I look back.

I have said this before, and this goes out to any person who wishes to invade the life of someone to the extent that it is ruined, destroyed and in tatters. If that is the case, and this is your wish just think about what you are doing, and what could happen as a result of you doing it. If a person hasn't got anything left, thanks to you and your involvement, and everything has been taken away by certain individuals, be that by their actions or worse, then just remember that they have nothing left to lose. So! - When a person is in that situation, with nothing to lose, they really do have *nothing to lose*. Think about it, I for one wouldn't want to be chased down by a man who has lost his family, house, maybe their job as well.

Live life nicely folks.

What I am building up to here is the wind down of certain CID officers that can happen at the end of a hard fought shift, or as a result of a well-planned day out. I think many would agree that officers these days spend very little time together after work. However, back then it happened quite a lot.

Tosh looked over quite a crowded office, his demeanour was positive for once, he had been quieter than usual, and a little grumpy at times. The kettle clicked off and boiling steam flew up behind him as he stood there in his olive green jacket and corduroy brown trousers..

'It's the big un Sat'dee boys and girls' he said loudly rubbing his hands together. He slapped Shakespeare on the back.

'Your in aint ya Hammers' Monty slapped him hard on the back again.

'Wolfie?'

'Aye, Aye Captain' Wolfie replied saluting from his desk.

He was gluing an Airfix spitfire with a large SOCO torch head set on to aid his vision.

'Karen dear?'

'Yes Sarge, you know I am coming'

'Barnesy boy, you is in ain't ya?'

Now whether I wanted to go or not it would be viewed very dimly if I didn't appear on the office outing. This was the way it was back then, to the extent if you didn't go you could easily be an outcast.

'Of course Tosh, I'll be there'

'I knows you will boy' he growled and walked over to the fridge and opened it.

'Right, where's me pot? He said. Hands on his hips he stepped back from the smell that always hit you from the office fridge.

'Fuck me' said Wolfie.

'That's getting worse, what is it?'

He knew … It was an office joke.

'It be the soul of the last Sarge that led two shifts on an office day out Wolf' Tosh laughed.

He waved his hands in front of his face towards him, searching out a smell.

'I can't honestly smell anything' Tosh announced smiling and started looking round the room.

'Now where's me fucking pot'

Tosh's pot was the stuff of legend. From within this pot was the list of names from the *'past'* Those officers who were also invited on the 'office outing' Those that had passed over to the other side, those that were no longer with us. People like *'Scrapper Lewis and Puncher Blake'*

Yes, their names clearly telling you of their hard earned moniker's and possibly how they got them. Like *'One eyed Carl'* and *'Basher Bates'* and my favourite – *'Dunking Dennis'.*

'He was a right cunt with a bucket full of apples' I was told once.

'Is Biffa coming this year Tosh?' Wolfie shouted across the room.

As if the smell from the fridge had with it a compound that sent everyone speechless the room fell silent. Wolfie looked embarrassed as Tosh roared 'He ain't coming nowhere near that river Wolf'

It was like a door being slammed.

BANG!

I was intrigued.

Brookesy and Lance were coming, that dashing pair of Detectives from E shift and add to that Tom Arkwright plus the four or five from the past (No, they weren't dead) and we were in for a big day out.

There were others.

And that day out for us would be this coming Saturday. The weekend when twelve, maybe twenty restless Detectives would be wobbling about on a boat on the river having been drinking since early doors enjoying the first warm rays of Spring.

'We meets at seven' Tosh announced.

'Bacon butties at The Royal Oak, then taxis over to the jetty to meet Wolfie's brother *'Fearless'* … Tosh looked pleased with himself.

'That won't happen' Wolfie whispered to me.

Tosh's pot was at the back of the fridge next to some ageing butter, it was kept there for fun.

This was the source of the smell.

The butter.

Rumour had it that this butter was first put there in 1979.

From the smell I had no reason to disbelieve it.

In fact 1969 was more believable.

The fact nobody had ever thrown it out told me more about camaraderie than any lengthy story, I mean, nobody breaks tradition, not back then. However the story I am about to tell you takes some beating. And at no time will I change anything, I can't, because if I do you would never forgive me.

*****

It was Saturday. 'So what is it with Biffa then Wolfie?' I said as we munched away on smoked bacon butties made by Mrs Cooper of the Royal Oak.

The plush carpet, smell of polish, bronzed brasses and hunting pictures decorated the room. We had been camped in there since just before seven.

I'm talking morning now.

'Fuck me youth, Let's not go there, Biffa has obviously not mended his time with us or indeed Tosh from last year'

'Yeah, but what happened Wolf? ' I said urgently but speaking in a lower voice.

Wolfie looked round, checking for listeners - as he moved in closer.

'It all went wrong after we got a couple of those boats that have punts with them'

He leaned in closer.

'By half past two in the afternoon we had two teams, full of beer, in two boats jousting each other at five mile an hour over by the weir'

I smiled.

Wolfie nodded and smiled.

He was loving this, almost salivating. He genuinely looked excited, eyes darting, looking at his watch and whispering.

'It was good fun Barnesy, plenty of beer on board as I said and just general larking about'

'Ok, so what went wrong?'

I was keen to get the full detail.

'Well, Tosh was leading the charge, as ever, he had this fucking big pole pointing at the other boat when Biffa side glanced him and knocked him clean out the boat, and I have to say – clean out.

'What? In the river?' I said.

Laughing.

'Yup, he disappeared under the boat much to the glee of everyone on the other boat but didn't reappear for ages'.

'Fuck' I said laughing.

'What happened?'

'Well youth, He eventually surfaced, but you could see he was distressed, all that river frog spawn stuff and weeds on his head, it was fucking hilarious'

Wolfie took a gulp of ale, he was in full swing.

'I have to say I laughed, but old Tosh didn't see the funny side and sort of floated to the river bank and staggered in to a tree and collapsed'

Wolfie did an impersonation of a staggering man walking.

Eyes all wonky, spilling a bit of ale on the carpet.

I began laughing uncontrollably as Tosh walked over holding a silver tankard of best ale.

'What's all the noise about Barnesy boy' he said with that menacing smile.

'Oh, nothing Sarge, just sharing a joke with Wolfie' I replied.

'Oh, that sounds funny Barnesy, tells me, what is the joke then?' Tosh asked.

He moved closer, the smell of fags and ale fresh on his breath.

'Tells me Barnesy boy, what makes ye laugh so loud'

Menacing.

He was growling in a whisper now.

Tosh glanced back and forwards between me and Wolfie.

Think Jack Nicholson in the Shining.

'I heard yuse both ya fools' he said. 'Laughing at the Sarge falling into the river were ya Barnesy?'

I looked at Wolfie.

And then I started laughing again.

'Ok Sarge, I give up, you got me'

Tosh glanced at Wolfie, and slammed his empty tankard in to his hand and said 'Your round Wolfie lad'.

Tosh looked over at me and smiled.

'It's going to be a long day young 'un, take care on your ale intake, we wouldn't want anything going wrong now would we?'

Tosh looked away and out the window towards the river.

'There's perils out there lad, perils'

A few faces arrived I didn't recognise.

'Wahay ya fuckers' shouted one of them as the other took his big jacket off and went straight to the bar the door banging behind him.

'Two pints of ale and two chaser's barkeep' he said.

Tosh looked back over to me menacingly.

'Since that day I have treated every day like it was my last young 'un' he said.

He glanced back out the window.

'Them rivers are cold and dark places let me tell you'

Tosh turned away again.

It was getting surreal.

One of the red faces that had just entered the pub came over.

'You all right Tosh you old misery'

It was Dunking Dennis.

A huge man, red face, woolly pully and jeans.

He had a big smiley face.

'Now I hope we don't get any problems like last year now Tosh son' said Dennis.

He looked at me, nodding towards Tosh and without introduction said 'The fella can't swim see, that's the problem, and last year he went fucking swimming in the drink, funniest thing I've seen in years'

'Aye and that Biffa has a lot to answer for' said Tosh.

Wolfie reappeared with a full tankard, he handed it to Tosh.

'Aye' replied Dennis' That's a fact, in fact I heard he was a right punt'

He laughed out loud and slapped Tosh hard on his back.

Ale was already being spilled and jokes were already being volleyed about the room as it filled some more.

It was only seven thirty in the morning.

This was going to be a long, long day.

*****

I naturally (as you would too) expected to be on the river come nine ish, maybe half past. But come that time we were still in the pub, music in full flow, more bacon butties being grilled and the ale flowing. Tosh was walking from group to group slapping backs and laughing so loudly he was most certainly the noisiest person in the room without talking. *'Turning Japanese'* by The Vapors was at full blast as certain folk started to get quite rowdy and started to dance around the bar. The oddest thing in amongst all this was various 'normal people' walking about outside going to work and such.

Some stopped to peer through the window at the party inside.

They were greeted with waves and cheers.

Karen and Lance were dancing, and in Karen's case she had already necked half a bottle of vodka, and Lance, a relative light weight in the drinking stakes was tie off, shirt undone doing some sort of Scottish jig.

It was 9.26am.

It was like a New Year's Eve party, truly incredible.

As is usual a few musical requests were shouted out.

Fags were lit, and more and more whooping and revelry continued as Scrapper Lewis and Puncher Blake arrived together, both decked out in boating wear, deck shoes, yellow wind-cheaters, new jeans and Millet's waterproof bags over their shoulders. The cheering continued as Mrs Cooper brought out more food and the ever increasing wad of money hung out of the till.

'Best day out of the year youth' Wolfie shouted in my ear as Men at Work, *Down Under* boomed out of the speakers.

Wolfie had this thing about making up words that offend to songs.

Previously he changed the chorus to Bee Gee's classic *'Night Fever, Night Fever'* to *'Wank me and toss me off'*

And yes folks, it works. Try it.

Men at Work continued.

'I took her home and fucked her sister' Wolfie sang as he held his drink above his head and danced away *'You come from a land down under'* pointing at Karen's middle. Lance was now sweating and breathless after running up and down the short flight of stairs in to the lounge continuously.

Like a kid at a birthday party.

Lance looked ill.

He was bent down breathless as Tosh ran up behind him and booted him quite hard up the backside. Further cheering ensued, Wolfie with both hands in the air and now shirt open shouted 'one nil, back of the fucking net'

Lance fell forwards on to the floor as Mrs Cooper stepped over him, still smiling with plates of butties held high to avoid spilling beer, fags and spit on her hard work from the various assembled lunatics.

'You cunt' he shouted loudly and faced up to Scrapper Lewis who just happened to be the closest person to him. Scrapper as I said was a retired, and as previously stated well turned out gent in complete yachting regalia.

'I ain't no cunt' replied a very gruff and shouty voice.

He leant forwards, white beard all frothy from ale.

Lance staggered towards him.

'You kicked me you fucking nonce' he slurred loudly; he was staggering forwards to meet him. Scrapper Lewis, a large and well-built man who I found out later wrestled for a living before joining the police calmly put his tankard on the bar. As I expected he tried to quell the situation with all the skills he had learned over this thirty years police experience.

Well, sort of …..

He walloped Lance with a huge glancing swipe, open palm round his ear before taking a hold of him and tipped him upside down. Scrapper was hanging on to him as if he were just about to slam the drunk bobby into the ground.

Wrestling styli.

'What shall I do with him lads' Lewis shouted and laughed Brian Blessed style as he turned round in the bar with Lance now held above his head.

'Throw him in the river' Wolfie shouted.

'Shag him' shouted another voice to much laughter.

'Make him dance like a clown' came the west country drawl from Puncher Blake.

Scrapper Lewis stopped in front of his ally.

'I can't do that Blakey' he said 'The boy is still learning'

'But he called you a nonce' came the reply from Blake.

'He did that aye, came a thoughtful response from Lewis.

'He did that aye'

The Scotsman threw Lance out of the big window to his right.

Fortunately for Lance the window was open and it was a large well-constructed patio type door design. He hit the top part of the door and landed about ten feet away in a big heap.

The 'ooohs' and aaaaagh's' from everybody were most evident.

'Now, now' came the response from Mrs Cooper, I don't want to go calling the police again now do I?' She laughed as she went back behind the bar to help out her husband who had not stopped serving and working throughout the melee'

Lance remained in his backside in the street. Shoppers just casually stepped round him and in one case over him.

Then 'Fearless' arrived.

Fearless was Wolfie's brother, and he was the spit of him if ever an older brother could be. He had a more battered look to him and was a bit wilier in appearance, maybe rugged, but he was definitely a Wolfie clan member.

'Fearless by fuck' Tosh announced very loudly, arms held out to greet him, as he walked in to the pub beaming, old sailors type blue hat on his head, pipe (unlit) in his mouth.

'Aye, Aye Tosh lad' said Fearless.

I put him at about 55 years of age, but definitely a man with plenty left in the tank.

Fearless glanced over at Lance.

'I see he hasn't learned' Fearless said chuckling.

Lance was still sat in a big heap on the decking floor rubbing his head and looking round, checking his pockets.

The music played on.

'Frankie boy' said Wolfie slapping his brothers back. 'How are you ship mate?'

'Oh I'm fine mucka came the reply

'Just dandy to be honest, things are good' he added.

'The day has already started Frankie' Tosh said smiling and raising his tankard.

'We be on the hops already'

More cheering as Lance vomited in the pub garden, trails of liquid leaving his head at a great rate of knots.

'Have you met Barnesy?' Tosh said pointing over to me.

Fearless held his hand out.

'You okay son' he said.

'Are you the new protégée then?'

I laughed.

'Well, maybe'

He's bloody rubbish Frankie, that's what Barnesy is' Tosh growled and smiled.

'Bloody hopeless and a lost cause'

'Old Frankie here was a serving member of Her Majesty's Royal Navy for twenty two years weren't ya son' Tosh leaned into me.

'He served with Uncle Albert from Only Fools and Horses you see'

Tosh laughed loudly as Fearless raised a fist in his direction.

'Twenty two years youth' he said.

'And never *once* did I go down with any ship. I did a lot of my time at Portsmouth, but I have to say I did enjoy my appearance in 'The Spy who Loved me' he added.

'We were extras in the old Bond film back in the seventies, and I did my bit in the Falklands too in 82.

That's still raw youth' he added.

Fearless looked at me, his eyes squinting.

'Still very raw'

The music hadn't rescinded, the laughter and noise were as loud as ever and *'I love to Love'* by Tina Charles was now at full blast.

'Oh I love to Love but all my baby just wants to shag' Wolfie appeared again in my vision changing the lyrics once more as he danced to his own sexual references and innuendo. Wolfie danced some more with Karen who had moved on to the Pernod, a most disgusting choice.

'So what ship did you serve on?' I said to Fearless.

He was walking away but stopped, paused and looked at me, he then cocked his head sideways.

'Are you taking the piss?' he said

'No mate, what ship? Is it a secret?'

I thought I had broken some old navy rule. Some untold *'never ask that question statement'*

Frankie Fearless looked at me and replied 'HMS Fearless you cunt'

He took a sip out of his glass and walked away shaking his head.

'Everybody ready for a days out boating' he shouted so very, very loudly. Fists were held high in the air, punching the sky and beers were downed quickly. The cheer was deafening, the movement towards the door was immediate and the day I felt was about to start in some style. Twenty four Detectives headed towards the riverbank where a long boat cum barge had been parked (do you park boats?) The chugging, engine noise from the long vessel told me that no punting would be done today. The middle of the old boat had seating inside a glass room, and long decking, albeit not very wide either side. I could smell freshly mowed grass, birds were evident for the first time that year, talking in tweets, there was no wind and little rain which made sure we had a perfect Spring Day.

Seated on the boat in a stripy deck chair was a Labrador dog.

He looked just like Fearless.

'Wait, wait' Fearless shouted with his hands held high towards the madding approaching crowd.

He turned to face everyone.

'Right listen folks, these are the rules. Important rules of the water you all should know okay?

Everybody nodded their heads and agreed in a loud murmur. All stood on the grass like a school trip day out, but for lunatics.

We all waited for this important information on safety and the like.

'Don't fucking vomit on me boat okay?'

Everyone looked at one another in agreement.

We all looked back at Captain Fearless.

He was walking away from us, pipe smoke bellowing behind him.

'Right folks, Let's get aboard' Fearless shouted as he jumped on to the deck undoing the ropes.

'Come on girls and boys, it's time for a trip on the river'

*****

I had been on a few boats, and this one looked *okay* on the surface, *okay* it had pools of water here and there and the smell of boat diesel was strong, but it looked *okay* enough.

As I stepped up onto the boat I said to Fearless 'I thought we were in for or a big briefing there boss'

Fearless was now puffing smoke from his pipe like a chimney, he stopped doing what he was doing and looked at me.

'If any of you dafties want to be told *what not to do* and *when not to do it* as members of the Queens constabulary then all hope is lost'

He looked heavenwards.

Again, he smiled and carried on prepping the ropes. Clearly Fearless was not as worldly wise as I thought he was when it came to the cops.

Contained within the inside area of the boat was a fruit machine and a big old bear, one of those huge things you often see in the foyers of hotels or grand old houses. The bear was at least seven foot high, on a big base, he was all brown fur with arms stretched outwards in a big huggy type pose. If it was real or not, I didn't know. I mean yes it was dead of course, but real in terms if it used to be alive.

Bench like white seating was around the edge of the room with a few old disco lights precariously placed on the edges greeted me.

It had a dance floor in the middle.

The floor was sticky, the windows dirty and the smell was of sick, pure vomitty sick was very evident.

'What's it to be land lubbers' shouted Tosh as the record decks sparked in to life with the music of Elton John and Kiki Dee.

It was loud.

A loud scratch of vinyl as 'Crocodile Rock' sprung in to life.

'That's the fucker' Tosh shouted like a pirate and laughed like a west country Scooby Doo. The beer crates were loaded on to the boat by a new addition to our group, *One eyed Carl*, and yes you guessed it he had one eye, and clearly had seen better days through the one he had left. A thin rake of a man, he had allegedly left the police in 1983 as a result of a misunderstanding with a flare gun and the Chief Superintendents Mrs. He now worked along the river, boating tourists across to the pub on the main island from a lay by on the carriageway adjacent.

'Twenty quid a go youth' came the voice in front of me.

Wolfie was standing in front of me with a sick bucket stuffed full with tens and twenty pound notes in it.

'What?' I replied.

'Its twenty notes for the trip, food and beer youth 'Wolfie replied.

'It isn't all free you know'

I tried to remind him of the initial arrangements for the trip but it was falling on deaf ears. The agreement being we wouldn't be paying. Not my idea, Wolfie's. I eventually saw his point, he was never going to see mine, and gave him the money, Wolfie walked away tutting.

It was becoming a trait.

The boat moved away from the river bank as Lance came running head long across the grassy bank from the pub.

'Oi, Oi, wait for me' he shouted as he scrambled on to the deck with the help of Scrapper Lewis.

As Lance dusted himself down Lewis towered over him and slapped his back noisily.

'You all right Sassenach?' he said laughing.

'You feeling better now we are friends?'

Lance smiled and although he looked pale, he looked happier.

Okay, Lance was covered in mud and looked like he had pissed himself, but apart from that he was fairing just fine. I went out on to the deck as another similar looking boat floated towards us on the opposite side of the river.

A cheer went up as the five occupants waved and shouted 'hello' in a rather posh put on accent. River etiquette taking over.

The response was typical and generally as I would have expected.

Twenty odd Detectives from Her Majesty's Constabulary showed them all their arses and cheered wildly.

Even Karen.

'Ave a lick of this chocolate tunnel' Tosh shouted, he was bent over and had inserted an empty bottle between his cheeks. Faces were covered as the boat drifted by; the occupants still probably talk about it today. Then the bear was placed on the main deck as people danced around with cans of light ale, lager and bitter held aloft to the tunes that Tosh continued to play.

The speakers now out on the deck as well for extra effect.

Andy Williams *'I love you baby and if it's quite all right'* as everyone joined in clapping and singing. Karen did the splits on the floor, legs akimbo, blue knickers hanging on to her skin like their lives depended on it.

Hamlet (to Tosh) had somehow relieved Fearless of his pipe.

He danced like a posh Johnny Rotten.

I sort of expected a more cultural day out, I had even brought my Jared Diamond bird spotting book. I had this ill thought out concept that today would be a quiet and relaxing trip down a sultry river spying wildlife and getting to know each other a bit better.

Well, the wildlife bit was sort of right.

But nothing sultry was occurring.

I know, I know, I knew really what the day would be like, but I still had some faith left in my colleagues. A large bell was rung as Scrapper Lewis, shirt off and now decked out in Lonsdale shorts took centre stage. His flab was hanging over his shorts as he 'Ali Shuffled' his way from one side of the deck to the other. From the other side came Puncher Blake, about the same size, but somehow containing the blubber better, he didn't quite spill out of his black long shorts as much.

Both had wellington boots on.

I had long passed being surprised at the way this day was going. Tosh was now acting as compere' to a boxing match as he roared out the rules and the betting got underway.

Things were fast paced now. I was stunned, was it me that didn't latch on to things as quick as I should?

'Are we really going to be betting on two sixty year old retired Detectives boxing?' I said to Shakespeare.

'Seemingly so' he said.

'Isn't this just great fun?' He added.

I wasn't so sure.

So I started drinking too.

Various chairs were positioned round the deck as people took their seats and odds were proffered and money changed hands. The opening of many a can and bottle could be heard as Fearless guided us further away from the watching eyes of the public.

'Ahoy there land lubbers' Tosh screamed in to his microphone as he now took centre stage.

A carnival tune, like the old fairgrounds used to have on their spinning rides accompanied him as a backdrop. Then from nowhere the theme tune from 'Rocky' burst out of the speakers.

Tosh roared.

'The confidentiality agreement of this trip make us all sworn to secrecy as the big match begins'

In the red corner etc. ……...

Tosh was in his element.

He introduced each man in turn, spitting and laughing (with intermittent slugs from his can) as they squared up to each other. I too was feeling a bit better, well, now I had quaffed a few quick tins, I was getting in the mood.

'I'll have a fiver on Scrapper' I said to Wolfie.

He was seated ringside on a crate, pencil poised, and book open.

Wolfie sucked inwards and propped his pencil behind his ear.

You sure youth?' He said.

'He is a rank outsider'.

'I've seen enough of him to know he is worth a punt 'I began to slur.

I heard a loud roar as Wolfie snatched my fiver.

'Done' he said looking over my shoulder, half standing up so he could see towards the two fighters.

I looked over too.

Scrapper was out cold on the floor as Puncher (the clue is in his name) Blake raised his arms aloft and shuffled like an overweight Teletubby.

'Oi Wolfie, that bet is null and void' I shouted.

'What youth? You jest me surely son, Scrapper was on his way down when I took the money and the rules clearly state that if a man is on his way down the bet is good'

'What rules?' I shouted again.

'My fucking rules Barnesy' came the growling voice to my left.

Tosh was smiling.

'Now pays yer dues Barnesy boy'

Whatever money had been made I had no doubt would be his and Wolfie's, and then split in Tosh's favour.

And the day went onwards and upwards.

Drinking, dancing, shouting and more drinking.

By mid-day Lance had got off the boat at some dodgy looking jetty at least five miles from home. He stated he had a lift booked with some nice young thing.

He collapsed on the river bank singing *'Come on Eileen'*

Shakespeare managed to make eye contact with a lady and a dog on the riverbank and wandered off with them across a field. As for Scrapper, once he was first aided, he lauded us with the funniest stand-up routine I have ever heard on any stage in any country in the world.

One eyed Carl sang Frank Sinatra songs as we drifted back to town with Fearless dancing to *'Mack the Knife'* and the watching brood of coppers sang together other ditties like *'New York, New York'* I tried to explain to some bloke whose name I forget now that *'Mack the Knife'* was about the London underworld and nothing to with the USA. He just blankly stared at me.

Start spreading the news.

Tosh drank himself in to oblivion as did I and everyone else.

Karen collapsed in a large heap and slept for two hours.

Brookesy and Tom Arkwright rolled about on the floor play fighting, although Brookesy would later claim he touched his 'willy'

As we docked back at the pub I walked as best as I could on to the grassy bank. My arms round Wolfie as we cheered our off duty colleagues from the boat.

'Well youth, did you enjoy the day out?' he asked.

He kept on hugging me as drunks do.

'Well, at the start I was a bit wary mate, but I think it was definitely one of my better days out' I replied.

It was dusk.

I had the beginnings of a severe headache. Just as we were about to walk into the pub for one last beer before home, I heard a loud shout and a scream followed by another one of those loud and boisterous cheers.

'What the hell was that?' I said to no one.

'Oh that was Tosh' came the reply.

'He head-butted that bear'.

I looked at the person telling me what had happened when Tosh appeared in the pub doorway. He had blood running down his face and that boyish smile with glistening blue eyes sparkling away.

Green farmers jacket still blowing in the wind as the night settled in.

'Now that's what I call a day out land lubbers' he shouted and raised his fist in the air.

'Now Let's all have a party, the beers is on me'

I got home the next day twenty four hours after we started.

Of course, as you would expect Mrs Barnes was kept abreast of my late arrival and safety. But it's probably only now, when she reads this chapter that she will understand all the reasons why. A day out on the river with a bunch of Detectives in Spring could only go one way. And as predicted the characters, and the times provided us with a story to tell, and yes, there are many more.

We didn't need a river to have a day out, and in fact we didn't need a boat or prescribed logistics as mad as water and alcohol to make it more interesting. What we had was the opportunity to get that pressurised release out of our systems, a day release for some! And of course, the inclination (albeit unwittingly) to recover from some upsetting times and even more upsetting investigations. We did it our way, or should I say for each individual concerned we did it 'My Way'.

Frank would be proud.

And yes, his first name was Fearless.

I don't think Sinatra is any good at driving boats ......

The Problem With Rape

THE PRINCIPLES OF INVESTIGATING A SEXUAL OFFENCE HAVE NEVER REALLY CHANGED.

The human belief system hinders that to an extent, the actual physical human and their background can kill any principles learned or otherwise.

These principles have rarely changed, not in my time as a police officer, nor I would hazard, have they for the many years before I started my journey. The main issues with the report of any sexual offence are not the offence itself, it is the person who is reporting. The police, no matter if they agree or not will always mentally grade a report by a number of factors. Personal bias, general prejudice, previous experiences and most certainly the class or otherwise of the victim. We ALL do it. The officer in the case will do this, the CPS will do this, the jury will do this as well any other legal mind involved. It's an unconscious filing system which has been explored for years, a 'Johari Window' into everyone's prejudices. Even the champagne socialists of our current times do it.

Now, I shouldn't do a disservice to stupid people here, but as soon as your victim starts lying you're stuffed in a rape inquiry. And of course, any witnesses or someone who can conform details or history. No matter how believable they are, if it actually happened or not, or if you have a thousand witnesses, it doesn't matter a jot. If the credibility of the reporting person is in question you may as well pack up and go home. This may start to assist your understanding of the state of play, and this is why any report like a *'good heart'* these days – is hard to find.

It just seems that for some (not all) genuine reports of sexual assault, and I mean in a lot of cases, there will be problems from the start. This generally happens as a result of the victim lying or making things up. They do this for a whole host of reasons, be that because of the person they were with, to cover up an affair or all manner of reasons connected to their behaviour. This will be the type of behaviour that they generally get away with as they lie their way through their general lives with others. These are *'the others'* who will eventually become witnesses, but sadly - who lie equally as much as they do. It becomes a continual problem for the investigator, when all along all we wanted was the truth, because no matter how bizarre or weird it sounds it's better to have the truth than to have to justify lies in court.

Juries don't like it.

And cases have been lost because of this, and in my experience more so than for any other reason.

The lies, the stories and the change of initial events will cloud the actual report to the extent whereby the actual event pales in to insignificance. Remember when I talked about making things up (responses by suspects) to suit the question being asked? Well, when a victim does this, it is curtains all round for the inquiry. I have to say some people do resort eventually to blaming the police for not taking their investigation seriously. And of course, I am sure you are thinking now, how can the police investigate anything properly when they are faced with a catalogue of lies that counteract what has been said before, or that was initially reported.

There is another element though and that is the initial misconception. That crucial time when the victim and the officer meet for the first time. I suppose it's here that the officer decides if what they are saying is the truth or not.

Apparently this takes about ten seconds.

Not a lot of time for either side to be convinced about each other.

What we have here I believe is what is known as a human reaction to a human situation brought about by human interaction. And I won't be swayed from this qualifier by anyone unless you have genuinely worked through thirty years of sexual offence investigation.

It is quite simply my view.

The police service will always start evaluating what information they have as a result of what information they have been given. And only after they have duly investigated further other 'investigative pathways' will a real conclusion be made. That is of course as long as the investigating officer isn't clouded completely by the five elements listed here.

If they are, we won't get a fit and proper investigation.

These officers are the reason why the police get such bad press at times regards sexual offence investigations. The preconceptions I refer to may well be argued against, but it is this sub conscious grading which when it is all boiled down, duly tasted and ready for the plate asks one question?

And that question is in police terminology.

'Is this a real one?'

And it still happens today as it did many years before I joined. This is why I stated at the start that little has changed when it comes to this type of inquiry. When I said that I meant attitude, because like in many fields of professional life it's the attitude that achieves the result. And it's the attitude, regardless of the times that will always surface at some point in any inquiry.

*****

I was cleaning out the shift CID car of crisp papers, chocolate wrappers and green mouldy sandwich cartons when Tosh appeared in the window of our old Sierra like a haunting vision. The back car park sometimes was a sanctuary away from prying eyes and supervisors, especially if you were noted as cleaning one of the cars, but not for Tosh.

'Ere young 'un, there's a young sort in reception wanting to speak to a CID officer' he announced.

'Okay Sarge, well why doesn't someone, preferably a CID officer go and speak to her then, I'm about to hoover the car' I replied, somewhat hoping there wasn't some ulterior motive to the conversation.

It was beginning to rain, and death by electricity is always heightened in water so I felt I may just have been swayed by the Sarge's thinking.

'Everyones' busy Barnesy boy' Tosh stood back, hands on hips looking at me.

Poised.

'I'll do that job as well then shall I Tosh?' I said

'Get it done then Barnesy it's only a car, then go and speak to her, she is all upset by all accounts, we don't want her hanging around for too long'.

Tosh walked off.

The rain increased.

I took a deep breath, I was sure there were at least six in the office when I took on the car cleaning duties, why always me? Of course there is an easy answer to this, it wasn't always me, it just felt like it, and when it was always me it was probably on the surface a shit job. I threw my wet cloth down, knocked the polish into the hot water in the bowl and tripped over the hoover.

'Fuck it' I said to no one in particular and headed towards the main reception.

I hated Sunday mornings.

If you weren't greeted by a table full of brown evidence bags and five hangovers in for fighting it usually meant some sort of other shit would head your way. For me Sundays were the worst day of a working week.

Seated in the main reception was a young woman, maybe twenty five years, slim with a brown waterproof mac type thing and belt at the front in a mini type skirt and ..... trainers. Her hair was brown, long and a bit matted, not dirty but giving the impression it hadn't been tended to that recently.

She was sniffy, holding a tissue and had with her a large overnight type bag.

She looked at me and smiled.

'Are you DC Barnes?' she asked.

I looked myself over.

'Er, I must be' I said sarcastically.

The reply prompted by the fact that one of those lazy bastards in the office had clearly told her who would be dealing with her when I was already doing something.

'Oh' she replied looking down and looking more upset.

I felt bad at my reaction.

'Hey only joking, Let's go in here'

I pointed to a grubby door which lead to a more private interview room.

I sat down, as did she and I offered her a drink, she declined.

The dark room, lit by a flickering fluorescent light I have to say was an embarrassment. The fact that joe public were invited in here most days as a first point of contact for any offence was simply wrong.

Something else that hasn't changed.

'So what brings you here?' I said. 'It's a bit early for a tour of the station' I said smiling.

This wasn't going well, what little people skills I had were not working.

I had my tie off, hardly professional, good for car cleaning, but not good for first impressions, and the splash from the water bowl displayed a damp crutch.

She noticed.

I looked down.

'Er, I was cleaning the car' I explained.

'Are you sure you're a Detective?' She asked.

She smiled slightly.

The light flickered.

I could see her point.

'Actually I'm not no, would you like to speak to a real one?' I laughed.

I was serious.

But it helped.

'Oh, the one who spoke to me first, the gruff one, said you were the best to speak to' she replied.

I bet he did I thought.

I nodded.

'Oh Tosh?' I said.

'Yes, the moody one'

'He actually isn't' I said.

I looked round the room, a tobacco stained and smoky smelling hell.

'It's a bit of an act, most of the time anyway' I said.

'His bark is worse than his bite, honestly'

She seemed more at ease now.

'So why are you here' I said.

She blushed a lot, looked down again and cried.

The wind hit the reinforced frosted window as did the rain.

I got that feeling you get when you feel uncomfortable and are fast heading out of your depth. I thought about the car, unlocked, the hoover, plugged in still and the keys in my pocket. Between the sobs and the tears, I heard her say 'Boyfriend, Nasty, Hit, Shout and Rape' If any of that lot in the office had left her in the reception after she had gathered the courage to come and report this, regardless of their rank, they would be hearing about it. Her name was Christina Jacobs and she had been raped five times since Wednesday.

****

Like every force of that time, we had very basic processes to put in place when a report of this type came in. Back then we had no referral centres or specialist teams and after care, well, not too many. And what we had then in the police was more about what the individual officer wanted to do and commit to, than a force wanting to do the same.

'We will have to go along to Prince Charles Way Christina' I advised her.

'We have an examination unit, I'll get a doctor out to speak with you, and then after that we can talk about a statement, is that okay?'

Christina nodded, sniffed and looked distinctly out of sorts as she stood up,

Slightly wobbly. We made our way to the CID car parked out back in the car park. As we approached the vehicle, I could see that someone had already tidied up for us after I left it to speak with Christina.

The hoover was on top of the car, the hose up the exhaust pipe and it had been wrapped in police crime scene tape. Of course, the police had a way of bringing us all back down to earth and certain individuals within it were pass masters, if not experts.

Busy my backside!

Christina looked a bit alarmed.

'Is this your car?' She asked.

Er, yes it is' I replied. 'Lovely isn't it'?'

We made our way to the examination suite, we called it a Rape Suite at the time, other names were bandied about, but that's what it was called.

'So young 'un, is it a real one?' Came the dulcet tones of Tosh over the phone.

'A real one?' I replied.

I was in the office of the examination suite whilst Dr Raymond did whatever Dr Raymond had to do with Christina next door. The police had set up some sort of examination area, it was grubby, and not that clean.

Forensics?

'Aye kidder, is she telling the truth or is it the usual bollocks' came the response.

I was slightly taken aback.

'She's with the doctor, I'm not too sure if she has her truth detector with her Sarge' I said.

There was a pause.

'Listen Barnesy, we have a few jobs in, once you've finished there get yourself over to to town, they have a need for a few Detectives on the Macari assault job'.

Tosh was on about a street fight with picks and axes, what would be described as a *proper job.*

'Okay Sarge, I'll get over there now, will someone be relieving me here or shall I ask the doctor to take her home to the guy who has meant to have done this?' I asked.

Another pause.

I expected a pause.

'Sarge' I said 'You still there?'

The phone clicked dead.

I assumed I was to carry on.

Remember the grading system we spoke about at the start of this chapter?

I was now in it, compliments of others.

I carried on.

Four hours after I initially met Christina the doctor reported vaginal bruising, anal bleeding, bite marks around the inner thigh, breasts and buttocks, a knife cut to her stomach and scratches, marks and abrasions over most of her upper body. The marks were well placed and not visible in clothing.

Well thought out some would say, and well placed too.

I decided to photograph all the injuries via a female SOCO (scenes of crime officer) and document the report from the doctor who also provided me with an examination book and a load of tubes from the examination for either freezing or chilling. I was to take these evidential tubes, note the reference numbers down, and then ensure the continuity was sound.

These would be stored in an old fridge freezer on the first to the floor of the examination suite. I once found the duty Inspectors sandwiches in there.

I sat down with Christina after we had eaten (not the duty Inspectors sandwiches) and she started to talk to me about her relationship with Derek Clinton, and the preceding five days of pretty awful treatment. It's odd now looking back because one of the questions you were often asked by fellow officers back then would be *'How long was the statement?'* It was as if somehow the length of the statement given by a victim would determine how important the job being investigated was to the police. I have never really got to grips with this price comparison by cops, and probably never will. I can reverse that by recalling a theft of fruit from Tesco's some years before where I took an eleven page statement from the manager and was met with some derision from my then Sergeant over the length of the evidence.

'That is far too long son 'I was told

'There is absolutely no need for that amount of clarification and information, it's almost as if you are there with the offender when you wrote this'

Are you thinking what I thought when he said this?

Isn't that the point?

Three months later the CPS were in the station on some training day. They used a statement to display a template as to what they wanted from officers submitting evidence from victims and witnesses.

The names were rubbed out, the signatures too, but I could see straight away who wrote that statement.

Yes, me.

I felt a warm glow and daggers from the Sarge from behind me.

Smug?

Yes.

Fuck him.

The police are odd at times.

By 7pm, some twelve hours after I had started work, and some ten hours after Christina first spoke with me we were on page twenty of her statement and had lots more to cover. However, I had enough information to get cracking and Christina had got a hold of her friend. They would be staying in a local hotel overnight to avoid any more issues with Derek. This would give me enough time to get over to their house and sort him out.

I intended to arrest him that evening.

I didn't need to think about seizing evidence, they lived together, what mattered was I seized him and pronto. Christina was sorted out and photographed I walked in to a dark and unattended CID office.

Everyone had gone home.

Everyone apart from the duty Detective who had a clear brief to advise at overnight scenes and manage handovers for the morning, he would be of no use to me. We called 'him' the crime car.

And anyway, he didn't look that bothered.

My next visit to the duty skipper's office revealed two special constabulary officers (specials) and a probationer available for the arrest.

No dog handler was on duty until the morning, they were on a control room call out, some sort of force initiative apparently.

Area B could help as could Area F, but only if it was an emergency or a response. I may as well have asked for Area 51!

Oh well, what we had was better than no Detectives I suppose.

We set off to Spring Vale Crescent a leafy and unassuming area of the town which at one time was all police houses and had a small station too. Since 1985 it had all been sold off and was now mostly rented properties purchased by a local Asian chap done good through profitable restaurants. I briefed the two specials to go round the back of the house and the probationer to keep eyeball on me and them from the side of the house. Basically, the four of us would have eyeball on each other from each corner and keep the whole house surrounded.

It was the best we could do.

Stick in hand I knocked on the door.

No answer.

I knocked again.

Still no answer.

Then a crash, smash (glass) and shouting from round the back.

The probationer ran to the back of the house followed by me.

We were met with the sight of our two specials all knocked akimbo and a smashed window with glass everywhere. It was dark of course; the lighting was poor and if it could be knocked over it was. Including the specials.

They looked like Laurel and Hardy all confused and dazed picking themselves up murmuring about *'he ran away'* and *'sorry mate, he's mad'*

I ran to the high fence, jumped up and over the top and gave chase.

It took me about two minutes of looking to understand I had lost him.

The three lads I brought with me were nowhere to be seen so I returned to the back garden.

All three were sat on a bench looking like the first bit part players in the picture *'Nine pints of the law'* This would take a bit of explaining once they started revealing to anyone who would listen about the one that got away.

It later transpired that the occupant, one Derek Clinton beckoned the two specials to the window whilst holding up a couple of choc ices to them. As they got close he threw a beer keg from inside the house outwards. He crowned one of the specials, showering both with glass and knocking them over as he ran outside through an unlocked door.

He then made good his escape over back gardens leading to fields and a carriageway to the town. I began to sympathise with Tosh over his dilemmas of police suitability for certain tasks. It wasn't that these two specials were bad officers because they were specials, I have worked with some really competent special constabulary officers. It was just that these two on a Sunday evening, should really be out and about elsewhere doing other things than playing cops and robbers for free at the age of twenty.

Well, at least that was my theory.

'Cheers lads' I said as we dusted ourselves down and went back to the car.

'At least we tried, eh?'

Plan A had most certainly backfired, but more importantly Clinton knew he was wanted, and it was just my luck he would locate his Mrs and escalate matters during the night. Yeah, that would be just my luck.

I managed to find the duty skipper (sgt) again and briefed her as to my plan for Christina, and what we had tried to do. Instead of being judgemental she seemed very co-operative, which between CID and uniform at times, even now, was unusual. We agreed police visits to the hotel car park overnight would occur, and I said I would be in at six in the morning.

I updated Christina, she wasn't best pleased, but I assured her we were on the case and the police would be looking after her overnight. This seemed to reassure her.

I went home, but didn't sleep well.

In seconds it was the next day.

'You fucking did what?' shouted a disturbed and spitting Detective Sergeant Tosh the next day.

We were in the CID office examining the biscuit barrel and tea bag situation as I appraised him of the previous evening's events.

It was just before 8am.

I had been in for over two hours researching a few things in an attempt to come up with some ideas on Clinton's capture.

'I lost him Sarge, he did a runner'

I was of course explaining in as few words as possible the escape of Derek Clinton.

'Why take two numb nuts and a bloke with six months in to arrest Clinton, he's a fucking nutter' Tosh raged.

'I know Sarge' I said. 'Problem was, no fucking CID were available, they had all gone home' I had raised my voice slightly. I thought this would make matters worse but Tosh surprisingly calmed down a bit.

'Listen young 'un, what have ye done with her, took her home?'

The biscuit barrel was placed on my desk.

'Er, no Tosh she is in the Beaumont Hotel with a friend, I couldn't take her home it could have been disastrous'

'They would have made up by now had ye done that Barnesy boy' Tosh said, he fiddled with the kettle.

'Er Sarge, the kettle is a bit iffy' I said.

He kept on fiddling.

'They always claims rape then before ye know it – it's all lovey dovey again and its all your fault'

Tosh fiddled some more with the kettle.

A bright spark and a loud blue flash bang accompanied a *'Fuck it'* from Tosh followed by a brief dance as he waved his hand in the air.

Then another loud bang, a few more sparks and a fizzing noise.

'What the fuck' shouted Tosh, leaping backwards.

Wolfie looked up from his newspaper and calmly pointed out 'That's fucked by the way Tosh, it needs chucking out, gives you electric shocks apparently'

'Right the fucking pair of you' Tosh was now angry again and looked slightly mad with drifts of electric hair sticking out above his head. 'Find Clinton, I don't care where he is or what it takes, find the fucker and let's repair this simple fucking job before we become a laughing stock'

'Sarge' I said.

I was interrupted.

Spitting and snarling he walked up to me his finger raised.

'Listen young 'un, it's your fuck up, all you needed to do was make her a cup of tea and drive her home. You're the first bloody attachment that has turned a quick kiss and a cuddle in to the Yorkshire Ripper inquiry that I am aware of. Now take ye away before I puts ye on traffic cone duty in the park'

His eyes were raging, his sleeves rolled up and he was definitely foaming from the mouth slightly.

It is fair to say Tosh was not having a good start to his Monday morning. Shakespeare walked in to the office whistling, looked at Tosh then at the kettle and placed down a new Kenwood box on the kitchen sink.

'You okay Skipper' Shakey inquired, looking at Tosh.

'You look a bit flustered'

Tosh said nothing.

'I've got the new kettle from Curry's, tenner off as well'

Shakey unpacked the box staring at Tosh whilst doing so.

'Bloody good un this one, has a blue light on the side instead of a red one, state of the art that means'

'Everything all right Sarge?' he asked as he took the kettle out of the box admiringly.

'You look out of sorts'

Tosh looked up.

He said nothing but looked at him.

'See lads, a beauty of a kettle' Shakespeare announced.

He held it up for all to see.

'Lovely job see Tosh, a great looker this'

He squinted his eyes slightly and looked deeper at Tosh.

'Your hairs all sticking up Sarge, had your hands in the sockets again?' he laughed and looked around.

Wolfie and I had already made for the door, car keys and radios in hand and ready to leave pronto.

As we left rapidly down the corridor Karen met us coming the other way.

'Steady, steady' Wolfie said as we approached her.

Wolfie grabbed my arm gently, we slowed down smiling.

Straight faces now Barnesy, opportunity knocks'

Karen smiled.

'You all right lads, how did that job go yesterday Barnesy' she asked.

'Oh, that's all done' Wolfie said for me.' Have you got a hair brush on you?'

Karen frowned.

'Yes, why?'

'Wolfie kept a straight face.

'Oh, it's just Tosh, he is moaning about not brushing his hair this morning, won't shut up about it, you know what he's like'

'I've got it here' Karen produced a hairbrush from her black leather bag.

'That should keep him quiet Wolfie said. 'He is a bit grumpy, just leave it on his desk'

Karen walked in to the office.

Wolfie and I ran away.

What happened over the next two days will stay with me until the day I report for duty with all those who have since passed over and left this mortal coil.

And it has nothing to do with Tosh, hair brushes or knackered CID office kettles.

Victim Care – There's Lovely

THE TAKING OF A QUALITY STATEMENT IS KEY TO ANY TRIAL that may lay ahead.

I was already aware of this as I hit page twenty with Christina in her continuing statement, and arranged at some point to conclude what was a very harrowing and disgusting attack on a defenceless person. Regardless of gender, this type of attack is the very worst that any person can experience. I will tell you some of the detail in due course, but of course I need to protect the identity of the victim as best I can.

I have learned much from Tosh and the crew.

I had already left a report on Karen's desk to make contact with

Christina at the hotel that morning and to recover 'some' of the rest of the evidence from her in writing. I was keen at the time in taking information from a witness about the impact of what had occurred and this statement would also contain her history with Clinton. Things like previous abuse, controlling elements of their relationship, and then seizure of medical records as evidence. Far easier back then than now, especially when you have permission. Karen was to try and locate the knife Christina alleged was used as well. Hey ! Look at me tasking my colleagues and making decisions, I sound like I know what I'm doing.

'Where do we start then youth?' Wolfie inquired as we sat down in the CID car and sparked up the engine – making a quick getaway.

'Over to to the CID in town?' He asked.

He was putting the ball in my court squarely.

'I reckon it's time to keep our heads down Wolf and use one of the smaller stations as a base mate. Then we can get some Intel rolling on Clinton, even if that means a bit of tasking to find out where he is'

Again I seemed to know what I was on about.

I had some hope I did anyway. Some time away from Tosh was needed and establishing ourselves elsewhere for a while, in peace

We whizzed out of town to 'Harry's Patch' a small station that generally took inquiries from holiday makers looking for chalet's down by the sea or a nice holiday barge on the canals. They still issued fishing permits from here as well. It was what we called back then a PC in charge station, a small outpost controlled by a senior PC and staffed in the daylight hours. This station had a lovely old cottage attached to it where PC Mike Bush, a roaring Geordie, ruled the roost with his wife and three kids. He was a bushy faced old timer, twenty five years in the job and ex-army too, he could go any time, any time he liked.

But who would give this up?

The village was a green land of serenity, rose bushes and old ladies, beautiful stone cottages and old style workers houses from industrial and farming days now long gone. Old mill houses and charming gardens all surrounding a green that saw cricket and warm summer days with ale.

Truly English in appearance some may say, but truly British would be more accurate. PC Bush's cider ridden glow and tarnished round glasses scooped off the side of his face welcomed us, a gruff portly copper of old, still wearing an old style nights coat laughing in the station doorway.

'Well, well, well, it's the CID, what the hell do we owe this pleasure, are you lost lads?'

A blue door behind him with the police sign in brass gleaming above a rounded frame finish painted a serene picture of country coppering. A burly man in old timers police kit welcoming the boys in suits.

Bushy always had a black badge on his police helmet. Generally uniformed officers would wear these on a night shift to prevent the steel glow of the normal custodian helmet catching the light. Some old boys just liked to wear them all the time. A sort of statement to new officers who in recent times had not been issued with a night helmet.

It was only taken off to pause for thought or scratch his large head or dampen down the moistened brow of his worried frown. That is if too many visitors asked too many questions about caravans or chalets.

He wore an old style white standard issue shirt, the type the job used to issue with removable collars pre 1978 so you could change the collar and not the shirt in times of quick change over's and long shifts. His tunic bore a whistle and his stick was of the old type black oak variety.

Bushy oozed 1955.

He wobbled a bit too much when he walked and he looked a tad unfit to say the least, but I knew and had seen, as did many a criminal that if he got a hold of you in the 'Bushy grip', you were for want of other words – fucked.

He puffed and wheezed a bit more these days though.

Beckoning us in to his abode cum station he pointed at the big wooden seats by the big wooden table that greeted us in the parlour area. He may have seen better and fitter days but Bushy could do a one man cell technique on any man quite easily, and was legendary for it. Quite possibly the strongest man I had encountered in the cops.

'You lads looking for some peace away from the tyrant?' Bushy joked as he put the kettle on to a hot AGA stove, a whistling silver type of vessel that would have suited us all in this environment. Mrs Bush came in to the kitchen, wearing an all in wrestling apron, a large woman who glowed as a result of healthy countryside living (or high blood pressure). She would bake and cook all day and then for hours consume what she made all evening with her family.

She was famed for her steak and Guinness suet pudding with runny gravy and caramelised onion topping.

That type of fame is worthy.

'You boys okay for a bit of nut cake?' she asked.

'I've got my old mums recipe, I've got drippers on the go too'

She looked at Bushy and tweaked his old style handle bar moustache.

'You be looking good for a nice bit of smoked pork for lunch love' she added.

Bushy smiled, shuffled slightly and bellowed out the laugh of a man with a big torso to fill. His forthcoming lunch would be a treat.

It was Heartbeat and The Darling Buds of May all in one.

'I think so dear' he said 'But it seems there's work on for these boys too mind, the CID don't come here that often'

For those unaware, in Scotland, the north and certain parts of the east coast and west country have a liking for drippers. Basically they are the most unhealthiest but gorgeous piece of honey (syrup) sultana (or fruit) laced cake you could ever wish for.

They harden your heart arteries in five minutes and could kill you in ten.

The dripper is best suited with a strong hot cup of Yorkshire tea, and fifteen minutes to spare, preferably with friends, mid-morning.

The ticking clock and wooden table with the warm AGA doing its best I felt drowsy and happy, I had no doubt about the fact that PC Bush would be carried out of here feet first before he would leave such an idyll.

You would have to be forced to move from this quite *literally* if it were in exchange for the ever changing confrontational life of town or city policing.

In fact that wasn't to be the case, four years later the station closed, and Bushy left as a thirty year constable, not including nine years in the military police as well. Old school he was, and the type I often see *not* getting a yearly honour or mention in despatches.

'We'll hole up in the main office Mick' Wolfie said.

'We need to track down one Derek Clinton, the Welsh wizard from look, you, see, territory, you know him mate ?'

Bushy laughed out loud again 'Know him ? Know him ?' he roared (think Brian Blessed here) 'By lord I recall Clinton when he first came here with his tribe back some fifteen year ago now, Christ he is never off the radar these days. I hear he has been running drugs over from Welshpool as well'

'Welshpool?' I asked

'Yes, a town in Wales mucka, Bushy went on ' I went there once in the army to collect a man who didn't fancy serving any more time in the mob, he'd gone AWOL see, it got nasty with the locals if I recall'

Bushy laughed out loud ' I liked that evening we had there, we had a right old tear up, and beers all round after, those Welshies like a good honest fight and a good old song afterwards that's for sure'

'When was this?' I asked.

'Oh, must have been' (pause) ….

A pronounced finger is offered in thought.

'I will tell you when it were, it were the year England won the World Cup, because they didn't like the thought of it see, England winning the big cup an all'

'Nineteen sixty six ?' Wolfie asked.

'Yes lads, nineteen sixty six, just before I got out, seems like yesterday'

The kettle whistled.

Wolfie nodded over to the door leading to the police office.

'Come on youth, there's work to be done, and when we've got a plan I'll let old Tosh know what's occurring'

'Wolfie' I said.

'Yes youth' he replied.

'It's my show mate, I'll call Tosh, when I'm ready mate, okay?'

Wolfie smiled and sat down at the main desk.

We set about our work, telephone calls to local Intel and force Intelligence, then a few calls to informants and then another local Intel check to see what was relevant and new. Nothing much turned up, he had a few contacts in Welshpool, old Bushy was right, and an officer over in a satellite station by the train station may well be speaking to him on an irregular basis for information.

That was one for later, but little more than that came forward.

Lunchtime was a feast of cheesy mash and hot smoked pork dripping in a mustard gravy and carrots from the station garden.

It was paradise.

If Bushy was going to die of a coronary he would die a full and happy man.

'Of course lads ' Bushy sat forward belching out some hot porky air.

'You could always go and speak with his step brother over by the Moon and Trumpet'

Silence.

Wolfie and I glanced at each other.

Just the odd clink of cutlery.

'He has a step brother?' I said

'Aye mucka, he has at that' Bushy went on 'Came over here about four year back, a decent guy as well, he obviously moved away because of problems in Wales, but he is a good lad is Ray, and pro the police as well'

Bushy whispered.

Moving closer.

'He has a few good old lock ins over the trumpet' he smiled. 'Bloody lovely ale he does there'

Bushy winked and shushed his lips looking towards the kitchen.

'I can hear you Mike Bush' came the loud voice from the kitchen 'I can hear you'

Bushy raised his eyebrows.

'Bloody hell lads, she has many great powers that woman, many great powers indeed'

It seemed we needed to take a chance and visit the Trumpet pub as suggested.

*****

IT'S JUST AFTER FIVE O' CLOCK AND THE MIST is drawing in and beginning to cover the moor over to our left as we walked the quarter mile to the Moon and Trumpet.

I was deep in thought about the ongoing issue regards tracking down Derek Clinton. Tosh would want an update no doubt too. I looked at Wolfie, he was looking ahead squinting at the sodium glow of the pub lights ahead. The welcoming sign that said *'Pub three hundred yards'* creaking slightly in the wind. It wasn't cold, but it wasn't warm when the chilled wind blew.

Our footsteps hurried forwards as a car drove in to the car park, a young couple jumped out laughing, slamming car doors, and ran in to the pub. The evening was dark now, but a light blue night sky showered the area with a grey and inviting light. Stars beginning to appear on high too, it was overall a lovely evening.

'Its nights like this Barnesy that make it all worthwhile' Wolfie said as he shoved his hands in to his pockets. There's a few pints in there too lad with our name on' Wolfie nodded towards the pub which was now twenty yards away.

'What shall I say to Tosh ? I asked, stopping and taking off my gloves.

Wolfie looked at me, he nodded towards the telephone box and patted me on the back.

'I'll get the beers in youth, you call Tosh, by all accounts it's your show'.

Yes, that came back to bite me.

Wolfie laughed and walked in to the pub, the door groaning slightly as he walked in turning left in to the public bar. The bright optics beyond the most welcoming thing I had seen for a long time.

I called Tosh, and his extension answered. I appraised him quickly, keeping it succinct and clear. He seemed calmer and gave us grace to move wherever we had to so we could track down Clinton. He also updated me on Christina Jacobs, she had moved over to her parents place in Little Channing, she was fine and had already got some form of restraining order out if he dared go near her. I knew she was strong enough for this.

Tosh also updated me that he had authorised a further interview which Karen had done, this time on the new-fangled video kit over at the 'Rape Suite'. I didn't know how to use it properly, in fact not many did, but Karen and another officer from the the CID who had done the training course had apparently cracked it.

He seemed more on board about things.

'Cheers Tosh' I said as we ended the call.

'She really does deserve our support Sarge' I added.

'I know son' he replied. 'I don't mean to be hard on yer like, but a lot of these jobs are all made up and too bloody hard to do in any case, but I've met her and seen what you have done so far. It's okay Barnesy, but find Clinton, and stop fucking about'

I sensed some form of conciliation in his voice and a smile.

'Aye Sarge' I replied. 'We are on to it'

I got in to the pub and Wolfie was clearly and already on pint number two.

'There ya go youth' he said. 'A pint of old best, the dogs bollocks'

He smacked his lips.

I sipped my pint and got a packet of KP, Wolfie was munching on Scampi Fries, they niffed of an old girls lower casing, they really smelled bad.

'Landlord, this pints a cracker' Wolfie said raising his glass.

'Another is it boys?' The question from the barman with a Welsh lilt told me this could well be Derek Clinton's step brother.

'Aye may as well' Wolfie responded. 'Youth, one for you?

'Er … driving Wolf, I think I'll stick'

'Not looking for digs tonight then boys' the barman interjected. Plenty of rooms here, we opened up bed and breakfast last July, but Tuesday's is quiet mind'

'Nah, were pretty local mate' I said. I raised my hand as Wolfie's next pint didn't touch the sides.

'Fucking hell Wolf, steady on mush' I said.

'Fuck em Barnesy, this is a moving inquiry, we are looking for clues and the job owes me a big glug of refreshments, now I don't know about you but I have been on duty for ten hours and I'm hungry. Now then Barnesy, its cold outside, and there's a warm bed upstairs. I suggest we do all we can to get this boyo on side and book it down to the job. What says you youth, are you an investigator reacting to this fluid (he pointed at his empty glass) and mobile investigation or are you just another young 'un' playing at it between nine and five wanting to get off home?'

Wolfie had a point.

I wasn't that used to investigating matters out of our metropolis, okay I had been on a few jobs but this was my first inquiry where I could take control, make decisions and form my own viewpoints.

I was in total control.

'So what did Tosh say then Barnesy?' Wolfie slowed his drinking down, sparked up a cigarette and blew blue smoke over my shoulder. 'What did he say?'

Wolfie's hand gesture prompted me to talk.

Beckoning.

'He just told us to get on with it Wolf, just said find him, it's our show'

'Well, that's what I suggest we do then youth' Wolfie remarked. 'It's time we did as the Sarge tells us then eh? We don't want to disobey direct orders do we? Now let's settle down and make some friends'

We took some corner view seats as the clock ticked on past six, the log fire was burning and the grey slate flooring reflected a dancing orange glow.

Make new friends eh ?

We did just that.

As the evening moved on we got chatting to Ray and his new wife Rosina, an Irish lady who ran the bed and breakfast side of things. She indicated that Ray's family were a bit iffy, which gave us an in. Ray also got chatty, it was a quiet evening, no more than six punters in the bar, and a few in and outs buying a carry out or crisps.

He also ran a video rental business from behind the bar and sold stamps.

Over the next three hours we chatted, Wolfie taking on the mantle of the chief chatter as the beer was downed. It was I suppose an added bonus for Ray on a quiet night. We downed a couple of steaks and shared a bottle of red as well. I have to say I wasn't a huge drinker so three pints saw me off, and then Wolfie threw his hat in the ring.

'Ray mate, I got to tell you this, we are the police and we are very keen to get a hold of your brother Derek'

Ray went a bit pale, his Mrs went a bit paler.

'Look, it's nothing to do with you, it's just that the local bobby told us you were related'

'What about my licence?' Ray asked.

'What?' Wolfie said looking confused.

'You're going to report me if I don't help you, aren't you?' Ray looked worried, he put his beer mat cum washing up cloth down. 'Come on boys, we are trying to make a go of things here' Ray sat down. He was very agitated.

Rosina walked behind the bar to serve a new customer. But she kept glancing over, looking very concerned.

'I'm not sure what you're on about Ray, but it's Derek we are looking for, not anything you may have done, well, not yet.' Wolfie laughed.

'Listen boys, it took a lot of convincing to make the brewery see I was good for this job when we took this over, I did proper time way back for a manslaughter, you understand this is really tricky for me?'

'I didn't realise' I said.

'What you didn't check me out before you came here?' Ray replied.

'No, we took you on face value mate ' I replied. 'That's what we do'

I leant forwards to gain his confidence and nodded slightly. My chair creaked.

Ray leant back and looked at us both. He looked pensive and studied us both.

'What will you tell the brewery then boys' He asked.

He leant forwards as well.

Wolfie smiled and leant forwards too.

Wolfie looked at me.

The fire crackled.

The cat who had strayed in an hour before stretched out in front of the warm glow. Wolfie took a sip of ale and nodded.

'Well, I'm not sure about you Barnesy' Wolfie replied. 'But all I can say is they do the best pint of best ale in the area and one of the finest steaks I have had in years' Wolfie raised his glass, and said ' Cheers'

Ray took a deep breath, and Rosina brought over the Brandy.

They told us all they could and it was enough to take us to midnight and an eight hour asleep upstairs. The next morning greeted us brightly with a fine breakfast and the inquiry, as fluid as Wolfie said, moved to Wales.

We were on the road.

To say it took a long time to get to Welshpool would be an understatement. Over six hours of driving, and a detour round Shrewsbury heading south was enough to make me feel as if we should have brought our passports.

Us big city Detectives weren't used to this.

The sheep, and there were many littered (that's what they do) the whole of the countryside, they wandered on to the road when they felt like it, and generally got in the way. Old tractors journeyed at twenty six miles per hour in front of us for far longer than the law allows and cows were also introduced at two points completely blocking the road.

At one point Wolfie, who had taken over the driving hooted the car horn angrily.

'Cunts' he shouted as we drove by a gaggle of farmers who gestured as we flew passed.

Fists were raised as Wolfie slowed down.

'Wolf' I shouted. 'No, this is their territory we are not scrapping in the middle of a country road in fucking Wales' I added.

'Fuck em, bogtrotters' he said.

I always thought the Welsh were sheepshaggers, and the Irish bogtrotters, but then this was all a part of my CID education. We made it to Welshpool by mid-afternoon stopping in a ramshackle old inn at first, and quickly bode our farewells as the first crusty old cockroach appeared in to view. In the town we located a decent pub which had rooms and settled in before making our first attempts at locating the local cops.

The police station was fairly large, a good few vehicles outside and surprisingly the building was all locked up. There was a sign on the door that said – *Out on patrol.*

We needed to locate a person who went by the name of Murray Humphreys, now this apparently wasn't his real name, and Ray wasn't too sure what it was, but he assured us the local police would know him. He could lead us to Clinton. Not a lot to go on, but enough to make the effort. I assumed Humphreys wasn't a name you would choose if you were a big-time gangster. That was odd. He was out now after a stint inside for possession of ecstasy at a rave two years before. It was one of those ad hoc raves that appeared in the late eighties and early nineties that attracted thousands.

Humphreys apparently was a lunatic, he once did things to a sheep and recorded it, showing it to the local young farmers one evening when there wasn't too much on TV. He seemed a nice chap, and clearly not a vegetarian.

My experiences of travel and the police was varied, but not varied enough to be able to deal with the next twenty four hours, in what I will describe as the Wild Wild West.

You definitely meet characters in the police.

There seems to be a huge difference between the mindset of certain city dwellers and those folk that choose the country lifestyle. The city type will aspire, on the surface at least, to display money and wealth quite openly, whereas the country person may not choose to do so. Success in the big city could mean the ability to buy champagne for all your mates after work in a flashy wine bar In the countryside a humble facial expression whilst two hundred sheep trot by could well suffice.

Therein lies the extremity of what we were about to encounter.

PC Mike Bush once told me that to understand a person you had better walk a mile in their shoes, he could never have been more right in this town. As I said we checked in at our lodgings, a welcoming landlady asked a few questions then showed us an idyllic country style twin room which quickly became two doubles. There was no way I was sleeping in the same atmosphere as Wolfie. She could have been the Welsh version of Mrs Bush but with less familiarity and much less flesh. As we left our comfortable rooms we made our way to the local cop shop, now it was occupied by the local Detective and a special constable.

The DC had an old grey suit on, a few too many creases for me and his receding hairline was testament to much head rubbing and pondering. He sounded cheery enough though and introduced himself as DC Dessie Davies.

'All right their boys, from the CID over the border, is it? '

'Yes mate' I replied. 'Took a few days to get here mind, plenty of challenging road manoeuvres were needed '

I looked at Wolfie.

Dessie smiled.

'Ah yes boys, the roads round this way can get cluttered with – Er ….non traffic Let's say, although I have seen one or two use sheep as a mode of transport, and other things too'

He laughed, I liked him straight away, a firm Welsh twang to everything he said, followed by that 'Is it' question at the end of each statement was endearing … 'Isn't it' ?

'So boys, what's this now?'

I assumed he meant 'What are you here for'

Dessie moved over to a cabinet and got out a bottle of whiskey and a few glasses. He held up the bottle to Wolfie who nodded in approval.

I declined.

The CID section of the station was clearly there to accommodate one or two Detectives and no more. Two desks with old style bat phones on, those big and black Dixon of Dock Green type phones and a computer in the corner, switched off and dusty.

Papers stacked high on cabinets and a few faces on a board with varying degrees of criminality attached to them.

'Well Dessie, it's a chap called Humphreys we are sort of interested in'

'*Whoa, Whoa*, hold it there boys'

Dessie raised a hand and stopped pouring.

'You means Murray Humphreys, is it?' He asked.

'Yes mate, apparently he may well have some information on the whereabouts of Derek Clinton' I added.

'Okay boys' A deep sigh.

He looked troubled. Dessie sat down and rubbed his chin. He went to pick his phone up but stopped.

He paused some more and looked at both of us. That ticking clock moment was happening again as the dust swirled round the window in sunlight. Our offices always attracted dust. A heater kicked in quite loudly outside and footsteps walked towards us down the corridor outside - and a door opened.

A big and burly suited gent with a fine Merv Hughes style tash entered the room. Twenty stone of colossus and bluster entered and stood before us.

'Jeez boys, all right?' He said loudly.

An ill fitting shirt, tomato stain it seemed with a huge belly wobbled in my general direction, a yellow unwashed tie halfway down his shirt created a clown like illusion.

He had mustard trousers on and golf shoes.

'These are the boys from England Sarge' Dessie said.

'Oh lovely job' the big man replied.

He coughed and got even more blustering as he moved across the room.

'English CID is it?' The Sarge asked.

That question on a question again.

'That's right Sarge' replied Dessie for us. 'They are here to speak to Murray Humphreys and locate our Derek Clinton'

The Sarge stopped, and looked round from the coat stand. He was standing by what was clearly his desk, and laughed inwardly.

'Humphreys is it?' he asked.

The Welsh version of that funeral directing Scotsman from Dads Army was definitely in the room now. Eerily.

I nodded.

So did Wolfie.

The Sarge's Welsh twang got heavier.

He sat down as did we, all of us waiting in earnest for the response to the facial expression that met us.

Tick, tock, tick, tock, tick ,tock.

The Sarge played with a pencil on his desk and then looked straight at me.

'Humphreys and Clinton is it boys, Humphreys and Clinton?' His voice was quiet, very Welsh and then he looked down.

'Yes Sarge' I replied. 'It's important we track them down'

'Oh, important is it?' He looked down up then down again.

'I'm sure it is, so boys, there is no problem getting to speak to Humphrey's he is always about, and always available. A bit of a local celebrity see'.

The Sarge coughed and looked even more intently at me.

'But he won't speak to no law boys, that's a dead cert'.

'Whys that?' I asked.

The Sarge cleared his throat. Well boys, see it's like this, unless you have brought a fucking (Welsh emphasis on the fucking should be noted, it created an aura) big fat army with you, you have got no chance, it's an army you need with Humphreys see, and not a man less'

He laughed.

But he looked concerned.

And I'm not being funny boys, but you two don't look like no army, and as your English to boot you have about as much chance of engaging with Murray Humphreys as I have running the London marathon next month'

Why's that Sarge?' I asked.

'Well to put it in as few words as possible lad its simple, the only person he likes is himself and to be honest I don't think he likes himself that much. If you want to speak to Murray Humphreys you will need that army I mentioned, and only then will that mean you have him in custody. But he still won't fucking speak'.

'Oh' I replied.

'Oh indeed boy' said the Sarge.

'Basically son he'll fucking kill you see, wrap you up and kill you, and then – (the Sarge looked at Wolfie) and then, he will eat you too, he likes a few courses on his menu'

'So what do you suggest?' I said.

'Listen boys' came the reply from the big Sarge. 'It's simple see, you don't want to go bothering Humphreys unless you have it well planned and all sorted, boxed off if you like. Hence the reason why we will need an army, and to be honest boys, we don't have one available this week'

Wolfie stood up and walked towards the CID office door.

'Where you going butt?' Dessie asked.

Wolfie glanced at his watch.

'I'm calling Tosh' he said. 'Wolfie turned to me. 'And you youth can tell these nice lads all about how this is your show'.

The door slammed.

It seemed we were about to take this up a notch or two.

Two hours later we all met in a friendly pub just outside the town. Dessie and the Welsh Sarge - Marty Thomas was his name, me and Wolfie. The pub was old, very old and virtually empty save a TV covering the golf in the corner. One old man, and yes his sheep dog burped and coughed as they watched. It seems the old mans habits had rubbed off on his sidekick.

'Pints is it boys?' Marty offered.

'Aye, all round boss' replied Wolfie.

We settled in to the snug corner, out the way.

The landlord polishing his glasses looked over at us.

'You the boys from across the border?' he asked.

I looked at him and smiled, jeez news travels fast in these parts.

'Er, well .....

The landlord laughed.

'I thought as much, you here for any good reason?'

It was as if he was judging whether the invading English should be resident in his town.

'Nothing much' I said.

'Oh, so just passing through then is it boys, on your way to Ireland is it?'

He laughed again and moved away to the kitchen where scampi and chips were being cooked.

'Just passing through Miriam' he said.

I couldn't see him, but I heard him.

Whoever Miriam was laughed as did he.

I looked at Wolfie.

'This place is fucking nuts mate' I said.

Wolfie didn't respond.

We swallowed a few big gulps and started to make some plans.

*****

Marty and Dessie had furnished us with the addresses of Humphreys and the family address of Derek Clinton. It all correlated with what Ray and his Mrs had told us back home. Clinton was of course our main objective, but if the Intelligence on these drug runs coming over from Welshpool to our city area was right then we had a two for one deal to look at. Wolfie got on the phone and touched base with the handler, (yes, I know) of Derek Clinton, well, the officer we felt may well be able to help locate him. Clinton like most villains needed the security of the police for all the reasons I've explained earlier.

I wasn't impressed.

'Wolfie' I whispered at the bar. 'What's all this about a handler?'.

Wolfie sucked in his breath and looked cynically at me.

'Listen youth, you spent a good few hours researching all this didn't you ?'

I nodded.

Wolfed continued. 'But you didn't think to look up our boys upstairs in local intelligence?'

'I did Wolf' I replied.

Wolfie had a slightly reddening face.

'You've got a fucking lot to learn youth. It isn't about ticking boxes; you develop your contacts within the police as much as you do outside. You need to think about your questions, who you are speaking to and what value there fucking isn't in speaking to the wrong people. You could have gone straight in to the DI, told him your issue and he would have helped you. He is the officer in charge of all the informants, he knows everyone remember. He is the all-seeing eye. All this cocking about because you think you're the bee's fucking knees has left gaps in your intel gathering. I've told you before. Keep it simple, stop, think and listen to yourself. Pause for thought. We are not racing about dealing with fucking cats up trees youth. We are in the business of making sure we go home safely and and nobody gets hurt. Got it … young un'

This was the quietest but hard hitting telling off I had received from Wolfie to date.

'Next time youth, and before go about shouting the odds that it's your show, you keep your mates updated. And beyond that do your due diligence properly, you are not a super cop, you are merely a 'temporary' and if you carry on like this big head, that's all you will ever be. Now stop pissing me off'.

I sort of got the point …

And Wolfie was right, I got too task focussed.

However, I still thought Wolfie hadn't told me because he wanted a jolly out of the county. The plan was simple, the officer would make contact if he could through any of the numbers he had for him. If he was lucky he would plead ignorance if Clinton mentioned the rape charge hanging over him - and talk him away by mentioning money.

It was a long shot.

Clinton would be well on his guard.

If only we could muster a few troops from these parts and then get a few uniforms over from our way things could be simpler. It was a long shot, but we just needed to be able to at least bring Clinton in, if indeed he was here. To enable this we needed to locate him and do some observations.

This would involve me and Wolfie treading the boards through the night, or at least until we could lodge him. At least if we could find out where he is life would get a bit easier. It could take five seconds it could take all night. Luckily, I had a half decent view of his back as he ran to freedom, and a very recent Intel photograph for an uncharged offence from two weeks before. We left the pub and sat up behind a conveniently placed bench towards the end of a small row of terraced houses where Clinton's family lived. They had three council houses next door to each other. Mum and dad were reasonable people apparently, they had the main family home, then his sister on one side and a cousin the other. The cousin was best mates with Murray Humphreys.

Two for one ?

I wasn't bothered at all about Murray Humphreys, or indeed what reputation he had, we had met many like him before. Big time gamers, full of local fandom and little else, trading their lives for the odd old wives tale that meant they were steeped in local folklore.

In the words of Tosh – Fuck him.

The problem of course in such a small area is being noticed, so what happened next was slightly alarming.

We had discreetly placed ourselves in the foliage area adjacent and opposite to Clinton's family home. What we were using back then was a bit of case law called *Regina v Johnson*. This allowed you to carry out observations once you had sourced a decent location. It came in for us around 1989. All you needed was a sarge to review the location, impact on neighbours, any obvious dangers and a form was signed, that was easy. I had spent some time in uniform as an Acting Sergeant, so I knew the score. I even recall a conversation on talk through on an operations channel where the control room asked if I needed a sarge to do the necessary.

Then my radio crackled again. 'Hey Barnesy, are you still acting'?

'No' I responded.

'Get yourself to a TK (telephone kiosk) and give us the number, ok?'

I agreed. They called me.

'Barnesy are you sure you're not acting'?

'Positive' was my reply.

'Well, you fucking are now youth, it's endorsed'.

The phone went down, and that was that. There were always a few questions surrounding this process, but that's how we went on. After all, ninety nine percent of locations are given the nod, so let's do it as easy as we can.

Even though the 'observations' brief at the time was always not to observe inside the premises, that's a serious interference of a person's private life, getting paperwork for that even then was difficult. It was pretty difficult not to see inside the house though that evening. The blinds and curtains were fully open as the bright lights and TV lit up the house, and indeed upstairs too. There were definitely more people in the house than the mum and dad.

A few pretty harmless looking sheepdogs roamed around the house too, but you could never tell with dogs.

There was no sign of Clinton.

The other two houses were in darkness, and clearly unoccupied at that point.

We must have been in the foliage for about an hour or so, and Wolfie was getting all fidgety when an old lady appeared near to the bench - and the bus stop we were hiding behind. She had a floral apron on and old lady tights, white cardigan, a brown skirt thing and she had fully permed bright white hair.

She must have been seventy if a day, probably a lot more.

'Shhhh' said Wolfie looking at me.

I looked back and frowned.

'Idiot' I whispered.

Shushing the obvious !

The old lady seemed to be looking at the timetable in the little shelter at the bus stop. She couldn't have been any more than eight yards away from us.

Then she put a packet of biscuits and a can of coke on the seat and walked off.

'What the fuck is that all about?' Wolfie said.

'I'm fucked if I know mate' I replied, but it was mystifying.

After ten minutes Wolfie moved out to the bench and looked at the biscuits and coke can.

He then unravelled a note.

He beckoned to me, so I came out of the hedge.

Wolfie showed me the note.

Officer, if I were you I would watch those houses from my cottage, it's going to be below freezing tonight.

There was a smiley face on the note.

'That's us scuppered' Wolfie said.

'What do we do mate?' I responded. 'This is a bit odd'

My thoughts were it could be a set up …. but then again we had been blown out by a local Miss Marple, so the least we could do was knock on the door.

Wolfie was reluctant, but what did we have to lose?

He wasn't best pleased. Wolfie wanted checks made properly, the occupant, relationships, intel, safety the lot. And that was a bare minimum.

'What checks Wolf?' I said. 'What fucking checks can we do here, least of all in the druids temple in town, they haven't turned the computer on since it was taken out the box'.

'I'm not happy' Wolfie said.

'Fuck it' I said.

The small house was to our right.

I made my way through the foliage and jumped the dodgy council fence.

I knocked on the door. Within a few seconds the door was opened, and the same old lady stood before us. The smell of baking and the warmth that hit us (Wolfie had followed me) from inside was enough to sway any thoughts of a mid Wales police massacre. The boiling kettle and the grey slate kitchen with the customary table was enough for me anyway.

'Oh' the old lady said.' I thought there was only one of you'

She smiled.

'Come in, you look freezing'

I showed her my ID, it didn't seem to compute.

'Sit down boys' she said, her Welsh dialect very strong, almost *scouse* and Welsh together, I hadn't heard anything of the like before.

'It's a cunt of a night' she said in her extreme accent as she put both hands on her hips.

'How about a strong brandy and a good cup of coffee?'

I will admit to a degree of shock in what was said.

'Pardon?' I said

'The old lady walked forwards, she was rubbing her wet hands from the sink down the sides of her apron,

'My accent a bit over the top for you young boy?' she asked.

'I said, it's fucking freezing out, freeze the lips of a moist fanny' the old lady reiterated.

Wolfie burst out laughing.

I am not sure if my mouth has shut properly since that first expletive.

Many would agree with me there mind.

'Edna' she said holding out her hand to me, then Wolfie.

'And don't worry, I won't blow you out, are you Miami Vice?'

She clearly liked her cop dramas.

For the next half hour whilst we warmed through Edna told us that she lived there alone, her husband had died seven years before.

She went on a bit. She saw us turn up because her night vision goggles which she left upstairs (so she could shoot the 'fucking' foxes) had clearly identified us.

'I assumed you were the police' she said pouring more coffee. 'Clinton is back in the neighbourhood, horrible little cunt of a man that he is' she said.

'I see' I said.

'Do you? Edna replied. 'I doubt it, he walked out the house just as you turned up, you have been watching sweet fanny fuck all since you arrived'

'Well, we did see someone leave' I said.

'Well that was Derek Clinton' Edna said.'He will be back around two I expect'

'Where does he go? I said.

Edna looked at me, stopping pouring.

'Well officer had you followed him you would have fucking found out wouldn't you? As you didn't your guess is as good as mine'

Edna turned to Wolfie.

'More brandy officer?'

Wolfie quaffed the remainder of his drink and nodded in agreement.

'Oh yes please Edna' he replied.

Yes please indeed! Edna smiled and shuffled off to the drink's cupboard in the corner of her warm kitchen. It was midnight. Now, taking stock as I did at that point it was still in our hands. If Edna wasn't some sort of local loon, and I guessed she wasn't, then we could easily snatch Clinton when he came back.

Plan A was to meet at 7am at the local nick, muster what troops we had and if we had tracked Clinton by then we were to take him out.

It seemed Plan A may work.

The worry with Murray, on the other hand, could wait.

From upstairs Edna furnished us with her night vision binoculars, bought for her by her grandson, who she described as a 'Lovely Boy' And we had a clear view across to the Clinton's.

And just after two in the morning Derek Clinton came back, got out of a car driven by another male and ran in to his mum and dads house.

'Bingo' Wolfie said.

'The cat is in the kennel'

With a few hours left for kip the plan was to sit tight and get some shut eye.

Edna was happy with that, afterwards we would then call the nick, wait at Edna's and liaise with Dessie and Marty as the doors across the road went in.

A perfect storm.

Sure enough as the sun started to peek its head round the corner two cars turned up and our radios crackled in to life.

The go-slow Welsh had turned up in quick time.

The voice of Marty came over the airwaves.

'Go, Go, Go' he shouted as eight figures ran towards the Clintons house.

Wolfie and I (unprofessionally, but without notice) joined them from the observation point as the door was pounded in. This job was done compliments of a big PC who was the same size as old Mick Bush back in Harry's Patch.

The first few figures ran in to the dark house, hall lights were switched on.

'Police, Police' came the loud cry as the officers ran upstairs.

The officer who had smashed the door, literally to smithereens turned round.

It was Mick Bush !

As the recognition hit me, I heard a loud shout from behind me.

'Chaaaarge' and I was knocked over by a flailing but familiar opened coated figure with the voice of the coast about him.

True enough, truncheon held high Tosh leaped over me like a steeple chase hurdler and in to the room to our right. The light came on and in bed was Derek Clinton. I got up and walked towards the room.

'Hello big boy' Tosh said grabbing him up by his long hair. His room was filthy, he was filthy, and I would suggest rather in shock.

'This officer has a few things to say to you'.

Clinton tried to struggle as Bushy joined us controlling his right arm whilst Tosh spun him round by his long hair.

'Listen Cunto, take it easy or I'll snap the fucker off' Bushy roared.

'Now quiet'

Just the job, and just what you needed in any trench you care to mention. Clinton looked breathlessly at Bushy and cleverly took the advice being roared at him.

He was naked and sweating.

He stunk.

I arrested him for the rape of Christina and her false imprisonment.

Clinton, still breathless looked down as he was held up by Tosh and Bushy. For him the game was up.

'What the hells going on?'

A dressing gown wearing much older version of Clinton appeared in the doorway. A bit like a Led Zep super fan.

'Are you Mr Clinton?' I asked.

'Yes I am' he replied.

I told him that his son had been arrested for rape as his mum appeared in the doorway too, I apologised for the damage but it was necessary.

'Oh Clint boy, what have you done this time?' his mum in tears asked. She was genuinely upset; she was at the end of her tether with the fruit of whatever loins and mixture she and her husband had concocted.

Clinton was led away in cuffs, just a pair of shorts on and a search was carried out of his room. A threatening letter was recovered from the room addressed to Christina at her mum's house, basically threatening all sorts if she gave evidence. We had done well, moved quickly and sorted this idiot out.

That was enough for me.

He was bang to rights.

Tosh slapped my back.

'You can't get it done proper like unless the old Sarge is with you can you Barnesy boy'

He laughed and patted Wolfie's shoulder.

'Old Wolfie here told me that you needed an English army to invade the Celts, so I brought old Bushy along, and Hamlet' (who appeared on cue in the doorway)

'Hello youth' he said.

Tosh went on.

'Looks a nice place this Kenny boy, I thinks we'll process our papers carefully today and as it's such a long drive back. I thinks we may well be stopping over, what you say Micky boy?'

Mick Bush was putting a few things in to an evidence bag.

'Sounds good to me boss' came the reply.

'I'll be getting home to the family' I said

'With all due respects there's only so much of landlady's and pubs I can take.' I added.

'Well, we have two cars Barnesy, and I agree the family is the best place to be' Tosh said.

'You be off as soon as you can Barnesy, it's a good job this un, and Clinton won't be seeing too much of the outside for a good five stretch, just update Karen before you take tomorrow off'

Tosh looked at Wolfie.

'You been drinking officer?'

'Well …. Wolfie said.

With that an elderly lady (yes our friendly neighbour) walked in to the hallway with a tray of tea's and a few glasses of brandy.

'Here we go' Bushy said rubbing his hands together.

'Thanks love'

Bushy reached out for a glass of the brown stuff.

'Steady on twat' the old lady shouted, right hand raised.

'These are for the Miami Vice twins'

Tosh was open mouthed.

She put the tray on the bedroom side table.

Looking round she looked at Tosh and Bushy and then at Shakey.

All three officers were transfixed on her.

Open mouthed.

Oh yes.

Edna faced Shakey, Tosh and Bushy.

'Okay boys, first things first, is this a crime scene?' Edna asked.

She peered at them all, those hands back on her hips.

'Well?'

'Er, yes love' Tosh replied.

Edna walked towards him and Bushy.

'Then I suggest you get the fuck out then boys, this is serious stuff, these two lads have been up all night'

Surprisingly all three retreated to the hallway.

Agog.

Edna shut the bedroom door as they all stood there looking at me and Wolfie disappear from view. She looked like a frail old lady, but what she did and said totally contradicted that concept.

'What a load of cunts' Edna said.

She laughed, sat down on the bed, rolled a fag and lit up.

'Now boys, let me tell you about my grandson, lovely boy that he is, I think he needs a talking to'

'Your grandson?' I said.

'Yes,' she replied. 'Lovely boy he is, but he is taking the drugs see, smoking the glue and stuff I think'

'Oh' I replied. Well maybe the local police can help you?'

'Fuck them' came the reply, her language no longer such a surprise.

'They are shit scared of him, no, its real coppers he needs, coppers not afraid to get stuck in is what he wants'

'Okay Edna, who is he?' Wolfie said.

Edna smiled and took a draw from her cigarette.

'Oh, I think you may know him' she said blowing out smoke. 'His name is Murray Humphreys, some name he has given himself after a Welsh gangster apparently, bit of a tossers name if you ask me'

Edna took further draws from her cigarette, holding it sideways like a school kid in the yard at break. Wolfie and I looked at each other.

'Murray Humphreys?' I said.

Edna smiled.

'Yes boy, you heard, he will be back this afternoon with his box of drugs looking to leave them in the house, I'm not happy about it'

I sat down next to Edna.

'Don't you worry Edna, I will make sure that Murray gets his talking to and doesn't bother you for a bit with all that worry'

'You're a good boy' Edna smiled.

She patted my leg and got up, as she did she farted really loudly about ten inches from my face.

'Better out than in' she said. 'Better out than in'.

As she opened the door she turned to us both.

'The big fat one, the officer who is big, what's his name?'

'Oh, Bushy' I replied.

'Bushy by fuck' Edna laughed. 'Bushy indeed!'

'Edna walked out of the bedroom as Bushy walked in through the front door of the house.

She patted his large stomach.

'Fuck me big boy' She stopped and pointed at him from a few feet away.

'You've ate all the pies, you've ate all the pies, you fat bastard, you fat bastard, you've ate all the pies' Edna sang shrilly as she walked back down the path towards her house across the road.

She laughed out loud and slightly cackled.

'What the fuck was that?' Bushy said holding a big box of tools in the doorway.

'Oh that's Edna' Wolfie replied. 'I think she would make a great Detective Inspector, what do you think youth?'

He looked at me. Wolfie laughed, I joined him. We both walked out of the house in to the cold and bright sunlight.

'Job done youth' Wolfie said' Job done'

I have to say, it certainly was.

*****

Murray Humphries was arrested later that day by three local CID / uniform officers (Tosh, Bushy and Shakespeare) and a horde of local police which took some effort as three officers were assaulted. *'Too much respect was paid'* was Tosh's judgement on the situation. Suffice to say it was a good arrest with two kilos of cocaine recovered and Humphreys, self-named after Al Capone's Cartel leader - Murray Humphries tied up like a turkey. By all accounts the real Murray Humphries was a local legend born at the turn of the century in mid Wales. Apparently the real Humphries controlled the American Cartels money matters, only resorting to violence when necessary.

He was Al Capone's enforcer.

His self styled namesake was hardly in the same mould.

He was beaten to death in prison two years later in a fight over a game of dominoes'.

No loss.

Derek Clinton finally admitted his guilt at the last minute, just before crown court trial and was sentenced to six years for rape and false imprisonment. He came out after four and a half years and was never seen again, well, not in our area. Christina rebuilt her life, and I saw her off and on throughout the next ten years. At one point she even joined a local training scheme that assisted police officers to understand the impact of rape and sexual assault on a person. I am sure great good came of it; she was an Intelligent and strong woman. Since that investigation to this very day I have always applied every rule many of us had to break to get justice for victims of sexual assault back in the late eighties and early nineties. Those broken rules have changed legislation and supported people through awful periods of their lives, and for me they were worth breaking.

They weren't cast iron rules, just the rules of mindset and personal opinion.

They are now set back in to the annals of policing history along with many other outdated opinions. Those opinions which sadly even today some people still have, especially when looking at having a go at the service, they still drag it up.

To deliver a public service you have to want to do it, to want to do it you have to know how to do it, and this only comes with experience.

For the likes of Christina she got what I would say is a good service based on the times and what I was prepared to do.

I did my best. Nowadays things are far, far better and rightly so.

But to see mindsets change and people change as a result of my actions, for the time was good enough for me.

As a footnote I have to say I did actually drive by Edna's house whilst on holiday with the family some eight years later. Purposely, and having promised myself we took our holidays that year, for the first time in Wales. I slowed down and looked over to the cottage where we first met Edna that cold night when Clinton got arrested. It was gone. The cottage had been replaced by two spanking new modern houses and the council houses opposite were the same, all new, or reasonably new.

For me there was little else to see or do.

I had no doubt that Edna had died and the land sold on for development.

I think you will agree she was some character, the type of character you will never forget. To have left this mortal coil but still be remembered affectionately for that reason isn't a bad way to leave matters.

Not a bad way to leave matters at all.

Internal Intrusion

BACK IN THE EARLY NINETIES internal investigations, or as my force called them *'Internal Affairs'* were always a consideration in my mindset when decision making.

Now why would this be? Well, quite simply, when you're a young cop trying to make his way in the job and not wanting to upset anyone, the last thing you need was that lot breathing down your neck. For me they created an aura of fear. They could lose me my job. Of course, back then I didn't think that I could fight them fairly (I mean I was and remained to the end an honest cop, purely driven by justice)

Trust me, no laughing.

Of course, being an honest Joe, when I think about it now, what did I have to fear? But I am sure you know what I mean. I was at that point, as I started my CID career in fear of them as people and as a department. They were split in to different strands, be that simple complaints, more major complaints, internal inquires (bent coppers etc.) and they also had a covert side which did god only knows what, but it would no doubt involve sneaking about in bushes, covert cameras and whispering.

As I am sure you can imagine Tosh wasn't a fan of Internal Affairs (he once said he had a run in with the Sarge there a few years before) and Wolfie just followed suit saying 'They ain't proper people youth, what type of person joins the job to lock up criminals and then starts locking up their own'.

Shakey and Karen were indifferent, and I, as I said was terrified of them. Now, admittedly I had just cause, I was accused of assault in uniform on several occasions. On one occasion the allegation was that I head-butted a bloke who I had arrested for stealing a kettle from Habitat. He stated that this happened in the doorway of the shop (the head-butt not the theft) whilst we were waiting for transport. A review of the tapes in store revealed he was lying. Now, back then I was just relieved I wasn't in any bother, but of course nowadays his backside wouldn't touch the ground, and he would be sued to his very last penny, and then some more. Back then I was advised just to *'crack on'* and put it down to experience. I had other complaints, we all did, usually incivility, people stating they had been told to 'fuck off' or sworn at more precisely. This type of complaint usually occurred as a result of small time arrests. Usually from people wanting to take the heat off themselves by lying in a complaint, clearly in the hope they would get away with it.

On the CID I realised quickly that the stakes were higher, more prison time was on the end of my arrests and investigations. More people would be affected, so I was always going to be more – *'game on'* to our criminal fraternity. As my time on the department was reaching its final assessment phase, we won ourselves a new Detective Inspector. His name was Clive Corn, a mid forties DI, overweight and a big drinker. Some would say old school, others would say stupid. He was at least eighteen stone and wore the obligatory grey long coat, grey suit, white shirt and red or brown tie. He was often sighted munching on a kebab in town after an evening out with colleagues (every night from what I could see) wowing them with tales of thirty years of coppering. He also had this little entourage' of what I can only describe now as sad and lonely idiots who hung on his every word. Tosh seemed to get on okay with him, but there also seemed to be an element of respect between the two. Wolfie did say 'They have a bit of history, but it's mended' And Shakey raised his eyebrows a lot. But that was as far as I could get with it. To be honest I wasn't that interested. My attachment was in a crucial phase, and the last thing I wanted was to be returned to uniform in disgrace. The CID office was quiet-ish, the activity by the kettle was orderly, the toaster was popping madly, and the microwave was dinging constantly with various porridges and the like being warmed up.

As usual the sunlight streamed through the blinds, the heating was on and it was at least seventeen degrees outside, the warm weather was definitely here. The heating wouldn't go off until May 1st, that was always the way.

'Tosh lad, any chance of a word?' The new Inspector was standing in the doorway, cup of tea in hand as the toaster popped and two pieces flew out and bounced on to the floor.

'Fuck' shouted Tosh, and the DI stood back a bit. 'Fucking toaster, it's meant to be state of the art' spat Tosh as he looked at Shakespeare.

'It is Sarge' he replied. 'It just needs a bit of love' Shakey smiled.

'Love? Love?' Tosh hit back loudly. 'There ain't be no love in a toaster Hamlet boy'

'In a minute then Tosh, in my office?' Came the voice from the doorway.

'Yes, yes boss' replied Tosh. 'Give me five'.

Wolfie stood up and stretched 'Another job you reckon boss?'

Tosh buttered his toast as it burned his fingers. His hair falling forwards as he stared crazily at his grub.

'How the fuck do I know Wolf, I'm not a clairvoyant am I?'

'A clairvoyant?' Wolfie laughed. 'We ain't investigating no more dead people'.

Tosh hurriedly buttered the rest of his toast, carrying it in his mouth he picked up his tea.

'Fucking pain in the arse this new un' Tosh moaned through sod ended toast as he left the room. The door slammed as he dragged it closed with his foot.

Tosh was gone for over an hour.

When he did come back he was with DI Clive Corn.

He looked desolate, totally knackered and shocked.

Corny had the same expression.

'They be suspending me boys' Tosh said. 'I have to be off, can't speak to any of you they says, it's fucking bonkers'.

'What the fuck for?' Wolfie stood up, eyes darting round back and forwards.

Papers fell on to the floor. Even the kettle clicked, the toaster once more spilling burnt toast onto the floor. Wolfie looked the most surprised I had ever seen him.

'Bloody hell Tosh' Karen said. 'What the hell is it all about?'

Shakey almost matched her word for word.

I was just stunned.

'He can't speak about it folks, now come on Tosh Let's get the formalities out the way' The DI guided Tosh by the arm away from the doorway.

And he was gone.

Distant voices as they walked down the corridor.

'Warrant card, suspension, no contact ' was all I heard.

It was one of those moments, you know, the silence, the clear dead quiet that will introduce itself to you uninvited when alarming things happen. We all just looked at each other. The shaking of heads, and the bewilderment is as memorable now as it was all those years ago. Within minutes DI Corn returned and quietly shut the door behind him.

He walked slowly and thoughtfully towards our team corner; *Team Tosh* was the sign above my desk. I had made it. Nobody had minded.

'Well, it's hard to know where to start, so I suppose I had better just come out with it' The DI said sitting down in Tosh's seat.

'Sadly folks, Tosh has been accused of sexual assault, report came in last evening, apparently he did it in the cells last Wednesday'

His Norfolk drawl getting more pronounced. Now, I could have understood a bit of angry shouting, maybe even the odd cuff in response to a criminal's threat, but no way, absolutely no way is Tosh like that, this was just not right.

'That's fucking bollocks boss' Wolfie said loudly.

'Yes, well, yes I am sure you feel strongly about it Detective' the boss replied. 'But rules is rules so no intervention and no counselling or going to see him, do I make myself clear?'

The boss looked round us all, I nodded as did everyone else.

'And I mean it officers' the DI added. 'No visiting whatsoever, or you may well find yourselves in the same boat' And this time I was certain it wouldn't be with Fearless on the river. The DI left the room and the silence returned for a short while.

'Fuck this' Wolfie said. 'Come on youth' he said to me' Let's go hunting'

The term 'Let's go hunting' was and still is used a lot, it can mean anything from going out on inquires to turning over some young criminal and signing them up as an informant. It can mean anything.

I didn't care, I needed to get out. We got in to the car and sped out of the nick.

'I don't fucking believe this youth' Wolfie kept saying 'What the hell is it all about, Tosh ain't no fiddler'.

'It can't be true' I said. 'This is made up it has to be'

'Of course it's fucking made up youth, of course it is, but I want to know who, and why, we owe him that much'?

'No Wolf, no way mate, the boss has already warned us'

I wasn't getting in too deep, not this time.

Wolfie slammed on the brakes and pulled over on the main High Road heading towards the town centre.

'Listen youth, we owe him, do you understand? We owe the man the right to know what the hell is going on, and to that end I am going to find out, now are you in or are you out?'

I took my time.

'Listen Wolf' ….

Wolfie shouted at me.

'In or fucking out youth, tell me now'

Cars whizzed by us, blurred metal whoosh, whoosh, whoosh. The sun the warmth and the determined look in Wolfie's eyes made my mind up.

'You know I'm in Wolf, you know I am'

*****

I made it clear to Wolfie that in no terms was I getting involved in anything illegal, this made Wolfie even worse. I had offended him by even thinking he would do such a thing, but we could still find things out, after all we were the police, and our job is to investigate. As long as that didn't affect any judicial pathway I was fine with it. The only thing we did do, advisable or otherwise, was not take any notice whatsoever of the DI. Three hours later after scratching around getting some information on another job we were sat in the Jolly Masters over on the road out to the north motorway. A wooden old style drinker with all day blokes and vodka cokes.

Tosh walked in.

'Aye, Aye Tosh mate' Wolfie said. 'What's your poison?'

Both of us had already supped a thirst quenching first pint of best ale and were on number two. I had parked my car at home and got the bus back in to town. I was on rest days after this, but I had the feeling there would be little rest.

'Fucking Marjorie Spencer's daughter, wasser name, Lisa .... is making an allegation I touched her tits for fuck sake' Tosh blurted out. 'I don't believes it boys, why would I touch they tits, she's a minger and she stinks, but the job has to do the right thing apparently'

Tosh shook his head and looked down, hands clasped together. Leaning forwards. 'I don't understand why they didn't tell her to do one' Wolfie said supportively.

'Yeah Tosh, why would they believe her?'

I was confused.

Tosh looked up.

'They want to believe her, it's that new Inspector on the internal affairs, he never did like me, I failed him his attachment because he couldn't investigate his own arsehole, he was always waiting for this chance, now the little twat has it'

'So he didn't need to suspend you then?' I asked.

Tosh sighed and took a gulp of ale.

'No lad, he didn't have to suspend me, he just wanted to'.

Wolfie shook his head.

A few office workers walked into the pub noisily.

And Wolfie said 'Cunt'

I tended to agree.

So as far as I was concerned that was it. Lisa Spencer had made a complaint, back then we had no video in the cells, and we relied upon witnesses, far too much I reckon.

This opened up the criminal to make all sorts of allegations.

And they often did. I have to say this wasn't the first time I had experienced a colleague under investigation for such an allegation, over the years a number of serious offences have been reported involving the police. I can also say that if any serious complaint came my way, maybe just to reinstate it, I wouldn't cease in the pursuance of that person. Every penny they had until their dying day, would have my name all over it.

Think on.

'What shall we do then Wolf?' I said as we left the pub and Tosh jumped the bus back home.

'I propose we meet up in the morning for breakfast youth and construct a plan having slept on it' Wolfie hopped across the road into the Beavers Arms.

'One more youth?' he asked doing the international drinking signage with his hand.

'No Wolf, I'm off home, the Mrs expects me to spend at least one night a week with her and the kids'

I laughed.

Wolfie tutted, raised his eyebrows and the swing doors swallowed him up as he walked into the bar. I got the impersonal yellow and grey bus back home and thought about Tosh. I really wasn't sure what we could do, but surely we could do something?

Next morning, and quite early we were in the local café out on Hardacre Road, it was a frequent haunt of the CID and the odd off duty cop looking for a bit of rest day midweek respite from the family. The early morning smell was always bacon and toast. The café had frying noises which always greeted you as you walked in. Radio on, Radio One, the latest tunes. The red check tablecloths, wipe easy coverings and compulsory red and brown sauce bottles completed the picture. I could never work out why tartar sauce was on the table as well.

What I can say is for at least four years the same tartar sauce bottle graced our usual table, I know this because Wolfie marked it with a pen.

I was enjoying a big fry up, a *'Big Boys'* as was the name for such a huge but fine meal. The full quota of black pudding, beans, tomatoes, four slices of bacon, two sausages, two pieces of toast, fried bread, two fried eggs with a large mug of tea. This could not be rivalled anywhere.

The staple CID breakfast, for the stable CID officer.

Four others were in the cafe, the on duty shift led by DS Poole.

'Hey up lads, what's the score with Tosh?

'Don't know' replied Wolfie. 'Thought you might know something?'

Wolfie unfurled his newspaper.

The DS shook his head.

'Probably had it coming, old Tosh though whatever it is'

I sensed that wasn't the best remark to make.

Wolfie leant over quickly.

'Fuck off prick' he said.

The DS flushed red, even redder than the sauce on his plate.

'I ain't on duty Pooler, and I ain't no dead head either, you know as much as I do his career may well be at stake, he don't deserve nothing of the sort'.

Wolfie's eyes flamed.

I looked at Poole.

He continued to flush red. His three sidekicks all looked down.

'He don't deserve to be spoken about in that way, you as much as anyone owe him a debt, and trying to impress your lads with wild talk will only get you in to trouble Pooler, that's a warning for ya'

Wolfie stood up, slapping his paper down spilling the salt.

He threw down his paper tissue too and moved his chair back noisily.

'Come on youth, the smell in here is too much for me to bear on a day off'.

I polished up my plate with toast, slurped my tea and followed Wolfie out the door, as I looked behind me DS Poole was still flushed red with embarrassment; his three DC's all looking shocked.

Wolfie barged back in to the café.

Pushing me aside.

'And another thing piss face, if you want to make this conversation official then go ahead, Tosh, I am sure will be happy to hear about the reasons why'.

Wolfie again pushed passed me and walked in to the street.

Turning round he gestured towards me.

'Cat got your tongue youth?' he said.

I smiled and walked towards my car.

'I thought you were doing just fine Wolfie, the only thing I could have added was a smack in his mouth'

'Well youth' Wolfie said 'Next time smack him hard'

Doors slammed we were off.

We travelled in silence, both knowing that we needed to get a CID car and book on, working on a job on a rest day wasn't that much of a shock. We did just that. The car was quickly secured, and our plan was to shake down a few informants and find out what the score was with Tosh. I suppose too it was an obvious course of action for us, we didn't have a lot to go on. A visit to Lisa's mother, the bilious and overweight fat *Marj* of Stanley's Gate was first on the list. Stereotypical of the time, her red brick free house littered with her seven spawn and six dogs. Government paid for shopping and all-inclusive bills were her life expectation as she spilled out kid after kid like a cavernous human slot machine.

I suppose that is the best way of describing her.

Her hairy boiled face, fat legs almost self pitying, trying to escape her frame, floppy large water bowl skin, wearing an apron type pinny, sleeves rolled up, gravy-stained woolly jumper, a jaundiced face with pinned eyes like a button doll.

She was a stinking benefits thief.

Now, this is how Wolfie described her to me, I recall it well, and I have to say his use of words on this occasion were spot on. As soon as we knocked on her door the dogs barked, the kids screamed and even from outside we could hear the TV.

Fat Marj answered the door.

'What the fuck do you want? She invitingly asked.

The smell of bum air and roast beef was almost over whelming.

In the flesh she was even worse than I expected.

'Morning Marj, any chance of a quick chat?

Wolfie smiled.

'What about?' Marj replied.

'Well love, if you invite us in we can talk off the street can't we?' Wolfie motioned forwards. 'I don't think the neighbours want to see the CID on your doorstep do they?'

Wolfie raised his eyebrows and smiled as he whispered and leant forwards with hands in pockets. Fat Marj stepped back, I looked at Wolfie.

Wolfie shrugged his shoulders and I sighed. It seemed we would be venturing into the house, and the thought didn't enthral me. Wolfie led the way following Fat Marj as the putrid smell of shitty nappies and talcum powder overwhelmed me. It wasn't the usual low glow of nappy smell; it was a putrid stench of bum matter.

I gagged. Gluk, Gluk, Yuk …. Gag, Gag.

'Steady youth' Wolfie said. 'Don't go throwing up lumps on the lovely carpet'

I looked down.

Dry dog shit engrained in to the carpet with slivers of what looked like saliva from kids or dogs. Crayons, food, newspapers and more shit as we entered the 'lounge' there we saw five kids aged between six and I would say twelve. All of them huddled round the TV chewing cheap sweets with dogs whining and wandering about sniffing themselves, the floor and the kids. It was half term, but I would hazard a guess this family picture would be no different in term time. The TV was huge, big backed old style Ferguson type with a light wooden panel, it was the only thing that was seemingly clean in the whole room. Various woolly jumpered loons with big letters on their fronts talked stupidly playing with large coloured blocks on the TV.

Kids TV.

'We are not talking in here' Wolfie said.

'Well, it's here or fucking nowhere big bollocks' replied Fat Marj. 'I'm not having you and him trying to shag me too'.

I looked away as the thought put more pressure on the bile as it was rising in my throat. The thought of even touching her made me wretch.

'Shag?' Wolfie said.

'Aye, shag is what I said' replied Fat Marj.

'Oh, I thought he touched her?' Wolfie moved forwards towards Fat Marj.

'I thought it was an assault not shagging?' Wolfie went on.

His head was turned slightly to his left as he talked.

'Yeah, well, shag, finger, fuck it's all the same' Fat Marj replied.

She lit up a cigarette from one of the three packets on the mantelpiece.

'My Lisa is a sensitive girl, she don't need that old man fingering her, does she?' Fat Marj looked at me for confirmation.

I stared back at her blankly. By Christ this was the mum of this fool who made a false complaint against Tosh. Wolfie smirked and pointed at the kids 'Well I am not sure how these were conceived but I am pretty sure it wasn't from your other half's middle fucking finger love, although'.....

Wolfie went on.

'It wouldn't surprise me'

Wolfie glanced at the kids sat across the room, none of whom took any interest in us.

'Fat Marj spoke.

'I've already given a statement of complaint, they calls it a statement of first complaint see' Fat Marj went on. 'I told them rightly what Lisa said, I told them Sergeant Tosh fingered her, that's what she told me'

'A fingering then' Wolfie said putting on a surprised voice.

'Well, by hell that's not nice is it Marj?' Wolfie picked up a packet of cigarettes and looked inside. 'When did you give the statement?' Wolfie inquired.

He looked at her intently.

'Yesterday' Fat Marj replied. 'Here, why don't you know, what you doing here if you don't know?'

'Well Marj, it's a bit like this, I don't believe that the Sarge fingered, fucked or even went anywhere near your decrepit stain of a daughter, in fact I would hazard a guess that very few if any have unless they were drugged, very drunk or very well paid' Wolfie seemed to be building up to a certain crescendo. 'I would also hazard a guess that the statement you have given to the police is somewhat different to the account that your lovely fucking Lisa has reported in the first instance. You see sweetheart.....already you have stumbled in to the age old problem with scum like you'

Remember the chapter on sexual offences reporting and witnesses? This was the whole thing in action, Fat Marj retreated as the TV seemed to lower and the kids on the floor melted out of the room as did one or two dogs. This didn't seem to be the best tact for Wolfie as far as I was concerned, and doing that in front of kids, who no doubt were used to hearing screaming most days wasn't that clever either.

Wolfie went on.

'You see fatty, the problem you have is the problem all types of fucking liars have, and it's just that – you lie so much you forget what you said, and then you forget when you lied and can't separate the truth from lies. In your case and indeed Lisa's it's pretty simple though, everything you said is a fucking lie'

'How do you know?' Fat Marj shouted back.

'Cos yer fucking lips are moving Marj, simple as that' Replied Wolfie angrily.

Wolfie was breathless, and, yes – he was shouting.

Fat Marj looked frightened, but she came back at Wolfie.

'You just wait till my Brian gets here, he'll knock you out copper, and your monkey sidekick here, and just you wait'

Wolfie smiled.

'Brian?' Don't tell me Damage is back in your life, Brian Damage?'

Wolfie laughed some more.

'Bring him on'.

Wolfie nodded towards the telephone in the corner.

'Go on, ring him and tell him Wolfie from the CID wants to speak to him'.

Fat Marj glanced back and forth from the phone to Wolfie.

'He, he's out, on a job' Fat Marj stammered.

Wolfie laughed again.

'Pah, he has never worked in his life no more than you have eaten a salad, unless you mean he is out grafting ' (stealing)

Wolfie turned to me.

'Brian Damage youth, now there's a name we both know'

I nodded as Fat Marj sniffled and sweated in the kitchen doorway, she was clutching a small shit stained puppy.

Wolfie looked at her.

'Right Marj, the games on, you tell Brian that Wolfie wants a word, and you make sure he rings me, he knows the number, and make sure it's before seven'

Marj sweated some more.

'You got it fatty?' Wolfie pointed at her. 'Because when you fucking lie like you have and I include that mess you call a kid of yours - and then put someone's career and life in jeopardy the gloves is off see, and these gloves have been off with bigger and fatter people than you'

Fat Marj sniffled some more.

'Come on youth, Marj here needs to change her nappy' He turned to her at the door' Now you think on chip girl, you think long and hard about how clever you think your being, and the consequences you are unfurling by doing what you are doing'

'Fucking hell Wolf, that was strong' I said as we left the address in to the street.

'Maybe so youth' he replied as we got in to the car quickly.

'Maybe so, but this is a bag of pants, the internal affairs Inspector is using these people to fuck up Tosh see, well he can fuck off youth, I'm on to him as well'

'I see Wolf' I said. 'This is all a bit heavy mate, she has given a statement'

I know she has youth, so she tells us, but how am I to know that?'

'She told us Wolf' I replied.

'Did she?' He responded.

Wolfie looked at me 'I really couldn't hear a great deal due to the yapping dogs, screaming kids and TV on volume ten youth'

Wolfie fired the engine. We headed straight into the nick, and hopefully to some sense and sensibility. The phone call did come, it could have been no more than ten minutes between us getting in to the office, DS Poole was still on duty (he just nodded and said nothing) and the caller was Brian Damage.

Wolfie fielded the call.

'Aye' he said.

'Ok'

'No problem Brian'

'Eight'

'Yes'

'Ok'

'I'll be there'

Wolfie looked at me and said 'Off duty mucker, it's time for a beer'

The pub we chose wasn't the healthiest of establishments, but as Wolfie pointed out Damage wanted an element of control in the meeting. I'll go a bit further the pub was a hive of criminal activity, a front for crime. Wolfie was happy to give him that control, I have to admit I wasn't, not at all. It was just after eight that Brian Damage and two others sprung into the bar looking here and there spotting the two of us quickly. All three bounced around the bar, chewing constantly and being noisy, making sure everyone knew they were there. Damage almost ran over to our table.

'What's the fucking problem piggy's' he roared.

Wolfie just looked at him. I was ready for a dust up, Damage's sidekicks both had their fists clenched, which I acknowledged and smiled. Gesturing enough for them to know it wouldn't be one way. I nodded and smiled some more.

The stand-off was on.

'Okay Brian, do your shouting so everyone else can see what a big man you are, then we'll talk' Wolfie was calm and indeed collected. He flicked the ash from his cigarette and inhaled some more. Wolfie waved his hand like the Queen. Damage went on almost playing the part.

'Come near my Mrs again and threaten her and I'll burn the fucking cop shop down you know I run things here' Damage shouted loudly.

Wolfie sat there and smiled, nodding his head.

Smoking.

He looked behind himself; people in the bar looked over, a few left, others were happy to watch the show. Most were smiling, some revelling in the police getting some lip and threats. Damage had his credibility intact and Wolfie put his hands up. Well, for now. As you may have gathered when I first met Damage and we rolled around on a dark night with Tosh. He wasn't the brightest.

'Okay big man, the shows done, get your goons to fuck off and we'll talk'

Damage hadn't finished.

'Now sit down and let me explain few things to you two' Damage shouted.

We both sat down, the goons left to go to the bar. I was intrigued.

Damage sat down too.

'All right Wolf, how's things youth' Damage whispered. 'All good?'

'Aye Brian, all is good, except of course that slapper step kid of yours has woven a trough of lies so bad Tosh has been suspended' Wolfie replied.

'Yeah I know' Damage replied. 'When I heard I gave her a slap an all'

Wolfie leaned forward.

'You knew but didn't tell me?'

'Listen youth, how was I to know it would be taken seriously, I thought it would just be a report and a bit of grief for him, not a suspension'

Wolfie looked peeved.

'Brian, whatever has inspired that useless piece of skin you call a step kid to lie like this needs rectifying, it isn't going to end well, why did she do it?'

Brian went a bit red.

'Well, she and her mum watched this old programme like, you know about compo, extra money from assaults, and they sort of hatched a plot to get Lisa arrested for a little bit of shoplifting and then take it from there'.

'Go on' Wolfie said.

'Well that's it guv, as soon as she got in the cells the plan was to get an officer to give her a tea or something, then she would make the claim. You know say he touched her. Thing is she lost her bottle and did it afterwards like, when she got home'

'This is fucking crazy' Wolfie said, his head in his hands.

'What can I do boys' Damage said, hands held out. 'I wasn't to know they would pick on the fucking CID did I? Damage looked uncomfortable. 'Had I known I would have put a lid on it straight away'.

I just sat there taking in the scene. The odd local kept looking over and smiling, believing the charade that Damage had created, his two goons too thick to know differently.

I eyeballed one of the locals on a stool.

A large lad, skinhead type, bulldog tattoo's.

I snapped.

'What's your problem mate?' I said.

I got up.

I walked towards him quickly, I felt anger rising so quickly inside. It was being channelled wrongly, and the stress of the past day or so was telling.

I get this at times.

'I've had enough of idiots like you coming across the big hard man, you believing in all this, you think that prick runs anything except taps in his kitchen?'

He looked confused. I walked towards him, so he had to back off further. He jumped down from his stool and backed off. He dropped his glass, pork scratching's falling on to the floor too. A noise to my left as the bar maid exited stage left. One of the goons walked towards me. I pushed him away and pointed at him.

'One more step and I'll snap you in two prick' I said.

Self-defence move there folks. Minimum amount of force used, the conflict continuum in action. It worked, he backed off. One goon moved off, the other kept looking over at Brian Damage.

'Don't look at him for help hard man, look at me, and I mean '..... I then shouted very loudly ' *Look at me, Look at me'*

The pub emptied. I felt his bowels were about to as well. Clattering chairs, doors squeaking, an emptying room – like a fire drill.

One goon had run off the other was still there but no threat.

I turned to Damage.

'Are you telling me that your kid made all this up?'

Damage looked around the bar, the empty bar, the last goon now scarpered.

'Answer the question mug' I said.

I was right in his face.

'Are you saying you sanctioned this by encouraging your fat Mrs and her last dump to orchestrate the end of a good coppers career?' I moved away slightly.

He did smell.

'Fucking answer me' I bawled in his face.

I meant it, I was furious.

Wolfie said nothing.

'Listen boss, Let's talk about this' Damage responded.

'Fuck talking' I said. 'You have literally twelve hours to put this right Damage or any credibility you think you have will be gone, dead in the water. You may even have to leave town mug. Got it?'

I left him in no uncertain terms that this was his job to mend.

I looked at Wolfie.

'Ring Wolfie first thing and get this put right Damage, if I don't hear from you by ten tomorrow I will be causing fucking havoc, and all for you mate, got it?'

Damage leant back and nodded. 'Papers get leaked' from the station you know.

'Okay boys, okay' Hands held up.

Wolfie pointed at Damage.

'Fucking sort it Brian, this is a step too far'.

As we left the owner came in to the bar.

'What the fuck are you two up to' he said.

'CID mucker' I said, 'Just paying you a visit, making sure everything is fine and dandy, you got any problems with that?'

The landlord gulped.

'No lads, all ok then?' He asked.

I pointed at the pork scratching's on the floor.

'One of your locals doesn't like the food mate' I said.

The landlord looked down at the mess.

'I'll clean it up officer' he replied.

'You need to clean all this place up mate' I said. 'We will be back'

'Okay lads' he responded. 'Cheers boys, cheers ' he stammered.

We left.

We got in the car and this time it was me smiling.

Wolfie looked at me. I was taking in large gulps of air.

'Now youth where did that all come from, almost old school that performance youth'

I looked at Wolfie.

'That was no performance Wolf, trust me'

As we sped off I said 'Listen Wolf, Tosh doesn't deserve this, had he done wrong then fuck him, he deserves all he gets, but he is a good un, a good copper, no scum bag is taking that away from him'

Wolfie said nothing – he just smiled.

And I meant it as well. Had Tosh done it I wouldn't have wasted a second let alone two days sorting this shit out.

*****

We returned from rest days to a beaming Detective Inspector and an even smilier Detective Sgt Tosh. Both were stood in the office as we got in just before eight in the morning.

'Oh, hello Sarge' I said. 'Fancy seeing you here'

Tosh smiled.

'Seems that complaint wasn't anything at all to worry about lads, thanks to some diligent investigation the Sarge here is clear' said the Inspector. I looked up from my desk as did Wolfie.

'You talking about internal affairs boss?' Wolfie asked.

'Yes Wolfie, they did a sterling job, took a retraction statement yesterday morning whilst you were enjoying your rest days'

'Did they now' replied Wolfie. 'What a credit they must be to the service sir' He added.

With that two kids ran in to the office, Detective Inspector Clive Corn smiled as they ran up to him.

'Daddy, can we go and get some ice cream now. … pleeeeeease'

Both hung on to his legs.

Yes, shush for now girls' he patted both of their heads.

'So lads, all is well and back together as it should be then is it?' DI Corn asked.

'It seems to be' replied Tosh rubbing his hands together. 'It seems to be'

Wolfie smiled as Karen came in to the room, she said a cheery *Hi* and put her bags on her desk.

'Lovely to see you Tosh' she smiled and pecked his cheek.

'They couldn't keep an old dog down then, didn't think they would' she said.

Tosh slightly blushed. Then Shakey came in.

Tosh pointed at him.

'Don't kiss me Hamlet'

He laughed.

'Good to see you Sarge, they didn't take long to clear you eh?'

Tosh beamed, and looked over to Wolfie and then me.

'It seems I have some good friends still in this here job boys and girls' he said. 'Some very good friends indeed'

With that DI Corn left with his two daughters.

'Come on kids' he said 'Let's get that ice cream'

As he left Wolfie nodded at the kids and the Detective Inspector.

'You know who they are Tosh don't ya?'

'What?' Tosh replied.

Wolfie nodded again in the direction of the departing DI and the two girls.

'Them Sarge, you know who they are don't ya?'

Tosh looked blankly as Wolfie got up and clicked the kettle on.

'Children of the Corn that's what they are Tosh – Children of the fucking Corn'.

The office once again resumed normality, if indeed this was in any way a normal way of earning a crust.

So, This Is the End

BACK WHEN I FIRST EXPERIENCED THE CID it wasn't for the faint hearted, and from what I believe, before my time it was even more discriminate. I *chose* to make the move to this particular department of policing, I could easily have walked a dog or driven a car, but I felt this was the best way for me to go. Many of my friends and colleagues have taken differing pathways and been a complete success, but that wasn't for me. Being a dog handler is a very specific role with many areas within the discipline, and it requires a particular type of police officer, as it does to be on traffic. Support group work or serial PSU (public order work) as well is very specific too. A more practical way of displaying your policing competency on traffic as an example is to drive to the police system of car control, that wasn't for me either. However, I did pass my advanced ticket, (eventually) but maybe that's more for another time.

I chose the CID because I wanted to investigate and solve crime, I wanted to be given the opportunity to display my worth as a specialist investigator, and in time it maybe did give me all those avenues to explore. The first four months or so since my selection to go on to the CID were eventful. I mean what job could have presented a young man with the things I became involved in, and indeed as I have described them in this book?

All I wanted was to be given a fair crack of the whip, to be able to display my competency by actually mixing it with the very best my force could throw at me. Competition for specialist places was hot. I thought I had done fairly well during my time on the CID, I haven't told you every story, and these are just a hand picked mixture of the long list I became involved in.

So what do you think?

From what you have read did I go above and beyond?

Should I have passed with glowing reports and even more glowing colours?

Would you have been happy with me walking up your path to investigate an horrific offence caused towards a member of your family?

I would like to think you would have been more than happy to have that service from me, but there will always be viewpoints other than my own of course. So, when I sat there on my last day on the CID, looking over all the work I had done and noting my last thoughts on paper for my portfolio I was quite pleased with myself.

After all, the big CID course wasn't attended then as a PC before your attachment. They weren't going to spend a whole load of money on you just to find out you were not suitable. Back then you passed the exam, and it was tough, then you had to wait via a selection interview, again with competencies displayed from your uniform work. It was then a case of waiting for an attachment. Pass that and your CID course followed, at some point. It was a long process. Nowadays it's very different, less personal and selection is a bit odd. There's these quick promotion people ticking boxes these days, they would never have made it through back when I did my tests and excruciating competency based proof of your ability.

The thing is, back then you didn't have an automatic pathway on to the CID, if you passed your attachment, nine times out of ten you went back to your old job or filled another role until you were selected. And often that selection was gained by sitting before, or through a series of interview panels with others going for one job. No rites of passage and no special treatment, well, not for me anyway.

It was spring, the office was being cleaned by the Detectives, and others rushed about gathering files and work together for a court case which was about to explode in the media and in crown court. I looked around as Wolfie whistled away as he cleaned round his desk and floor space, the banging of desk drawers and laughter filled the room. The yellow dusters and Mr Sheen all over the shop as moving chairs and the bangs of moving steel cabinets relentlessly filled my ears.

The wire constructed in-trays and out-trays all spewing out paperwork were carefully carried and stacked as dust and caked dirt was blown away once again as the days were about to get longer. The sun shining through the window as the dust flew about the office, the smell of polish and laughter, and most importantly camaraderie. I loved the changing seasons I had witnessed on my attachment. It was a hive of activity.

'This is the big day then young 'un, you have avoided our 'bull' day too' said a smiling Tosh, hands on hips, yellow duster in hand staring down at me as I perused my work.

'Seemingly so Sarge' I replied. I leant back. 'I just hope its good news' I added with a sigh, and yes the butterflies were with me big time. Those churning butterflies, no better an explanation to describe those fluttering moments we all get when highly charged and nervous.

'Just remember when you go in to see the Detective Superintendent, stay calm, don't argue, just agree and then come out, don't get involved in emotions, he don't do emotions'

Tosh slapped my back. 'And don't bribe him either' He laughed as he walked away.

'Wolfie, rub it harder lad, you may get a genie to grant you a wish ' shouted Tosh across the office.

My review was due at eleven and it was ten to the hour.

I decided to arrive a few minutes early and wait outside his door, his PA would let him know I was there I was sure. I duly arrived with those few minutes to spare in the well carpeted corridor leading to the Superintendents (Supers) office. A sumptuous blue carpeted walkway leading to a large brown door with the name Detective Superintendent Alfie Wright written on it.

It all seemed splendid.

No PA was evident. However I could smell the waft of perfume, so she was lurking somewhere, probably in the shitter I thought. We all do it, send down curly ones, but you wouldn't have guessed back then that these ladies did. I sat down outside; the door had a sign on it.

'Knock and Wait'

I knocked, I sat down, I stood up, and sat down again, I was fidgety, but mostly I did exactly as the sign demanded - I waited. The smell of polish was overbearing, it was bloody hot, and I put this down to the fact my nostrils were still suffering from the Pledge attack in the main office. Then the door opened quickly.

'Ah, Barnes, er .. Right, come in lad'

Stood before me was the small frame of Alfie Wright, a brown suited very well-groomed officer with an unlit pipe in his mouth. Ginger hair on his head and face - and a pokey nose.

'If you want to smoke lad, please do so' the Super added as he ushered me in, to me that was just looking for endorsement to smoke yourself.

'I don't smoke sir' I responded.

'Oh, I see' he responded.

'Well sit down lad'

As I walked in I saw the many photographs around the room of a senior Detectives career, from the CID course in 1965 to the specialist courses and awards from the various investigations he had headed.

A black and white timeline of a career reinforced.

It was almost as if any visitor to the office would see these pictures and framed awards and have their faith restored that before them sat an officer who didn't frequent his office all day waiting for home time.

The room screamed out to me *'Look what I have done'*

It didn't impress me, maybe I was gaining that cynical edge that the CID required of me to be that extra special in investigations? I also noticed my nerves were gone, no butterflies, no edginess, I was calm confident and focused.

'So lad, you have finished your attachment unscathed' laughed a slightly nervous Super.

He had a pencil sharpener fitted to the end of his desk, the type your teacher had in school on their desk. The one with the winding handle. In fact I hadn't seen one since school. He looked at me and then looked down again at some papers that I assumed were a reflection of my time on the CID.

'It's been very pleasurable sir' I replied very much regretting the response as I said it.

'The varied investigations have been very challenging and inspiring' I added smiling. What a twat I must have sounded!

The Super smiled. 'You have certainly had a variety of things to do, and to some extent have impressed the sergeant too, er (he looked down again at his papers)… Oh yes, DS Tosh'

I nodded.

'And your tutor was DC Wolf I see, how was that for you?'

I hesitated.

'Well sir, he was er … Well, he is very experienced sir, knows his way round an investigation'

'I see' replied the boss. 'I see, so you found it all quite rewarding then?'

I nodded.

He sucked on his pipe, unlit, as he pondered some more.

'I see' he said again. Pushing some papers around, all brown suited, 'mmmmmm' he added as he looked down and flicked through the folder on his desk.

He added another 'mmmmmm' again.

He looked up.

'Okay, good, good, well done lad, you survived it'

I nodded.

He smiled.

The Super stood up and beckoned me to the doorway.

'Well, I look forward to seeing you again in the future then lad' he said.

I got up and walked to the door.

'Is that it?' I said.

'Is that it what?' replied the Super.

'Is my interview over sir?'

I must have looked surprised because he stopped in his tracks.

'Well, yes it is officer, what more would you like?'

Well, nothing sir if that's it ' I responded.

I turned round and headed to the office door.

Next to the light switch was a picture of Alfie and the Queen, he was holding up what looked like a Tesco bag, like he had just won a prize on Tiswas - he looked even smaller in that picture than he did in real life.

I left the room.

I shook my head and sighed again, not for the first time that day. The door closed behind me as I stood still in the corridor. The soft carpet was bouncy under my feet as I walked away. A creaky wooden floorboard walk. Now seated at her desk was his PA a snooty looking woman, all prim and proper pampering herself with some spray and looking in to a vanity mirror.

'Oh, I didn't know you were in there' she said.

'Neither did I' I responded and walked on by, down the stairs and went to the pub.

✳✳✳✳✳

'He's a fucking cock youth' laughed Wolfie as he sipped his from a pint of best ale. 'Always has been' He added.

I nodded.

'It was just so surreal Wolf' I said. *'He just ummed and arred* and then said *'good, good'* and it was over. It was the most bizarre interview I have ever had. He didn't tell me how I had done, what I had scored, where I could develop or what happens next. It was pointless!'

'I'm none the wiser at all' I must have looked as surprised as I did when I left the office as Wolfie was looking right at me. Wolfie laughed out loud, a froth of beer on his top lip as Tosh walked into the busy boozer.

'Oi there shipmates' he shouted and walked over, green Barbour flying out behind him. 'How did it go lad?' he asked sitting down.

'I don't know how it went Tosh, the man is weird, didn't say anything' I replied.

Tosh smiled. 'He never has Barnesy, he has spent his whole career saying fuck all and getting through the day, that's how he has survived. Bloody useless is what he is'

Tosh laughed, Wolfie joined in and pints were raised.

'Never a better way to spend the day' Wolfie said as he motioned to us both for more beer.

I declined.

'I'm off home Wolf, I suppose that's it, I'm back on shift on Thursday morning early turn'.

Both Tosh and Wolfie seemed to stop what they were doing. The metal bar framework and dark oak of our pubs in the area around that time were always an invitation to sup some more and take your time, I was tempted.

'You haven't told him have you Tosh?' Wolfie said looking dismayed.

Wolfie stood part way between the bar and our table.

I turned to Tosh seated next to me.

'Told me what?' I said.

Tosh looked uncomfortable and shifted in his seat.

'Listen lad' he said.

I knew something was coming. That much was patently obvious.

'It isn't always that everyone of us is suited to the post of Detective see, it's not as if we can all do it'

I felt a rising surge through my stomach and chest, a travelling horror moment. I went a bit blurry too and I felt the start of anger.

'Listen Barnesy, you ain't going back to your shift, you're going to spend a few weeks on traffic as a relief dispatcher over at their training centre, they can't fill the role so it's all loose hands to the pumps. Sadly, you is a loose hand chum'

Tosh looked down and shook his head.

'There ain't be many officers available, sorry mate' He added.

'I'm really sorry Barnesy boy, you're out, you gave it your best shot and it didn't come off, I am really sorry'

I wasn't happy, I wanted more of an explanation.

'Listen Tosh, if I was going wrong you should have told me, I thought we were going good, I was doing everything you asked of me, why didn't you point me in the right direction – or you?' I looked sternly and pointed at Wolfie who had his head bowed with two pints in his hand. He spat out the bags of crisps from his mouth on to the table and turned to Tosh.

'I told you the lad was needing to speak with you, why didn't you say anything Sarge' Wolfie said.

Tosh held his hands out.

'It's hard sometimes Wolf' Tosh replied.

Both were now seated and looking at me, and Tosh handed me a piece of paper.

'I'm sorry son, here is your order to move, report to Traffic at 8am tomorrow morning, your rest day is cancelled, and they will put you on a different shift pattern, sorry mate'.

'This is fucking not on' I shouted. 'I thought we were mates, I thought I was doing okay'

'Okay, okay youth' Wolfie interjected. 'It isn't okay to go off on one in here is it? Now settle down, get yourself sorted for the morning and apply again, you never know they might let you do another attachment'

'Fuck you and fuck your attachment ' I replied.

Red mist. I stormed out of the pub.

Both Tosh and Wolfie, and of course the rest of our small shift will never know just how upsetting it was to be told in that way that I had failed my attachment. And in the way I was told - I was furious. Over the afternoon and evening I sulked in my house, not understanding why this had happened. Just what had I done wrong, and why was it handled so badly?

All I knew then was I was right to believe the bad stories and the poor management of people in the police - that I often heard from many officers.

In the end I resorted to blaming myself, I clearly wasn't cut out for it. I really thought I was, but my own perception clearly wasn't everyone else's. I told a few mates on the phone, they all agreed it was a wrong old do, and could have been handled better. Mates do that, they agree with you regardless.

The next morning I drove over to traffic, a big old traffic unit based on the edge of various motorways, and a few more close by, a real old traffic place, full of traffic people and traffic ideals. I couldn't have been further away from where I wanted to be, both in location and mindset. I have nothing against traffic at all, but we all choose our way in our police life, and this wasn't mine. I wandered in to the trim and clean despatch office overlooking the main roads as the green screened computers jumped out at you, all over the place. They reflected in the dark mirrored glass and on the glass partitions separating each dispatcher.

It was office hell.

I just stood there, PC Barnes, an officer without a cause.

A uniformed Inspector I had never seen before came over. He held out his hand. We shook.

'Ken isn't it? he said.

I nodded. 'Yes Inspector, I'm Ken Barnes' I replied.

I looked round for some inspiration, and had never felt so deflated.

'Listen mate, you choose one of those two seats and a screen, I'll be over later, get acclimatised and we'll speak in half hour okay?

He patted my shoulder and went back in to his office glancing over as he sat down. I looked round again, not a sign, nobody saying 'hi' just earphones plugged in, gazing at screens and no soul. Chatter, chatter, was all I could hear. I sat down too and noticed the Inspector looking over whilst on the telephone, he looked concerned. His separate office and blinds no mask to what I could see on his face. If I was him, I would be concerned. I was the most pissed off officer in the world right now.

I decide to ring my old skipper who was on duty in town, he may have an answer for me. As this thought crossed my mind my telephone rang, I left it.

It stopped and rang again.

I looked at it. It stopped and rang again.

I answered it.

'Er, hello PC Barnes' I said.

'PC who?' came the reply. A male voice, high pitched and sounding daft.

'PC Barnes' I said again.

Giggling.

'Hello' I said. 'Can I help you?'

I was about to put the phone down when I heard giggling again.

'Who is this?' I demanded.

'Who is this what? came the reply, and now a voice I recognised.

'Ere Barnesy what you be doing there, all dressed up like a cartoon clown in your best bib and tucker'

It was Tosh.

'I don't need this Tosh, give me a break mate' I said. 'And anyway, I will be putting in a complaint about the way you dealt with my report and end of attachment, that was out of order' I added.

'Complaint' Tosh asked. 'Why?'

'Because you treated me like a mug mate that's why, and you know it, I deserve better than this' I replied. I wasn't happy and was shouting, a few staff close by looked over to me.

'Listen Tosh, go away, I have had enough' I said.

'NO, you go away' said Tosh. 'And get that Detective backside of yours over this office now boy, and don't speak to me like that either'

'Fuck off' I replied and put the phone down.

I felt out of breath, how dare he gloat, he may well be an old school skipper, but this is pushing piss taking too far, he always took piss taking too far. That's all he ever did. I put my head in my hands. He took piss taking too far. Always pushing those he knew well to the hilt for a laugh.

I thought about what he said.

And then I realised.

'Detective' I said.

I looked up.

I thought it and said it again.

'Detective'

The phone rang.

I picked it up.

'DC Barnes, if you tell me to fuck off again I will kick yer ass all over the country, now gets that backside over here and help Wolfie out. He's all cold and lonely without ye'

I thought 'You passed you bloody fool, why do you take things so seriously'

I didn't know whether to laugh or cry.

'Tosser' I said and put the phone down.

The Inspector I had just met came out of his office.

'He wanted to keep this up all day Ken' he said. 'I called him and told him to call it a day, a laugh is a laugh, but I couldn't have you committing suicide in the toilets youth'

He laughed.

I sat there for a few minutes; I shook my head and smiled. It was just like Tosh to go the extra mile, not only in the job itself, but in his wind ups and indeed camaraderie. I got up, picked my bag up and walked out of the dispatch office.

I don't think I have ever felt such a huge sense of relief since that day.

*****

I went home and got changed, my new suit that I had bought just the week before seemed a fitting garment for my first day in the office. Fair play they had got me hook, line and sinker, it would take some living down that one. However, there would be plenty of opportunities ahead that's for sure to get my own back, and trust me I did, many times over and more. Nowadays the CID is a completely different beast to the one that I joined back all those years ago, I haven't excelled but then again I haven't let anyone down. I have just detected I suppose, in the way a Detective is expected to do.

I have worked on hundreds of jobs, led teams as an acting Sarge and made temporary Sarge too. Some of those jobs were small, some average and a few huge. I do hope that I made a bit of a difference to those people I met, either directly or indirectly. They would know better than I. It depends I suppose how you quantify it. I walked into the station and turned the corner towards the main CID office. The reception I received in the office from all ranks and more gave me a bit of a lump in the throat. The loud cheer and party poppers were deafening for a few seconds as I walked into the office that afternoon having composed myself enough to start work. The back slapping and cheering is something I will remember for ever. I forgave Tosh immediately, and Wolfie, as I did Karen and Shakespeare, and indeed Alfie Wright.

He came along too, smiling, all in on the joke. The joke of the year if the rumours thereafter would be believed. It spread like wildfire. In time these things are forgotten, people move on and indeed the death of a colleague is as quickly forgotten now as anything else, such is the climate change we have undertaken as a service. However, I have to add this, there is the small matter of twenty odd years CID service for me to recollect and record. And well, you never know, if ever again you feel like a little journey through the life of Detective Ken Barnes, you may feel the desire once more to join me as we roll along the criminal road of my policing life.

I remain hopeful we will hook up soon, it would be a shame not to now – wouldn't it?

To go in to or into? That is the question.

Printed in Great Britain
by Amazon

39508150R00175